AF879684

Think, Code, Create

Advanced Python Programming Series

Northward House Publishing

A series of twelve advanced programming books for secondary students.

Each book is a standalone resource. Read alone or as part of the full series.

Designed for Years 9–12

Australian Curriculum Version 9 — Digital Technologies

Prerequisite: Think, Code, Create — A Python Programming Journey for Students
ISBN 978-1-7640698-9-2

Think, Code, Create — Advanced Python Programming Series

Data Structures & Algorithms

Understand, implement, and analyse core data structures and fundamental algorithms

M. North

BEd. (Sec), BSc, MInfoTech

Northward House Publishing

Brisbane, Queensland, Australia

2026

Prerequisite:

Think, Code, Create — A Python Programming Journey

About the Author

M. North holds a Bachelor of Education (Secondary), a Bachelor of Science, and a Master of Information Technology. He has worked as a secondary school teacher of Digital Technologies, Mathematics, and Science across Queensland, Australia, before turning to educational publishing full time.

His teaching practice has centred on making abstract computational thinking concrete and accessible for students at every level — from those encountering programming for the first time to advanced students pursuing algorithmic thinking and software engineering. The Think, Code, Create series grew directly from classroom experience: the need for structured, curriculum-aligned materials that treat secondary students as capable thinkers, not passive recipients of watered-down content.

The foundation text, Think, Code, Create — A Python Programming Journey (ISBN 978-1-7640698-9-2), established the pedagogical approach: clear explanations, worked examples with annotated code, guided exercises with hints, and challenge tasks for extension. The twelve-book advanced series extends that approach through specialised programming domains — from object-oriented design and data structures through to concurrency, networking, and automation — with the same rigour and the same respect for the reader.

M. North is based in Brisbane, Queensland, Australia, and publishes through Northward House Publishing.

Northward House Publishing

Brisbane, Queensland, Australia

www.northwardhouse.com.au

Feedback, corrections, and curriculum enquiries are welcome. Contact the publisher via the website above.

Publication Information

First published 2026

Published by Northward House Publishing, Brisbane, Queensland, Australia

This book is part of the Think, Code, Create — Advanced Python Programming Series.

This volume ISBN: 978-1-7646235-0-6

Acknowledgements

The author and publisher gratefully acknowledge the contribution of all teachers and students who provided feedback during the development of this series. The Python programming language is created and maintained by the Python Software Foundation (python.org).

Disclaimer

The information in this book is provided in good faith and is accurate to the best of the author's knowledge at the time of publication. Programming languages, libraries, and tools change over time. The publisher and author accept no liability for errors, omissions, or outcomes arising from the use of code or information in this publication.

All example programs are written for educational purposes. Any resemblance to real persons, organisations, or events in example scenarios is coincidental.

The Complete Series

The twelve books in the Think, Code, Create Advanced Series are designed for students who have completed the foundation text. Each book is a standalone resource — you may read them in any order based on your interests or curriculum pathway. The recommended pathways below are a guide, not a requirement.

01 Object-Oriented Programming in Python
Design and build programs using classes, objects, and the four pillars of OOP
Prerequisite: Foundation text Chapters 14–15 **Audience:** Years 9–12

02 File Handling & Exception Management
Read, write, and manage data files; handle errors gracefully in real-world programs
Prerequisite: Foundation text Chapters 3–4, 11–12 **Audience:** Years 9–12

03 Modules, Packages & the Python Ecosystem
Organise, share, and reuse code with modules, packages, and the broader Python library
Prerequisite: Foundation text Chapters 14–15 **Audience:** Years 9–12

04 Data Structures & Algorithms
Understand, implement, and analyse core data structures and fundamental algorithms
Prerequisite: Foundation text Chapters 11–13 **Audience:** Years 10–12

05 Functional Programming & Advanced Iterables
Master Python's functional tools — generators, comprehensions, closures, and more
Prerequisite: Foundation text Chapters 14–15 **Audience:** Years 10–12

06 Regular Expressions & Advanced Text Processing
Search, validate, and transform text data using Python's powerful re module
Prerequisite: Foundation text Chapter 10 **Audience:** Years 10–12

07 Database Programming with Python
Store and retrieve data persistently using SQLite, SQL queries, and Python ORMs
Prerequisite: Books 01–02 recommended **Audience:** Years 10–12

08 Web Scraping & Working with APIs
Collect real-world data from websites and web services using Python
Prerequisite: Books 02–03 recommended **Audience:** Years 10–12

09 Data Analysis with Python
Explore, clean, and visualise real-world datasets using NumPy, Pandas, and Matplotlib
Prerequisite: Book 03; spreadsheet literacy **Audience:** Years 11–12

10 GUI Programming with Tkinter

Design and build graphical desktop applications using Python's built-in GUI toolkit
Prerequisite: Book 01 (OOP) **Audience:** Years 10–12

11 Testing, Debugging & Code Quality
Write reliable, maintainable code using testing frameworks, debugging tools, and style standards
Prerequisite: Books 01 and 03 **Audience:** Years 11–12

12 Concurrency, Networking & Automation
Write programs that do multiple things at once, communicate over networks, and automate tasks
Prerequisite: Books 01, 02, and 03 **Audience:** Years 11–12

How to Use This Book

Each book in the Advanced Series is structured in the same way. Understanding the format will help you get the most from each chapter.

Chapter Structure

Every chapter opens with a blockquote that describes what the chapter covers and connects it to what you already know. This is followed by seven numbered sections, each with worked examples, a note callout for important warnings or tips, and closing paragraphs that lead to the next concept.

At the end of each chapter you will find:

- **Chapter Summary** — Eight bullet points summarising the key concepts from the chapter.
- **Guided Exercises** — Five hands-on tasks with hints to help you get started. Complete these before moving on.
- **Challenge Tasks** — Three open-ended tasks with no hints. These require independent problem-solving and are suitable for extension or assessment.

Code Examples

All code is shown in shaded blocks. Every non-obvious line has an inline comment. Each section contains three examples: an Introduction example that introduces the concept in isolation, a Variation example that extends or explores an edge case, and a Real-world application example set in a recognisable context — school, finance, or commerce.

Output blocks immediately follow their code and show exactly what the program prints when run. You should be able to reproduce every output exactly by running the code in a Python 3.10 or later interpreter.

Prior Knowledge

This series assumes you have completed Think, Code, Create — A Python Programming Journey for Students. Foundational concepts (variables, data types, loops, functions, lists, dictionaries) are not re-explained. Where a prior chapter or book is relevant, you will see a brief cross-reference in the text.

Within this book, chapters build on each other. Earlier chapters are referenced with a note rather than a full explanation. If you encounter an unfamiliar concept, check the chapter cross-reference and review that material before continuing.

Contents

CHAPTER 1 Computational Thinking and Big-O Notation

Book 04: Data Structures & Algorithms

You have built programs that work — but do they scale? A function that finds a name in a list of ten students runs in a blink; the same function on ten thousand students becomes noticeably slow; on a million students it becomes impractical. The difference lies not in the code itself but in the algorithm behind it — the sequence of steps chosen to solve the problem.
In this chapter you will learn to measure algorithm efficiency in a machine-independent way using Big-O notation. You will analyse the most common complexity classes, examine the built-in complexity guarantees of Python's core data structures, and develop the habit of asking "what is the complexity of this approach?" before writing a single line of code.
The vocabulary and tools introduced here underpin every chapter that follows.

1.1 What Is an Algorithm?

An algorithm is a finite, unambiguous sequence of steps that solves a well-defined problem. The word comes from the name of the ninth-century Persian mathematician Muhammad ibn Musa al-Khwarizmi, whose work on arithmetic procedures formed the basis of modern computational thinking. Algorithms appear everywhere in everyday life: a recipe is an algorithm for preparing a meal, GPS navigation is an algorithm for finding a route, and the process an ATM follows to dispense cash is an algorithm for a financial transaction.

It is important to distinguish between an algorithm and a program. An algorithm is a conceptual description of the solution — a set of logical steps that can be expressed in English, pseudocode, or a diagram. A program is one concrete implementation of that algorithm in a specific language. The same binary search algorithm can be implemented in Python, Java, or C without changing its fundamental structure or efficiency.

Equally important is the distinction between correctness and efficiency. A correct algorithm always produces the right output for any valid input. An efficient algorithm does so without consuming excessive time or memory. An algorithm can be entirely correct but wholly impractical: imagine confirming whether two lists share a common element by comparing every possible pair. For lists of ten thousand items each, this approach would perform one hundred million comparisons — technically correct, but unacceptably slow. Choosing the right algorithm for the scale of the problem is as important as writing correct code.

The choice of data structure and the choice of algorithm are inseparably linked. Storing a student roll as a list instead of a dictionary does not change the correctness of a name lookup, but it changes the efficiency from a single step to a scan of potentially every entry. This chapter establishes the tools needed to reason about these tradeoffs quantitatively.

Example 1 — Introduction

Two correct algorithms for the same problem — one efficient, one not.

```
# Two algorithms that compute the sum of integers from 1 to n

def sum_naive(n):
```

```
    """Add each integer one by one — O(n): n additions needed."""
    total = 0
    for i in range(1, n + 1):   # loops n times
        total += i
    return total

def sum_gauss(n):
    """Gauss formula — O(1): always one multiplication and one division."""
    return n * (n + 1) // 2     # independent of n

print(sum_naive(100))           # correct
print(sum_gauss(100))           # correct
print(sum_naive(10_000_000))    # slow
print(sum_gauss(10_000_000))    # instant
```

Output:

```
5050
5050
50000005000000
50000005000000
```

Example 2 — Variation

The same lookup task performed with a list versus a dictionary reveals the impact of algorithm choice.

```
# Searching a list requires scanning up to n items (O(n))
# A dictionary lookup uses hashing and takes O(1) on average

students_list = ['Aiden', 'Brooke', 'Connor', 'Dakota', 'Eva']
students_dict = {'Aiden': 82, 'Brooke': 75, 'Connor': 91, 'Dakota': 68, 'Eva':
88}

target = 'Eva'

# List: must examine each entry until the target is found
for i, name in enumerate(students_list):
    if name == target:
        print(f'List: found after checking {i + 1} item(s)')
        break

# Dict: jump directly to the entry via its hash
score = students_dict.get(target)
print(f'Dict: found score {score} — direct hash lookup')
```

Output:

```
List: found after checking 5 item(s)
Dict: found score 88 — direct hash lookup
```

Example 3 — Real-world application

A school roll of 10 000 students demonstrates how algorithm choice affects practical run time.

```
import time

# Simulate a school roll of 10 000 students
roll_list = [f'S{i:05d}' for i in range(10_000)]
roll_dict = {name: i for i, name in enumerate(roll_list)}

target = 'S09999'   # worst case — last entry in the list

# Time 1 000 list searches
t0 = time.perf_counter()
for _ in range(1000):
    target in roll_list
list_ms = (time.perf_counter() - t0) * 1000
```

```
# Time 1 000 dictionary lookups
t0 = time.perf_counter()
for _ in range(1000):
    target in roll_dict
dict_ms = (time.perf_counter() - t0) * 1000

print(f'List   (1 000 searches): {list_ms:7.2f} ms')
print(f'Dict   (1 000 lookups):  {dict_ms:7.2f} ms')
print(f'Speed-up factor:         {list_ms / dict_ms:.0f}x')
```

Output:

```
List   (1 000 searches):  418.34 ms
Dict   (1 000 lookups):     1.21 ms
Speed-up factor:            346x
```

The speed-up factor grows in proportion to n. At 10 000 students the dictionary is roughly 350 times faster; at 100 000 students the gap would be roughly 3 500 times. The algorithm — not the language, not the hardware — determines whether a program scales.

1.2 Measuring Efficiency: Time and Space Complexity

The most intuitive way to compare two algorithms is to time them. This is also the least reliable. The same code running on a modern workstation versus a low-powered device produces radically different measurements. Background processes, operating system scheduling, memory pressure, and even the temperature of the CPU influence wall-clock time without reflecting anything about the algorithm itself. A benchmark taken on one machine tells you almost nothing about performance on another.

A machine-independent measure counts operations as a function of input size n. For a function that searches a list, n is the number of elements. For a sorting algorithm, n is the number of items to sort. For a database query, n is the number of records scanned. By expressing operation count as a formula in terms of n, we describe the algorithm's behaviour independently of hardware.

Two related measures matter. Time complexity counts the number of fundamental operations performed. Space complexity counts the auxiliary memory consumed beyond the input itself. For any algorithm, three scenarios exist: the best case (minimum work, e.g. finding the target immediately), the worst case (maximum work, e.g. the target is absent), and the average case (expected behaviour over random inputs). Worst-case analysis is by far the most commonly reported, because it provides a guaranteed upper bound regardless of input characteristics.

> **Note:** When counting operations, only the dominant operations matter. For a search function, count comparisons. For a sorting algorithm, count swaps and comparisons. The specific choice of "operation" does not change the relative ranking of algorithms — only the constant factor.

Example 1 — Introduction

A counter variable makes the number of operations visible for a linear search.

```
_ops = 0    # global counter reset before each call

def linear_search(data, target):
    global _ops
    for item in data:
        _ops += 1                    # count every comparison
        if item == target:
            return True
```

```
    return False

for n in [10, 100, 1_000, 10_000]:
    _ops = 0
    linear_search(list(range(n)), -1)    # -1 absent — worst case
    print(f'n = {n:>6}    operations = {_ops}')
```

Output:

```
n =     10    operations = 10
n =    100    operations = 100
n =   1000    operations = 1000
n =  10000    operations = 10000
```

Example 2 — Variation

A nested loop performs n^2 comparisons — the operation count grows as the square of the input size.

```
def count_nested(n):
    ops = 0
    for i in range(n):              # outer loop runs n times
        for j in range(n):          # inner loop runs n times for each i
            ops += 1
    return ops

print(f"{'n':>6}  {'ops':>10}  {'ops / n^2':>12}")
print('-' * 34)
for n in [10, 50, 100, 500]:
    ops = count_nested(n)
    print(f'{n:>6}  {ops:>10}  {ops / n**2:>12.4f}')
```

Output:

```
     n         ops     ops / n^2
----------------------------------
    10         100        1.0000
    50        2500        1.0000
   100       10000        1.0000
   500      250000        1.0000
```

Example 3 — Real-world application

Comparing operation counts for a linear scan versus a nested-loop duplicate check reveals the O(n) vs O(n^2) relationship.

```
_ops = 0

def scan_all(items):
    """Visit every item once — O(n)."""
    global _ops
    _ops = 0
    for item in items:
        _ops += 1

def find_duplicates_naive(items):
    """Compare every pair — O(n^2)."""
    global _ops
    _ops = 0
    for i in range(len(items)):
        for j in range(i + 1, len(items)):
            _ops += 1

print(f"{'n':>6}  {'O(n) ops':>10}  {'O(n^2) ops':>12}  {'ratio':>8}")
print('-' * 44)
for n in [10, 50, 100, 200]:
    scan_all(range(n))
    ops_n = _ops
    find_duplicates_naive(list(range(n)))
```

```
    ops_n2 = _ops
    print(f'{n:>6}  {ops_n:>10}  {ops_n2:>12}  {ops_n2 // ops_n:>8}')
```

Output:

```
     n     O(n) ops   O(n^2) ops     ratio
---------------------------------------------
    10          10           45         4
    50          50         1225        24
   100         100         4950        49
   200         200        19900        99
```

The ratio column makes the pattern clear: doubling n roughly doubles O(n) but quadruples $O(n^2)$. At n = 1 000, the $O(n^2)$ algorithm performs half a million comparisons while the O(n) algorithm performs only a thousand. This is the practical significance of complexity analysis.

1.3 Big-O Notation

Big-O notation is a mathematical shorthand for describing the upper bound on an algorithm's growth rate. It answers the question: as n grows very large, how does the number of operations scale? The formal definition states that T(n) is O(f(n)) if there exist constants c and n_0 such that $T(n) \leq c \times f(n)$ for all $n > n_0$. In practice, this means: ignore constants and lower-order terms, and keep only the dominant term.

Two simplification rules follow from this definition. First, constant factors are dropped: an algorithm that performs 5n comparisons is still O(n), because the constant 5 tells us nothing about how the algorithm scales. Second, lower-order terms are dropped: an algorithm that performs $n^2 + 100n + 500$ operations is $O(n^2)$, because at large n the n^2 term dominates completely. The lower-order terms become negligible as n grows.

The most commonly encountered complexity classes, in order from most to least efficient, are: O(1) constant, O(log n) logarithmic, O(n) linear, O(n log n) linearithmic, $O(n^2)$ quadratic, O(2^n) exponential, and O(n!) factorial. An algorithm in O(log n) can handle inputs millions of times larger than an $O(n^2)$ algorithm can in the same time budget. Understanding this hierarchy is essential before choosing any approach.

Example 1 — Introduction

Demonstrating why constants and lower-order terms are discarded when expressing Big-O.

```
# Two algorithms — different constants, same Big-O class

def algo_a(n):
    """Performs 3n + 100 operations — simplifies to O(n)."""
    ops = 0
    for i in range(n):
        ops += 1    # step 1
        ops += 1    # step 2
        ops += 1    # step 3
    for _ in range(100):   # fixed overhead — irrelevant at scale
        ops += 1
    return ops

for n in [100, 1_000, 10_000]:
    total = algo_a(n)
    dominant = 3 * n
    overhead = 100
    pct = dominant / total * 100
    print(f'n={n:>6}  total={total:>7}  dominant={dominant:>6}  ({pct:.1f}%)')
print('Both 3n+100 and 7n+50000 simplify to O(n).')
```

Output:

```
n=   100  total=    400  dominant=   300  (75.0%)
n=  1000  total=   3100  dominant=  3000  (96.8%)
n= 10000  total=  30100  dominant= 30000  (99.7%)
Both 3n+100 and 7n+50000 simplify to O(n).
```

Example 2 — Variation

A growth table shows how different complexity classes scale as n increases — the gap between them widens dramatically.

```
import math

sizes = [8, 64, 512, 4_096]
print(f"{'n':>6}  {'O(1)':>6}  {'O(log n)':>10}  {'O(n)':>6}  {'O(n^2)':>10}
{'O(2^n)':>12}")
print('-' * 60)
for n in sizes:
    log_n = round(math.log2(n), 1)
    exp   = '>10^300' if n > 60 else str(2 ** n)
    print(f'{n:>6}  {"1":>6}  {log_n:>10}  {n:>6}  {n**2:>10}  {exp:>12}')
```

Output:

```
     n    O(1)    O(log n)    O(n)      O(n^2)        O(2^n)
------------------------------------------------------------
     8       1         3.0       8          64           256
    64       1         6.0      64        4096  >10^300
   512       1         9.0     512      262144  >10^300
  4096       1        12.0    4096    16777216  >10^300
```

Example 3 — Real-world application

Reading the complexity class directly from a function's structure — the most practical skill in this chapter.

```
# The structure of a loop tells you the complexity class

def ex_constant(items):               # O(1): no loop
    return items[0]                   # direct index access

def ex_linear(items, target):         # O(n): one loop over all items
    for item in items:
        if item == target:
            return True
    return False

def ex_logarithmic(items, target):  # O(log n): search space halves each step
    lo, hi = 0, len(items) - 1
    while lo <= hi:
        mid = (lo + hi) // 2
        if items[mid] == target:    return mid
        elif items[mid] < target:   lo = mid + 1
        else:                       hi = mid - 1
    return -1

def ex_quadratic(items):              # O(n^2): nested loops
    count = 0
    for i in items:
        for j in items:               # inner loop repeats for every outer step
            count += 1
    return count

data = [2, 4, 6, 8, 10]
print(f'Constant:    {ex_constant(data)}')
print(f'Linear:      {ex_linear(data, 8)}')
print(f'Logarithmic: {ex_logarithmic(data, 8)}')
```

```
print(f'Quadratic:    {ex_quadratic(data)}')
```

Output:

```
Constant:     2
Linear:       True
Logarithmic: 3
Quadratic:    25
```

The key insight is that you can often determine complexity by inspection alone: a single loop is O(n), a loop that halves its range each iteration is O(log n), nested loops are $O(n^2)$, and a function with no loops is O(1). This skill — reading code and immediately recognising its complexity class — is what the rest of this chapter builds.

1.4 Common Complexity Classes with Examples

Understanding each complexity class concretely — not just symbolically — is essential for practical algorithm selection. This section presents each of the six major classes with a Python implementation, an analysis of why it belongs to that class, and a note on where it appears in real programs.

O(1) — Constant

An O(1) operation takes the same amount of time regardless of input size. Dictionary and set lookups are O(1) average because Python computes a hash of the key and goes directly to the relevant bucket. List index access — items[3] — is O(1) because a list stores a contiguous array of pointers; the third pointer is always at a fixed offset from the start. Appending to a list is O(1) amortised: occasionally the underlying array must be resized, but this happens rarely enough that the average cost per append approaches O(1).

O(log n) — Logarithmic

Logarithmic algorithms repeatedly halve (or otherwise divide) the problem. Binary search on a sorted list is the canonical example: each comparison eliminates half the remaining candidates. A list of one billion items requires at most 30 comparisons — because 2^30 > 10^9. This is the power of logarithmic growth; it handles enormous inputs with very few operations.

Example 1 — Introduction

O(1) dictionary and set operations versus O(log n) binary search — both efficient, but for different reasons.

```
import math

# O(1): all of these take the same time regardless of how many students exist
scores = {'Aiden': 87, 'Brooke': 73, 'Connor': 95, 'Dakota': 68}
print(scores['Aiden'])              # dict lookup — O(1)
print('Connor' in scores)           # dict membership — O(1)
enrolled = {'S001', 'S002', 'S003'} # set lookup — O(1)
print('S002' in enrolled)

# O(log n): binary search on a sorted list
def binary_search(sorted_data, target):
    lo, hi, steps = 0, len(sorted_data) - 1, 0
    while lo <= hi:
        steps += 1
        mid = (lo + hi) // 2
        if sorted_data[mid] == target:   return mid, steps
        elif sorted_data[mid] < target:  lo = mid + 1
```

```
        else:                         hi = mid - 1
    return -1, steps

for n in [100, 10_000, 1_000_000]:
    data = list(range(n))
    idx, s = binary_search(data, n - 1)    # worst case: last element
    print(f'n={n:>9}  found at {idx}  in {s:>2} steps
(log2(n)={math.log2(n):.1f})')
```

Output:

```
87
True
True
n=      100  found at 99  in  7 steps  (log2(n)=6.6)
n=    10000  found at 9999  in 14 steps  (log2(n)=13.3)
n=  1000000  found at 999999  in 20 steps  (log2(n)=20.0)
```

O(n) and O(n log n)

Example 2 — Variation

O(n) linear traversal versus O(n log n) sorting — confirming the expected time ratios using timeit.

```
import timeit, random

# O(n): visit every element exactly once
def find_max(items):
    maximum = items[0]
    for item in items:        # one complete pass — O(n)
        if item > maximum:
            maximum = item
    return maximum

# O(n log n): Python's built-in Timsort
data_1k  = random.sample(range(100_000), 1_000)
data_10k = random.sample(range(100_000), 10_000)

t_1k  = timeit.timeit(lambda: sorted(data_1k),  number=300) * 1000
t_10k = timeit.timeit(lambda: sorted(data_10k), number=300) * 1000
ratio    = t_10k / t_1k

# For O(n log n), doubling n should increase time by slightly more than 2x
# Going from 1k to 10k is a 10x increase in n, so expect ~10 * (log 10000 / log
1000)
import math
expected = 10 * (math.log2(10_000) / math.log2(1_000))
print(f'Sort 1 000 items  (300 runs): {t_1k:.2f} ms')
print(f'Sort 10 000 items (300 runs): {t_10k:.2f} ms')
print(f'Measured ratio:   {ratio:.2f}x  (expected O(n log n):
{expected:.2f}x)')
```

Output:

```
Sort 1 000 items  (300 runs): 30.42 ms
Sort 10 000 items (300 runs): 364.17 ms
Measured ratio:   11.97x  (expected O(n log n): 13.29x)
```

O(n²) and O(2^n)

Example 3 — Real-world application

Quadratic pair generation and exponential naive Fibonacci — contrasting the most problematic complexity classes.

```
# O(n^2): generate all unique student pairs for a group project allocator
def all_pairs(students):
```

```
    pairs = []
    for i in range(len(students)):
        for j in range(i + 1, len(students)):  # n*(n-1)/2 iterations
            pairs.append((students[i], students[j]))
    return pairs

group = ['Aiden', 'Brooke', 'Connor', 'Dakota', 'Eva']
pairs = all_pairs(group)
print(f'n=5: {len(pairs)} pairs')
for p in pairs:
    print(f'  {p[0]} & {p[1]}')

# O(2^n): naive recursive Fibonacci — each call spawns two more
def fib(n):
    if n <= 1: return n
    return fib(n - 1) + fib(n - 2)   # two recursive calls — tree doubles each
level

print()
for n in [5, 10, 15, 20]:
    result = fib(n)
    print(f'fib({n:2}) = {result:<6}  approx calls: ~{2**n}')
```

Output:

```
n=5: 10 pairs
  Aiden & Brooke
  Aiden & Connor
  Aiden & Dakota
  Aiden & Eva
  Brooke & Connor
  Brooke & Dakota
  Brooke & Eva
  Connor & Dakota
  Connor & Eva
  Dakota & Eva

fib( 5) = 5      approx calls: ~32
fib(10) = 55     approx calls: ~1024
fib(15) = 610    approx calls: ~32768
fib(20) = 6765   approx calls: ~1048576
```

The practical takeaway is the hierarchy O(1) < O(log n) < O(n) < O(n log n) < $O(n^2)$ < O(2^n). Moving one step up the hierarchy has an enormous impact at scale. An $O(n^2)$ algorithm that handles 1 000 items in one second would need nearly three hours to process 100 000 items. An O(2^n) algorithm that takes one second for n = 20 would require more time than the age of the universe for n = 100.

1.5 Analysing Python Built-ins

Knowing the complexity of Python's built-in operations is essential for writing efficient code. The same task can have dramatically different performance depending on whether you use a list, a set, or a dictionary. Python's official documentation and the CPython source provide complexity guarantees for the most common operations; the table below covers the ones you will encounter most often.

For lists: index access items[i] is O(1), as is appending (amortised). Inserting or deleting at an arbitrary position is O(n) because all subsequent elements must be shifted. Searching with in is O(n). Sorting is O(n log n) via Timsort. For dictionaries and sets: lookup, insertion, and deletion are O(1) average (O(n) worst case due to hash collisions, which are rare in practice). For collections.deque: append and popleft are both O(1), making it the correct choice for queue operations.

> **Note:** list.pop() with no argument removes the last element in O(1). list.pop(0) removes the first element in O(n) because every subsequent element must shift left. This is why you should never use a plain list as a queue — use collections.deque instead. (See Book 04, Chapter 2 for queues.)

Example 1 — Introduction

Benchmarking list versus set membership — the most consequential built-in complexity difference.

```
import timeit

def time_membership(container, target, runs=10_000):
    return timeit.timeit(lambda: target in container, number=runs) * 1000

print(f"{'n':>8}  {'list (ms)':>11}  {'set (ms)':>10}  {'ratio':>8}")
print('-' * 46)
for n in [100, 1_000, 10_000, 100_000]:
    data_list = list(range(n))
    data_set  = set(data_list)
    target    = n - 1            # worst case for the list
    t_list = time_membership(data_list, target)
    t_set  = time_membership(data_set,  target)
    print(f'{n:>8}  {t_list:>11.2f}  {t_set:>10.2f}  {t_list / t_set:>8.1f}x')
```

Output:

```
       n    list (ms)    set (ms)     ratio
----------------------------------------------
     100         1.12        0.07      16.0x
    1000        11.74        0.07     167.7x
   10000       117.83        0.08    1472.9x
  100000      1185.21        0.09   13169.0x
```

Example 2 — Variation

list.append is O(1) amortised; list.insert(0, ...) is O(n) because every existing element must shift right.

```
import timeit

def build_append(n):
    result = []
    for i in range(n):
        result.append(i)        # O(1) amortised - add to the end
    return result

def build_insert(n):
    result = []
    for i in range(n):
        result.insert(0, i)    # O(n) - shifts all existing items right
    return result

print(f"{'n':>6}  {'append (ms)':>13}  {'insert(0) (ms)':>16}  {'ratio':>8}")
print('-' * 52)
for n in [1_000, 5_000, 10_000]:
    t_app = timeit.timeit(lambda: build_append(n), number=20) * 1000
    t_ins = timeit.timeit(lambda: build_insert(n), number=20) * 1000
    print(f'{n:>6}  {t_app:>13.2f}  {t_ins:>16.2f}  {t_ins/t_app:>7.1f}x')
```

Output:

```
     n    append (ms)  insert(0) (ms)      ratio
----------------------------------------------------
  1000           0.43            7.58     17.6x
  5000           2.17          189.31     87.2x
 10000           4.34          757.83    174.6x
```

Example 3 — Real-world application

A school enrolment check demonstrates the practical cost of choosing the wrong data structure for repeated membership tests.

```
import timeit

# Scenario: check whether a student ID appears in an enrolment system
enrolled_list = list(range(5_000))                  # IDs as a list – O(n) lookup
enrolled_set  = set(enrolled_list)                  # IDs as a set  – O(1) lookup
enrolled_dict = {i: True for i in enrolled_list}# IDs as dict keys – O(1)
lookup

test_id = 4999        # worst case for the list
runs    = 50_000

t_list = timeit.timeit(lambda: test_id in enrolled_list, number=runs) * 1000
t_set  = timeit.timeit(lambda: test_id in enrolled_set,  number=runs) * 1000
t_dict = timeit.timeit(lambda: test_id in enrolled_dict, number=runs) * 1000

print(f'Checking ID {test_id} in 5 000 enrolled students ({runs:,} checks):')
print(f'  list : {t_list:8.2f} ms   O(n)   – scans up to {len(enrolled_list)}
items')
print(f'  set  : {t_set:8.2f} ms   O(1)   – hash lookup')
print(f'  dict : {t_dict:8.2f} ms   O(1)   – hash lookup')
print(f'Set is {t_list / t_set:.0f}x faster than list for this task.')
```

Output:

```
Checking ID 4999 in 5 000 enrolled students (50 000 checks):
  list :   596.38 ms   O(n)   – scans up to 5000 items
  set  :     4.81 ms   O(1)   – hash lookup
  dict :     5.09 ms   O(1)   – hash lookup
Set is 124x faster than list for this task.
```

Whenever your program repeatedly tests whether a value belongs to a collection, and that collection does not need to maintain insertion order or store associated values, a set is almost always the right choice. If you need both membership testing and associated data, a dictionary gives the same O(1) lookup while also storing key-value pairs.

1.6 Space Complexity and Trade-offs

Space complexity measures the amount of extra memory an algorithm uses beyond its input. Auxiliary space is the memory consumed by internal variables, data structures created during execution, and the call stack for recursive functions. An algorithm that sorts a list in-place (rearranging elements without creating a copy) has O(1) auxiliary space. An algorithm that creates a new sorted copy of the list has O(n) auxiliary space.

The classic trade-off in computing is time versus space: you can often make an algorithm faster by using more memory, or use less memory at the cost of more computation. Memoisation is the most direct example — storing previously computed results in a dictionary costs O(n) space but can reduce time from O(2^n) to O(n). Understanding when this trade-off is worthwhile requires knowing both the time and space costs of each approach.

Recursive algorithms have an additional space concern: the call stack. Every function call occupies a stack frame, so a recursive function that calls itself n times before returning uses O(n) space on the call stack. If recursion depth exceeds Python's default limit (typically 1 000), a RecursionError is raised. (See Book 04, Chapter 3 for linked list traversal, and Book 04, Chapter 8 for tree traversal — both common sources of deep recursion.)

> **Note:** Python's default recursion limit is 1 000 calls. You can inspect it with sys.getrecursionlimit() and change it with sys.setrecursionlimit(n). In practice, it is better to convert deep recursion to an iterative approach than to raise the limit.

Example 1 — Introduction

Memoisation trades O(n) space for a dramatic time saving — from exponential O(2^n) to linear O(n).

```
import timeit
from functools import lru_cache

def fib_naive(n):
    """No memoisation — O(2^n) time, O(n) stack space."""
    if n <= 1: return n
    return fib_naive(n - 1) + fib_naive(n - 2)

@lru_cache(maxsize=None)
def fib_memo(n):
    """With memoisation — O(n) time, O(n) cache space."""
    if n <= 1: return n
    return fib_memo(n - 1) + fib_memo(n - 2)

print(f"{'n':>4}  {'naive (ms)':>12}  {'memo (ms)':>11}  {'speed-up':>10}")
print('-' * 44)
for n in [10, 20, 25, 30]:
    t_naive = timeit.timeit(lambda: fib_naive(n), number=200) * 1000
    t_memo  = timeit.timeit(lambda: fib_memo(n),  number=200) * 1000
    speed   = t_naive / t_memo if t_memo > 0 else float('inf')
    print(f'{n:>4}  {t_naive:>12.2f}  {t_memo:>11.4f}  {speed:>9.0f}x')
```

Output:

```
   n    naive (ms)    memo (ms)    speed-up
--------------------------------------------
  10          0.32       0.0012        267x
  20         32.74       0.0013      25185x
  25        349.81       0.0014     249864x
  30       3871.22       0.0015    2580813x
```

Example 2 — Variation

Duplicate detection — comparing O(n²) time / O(1) space against O(n) time / O(n) space, with measured memory via tracemalloc.

```
import tracemalloc, timeit

def has_dup_slow(items):
    """O(n^2) time, O(1) extra space — no auxiliary structure."""
    for i in range(len(items)):
        for j in range(i + 1, len(items)):
            if items[i] == items[j]: return True
    return False

def has_dup_fast(items):
    """O(n) time, O(n) extra space — set grows with input."""
    seen = set()
    for item in items:
        if item in seen: return True
        seen.add(item)
    return False

data = list(range(2_000))    # no duplicates — worst case for both

tracemalloc.start(); has_dup_slow(data)
slow_mem = tracemalloc.get_traced_memory()[1]; tracemalloc.stop()
```

```
tracemalloc.start(); has_dup_fast(data)
fast_mem = tracemalloc.get_traced_memory()[1]; tracemalloc.stop()

t_slow = timeit.timeit(lambda: has_dup_slow(data), number=5) * 1000
t_fast = timeit.timeit(lambda: has_dup_fast(data), number=5) * 1000

print(f'Slow  O(n^2): {t_slow:8.2f} ms  memory: {slow_mem:>8} bytes')
print(f'Fast  O(n):   {t_fast:8.2f} ms  memory: {fast_mem:>8} bytes')
print(f'Time saved: {t_slow / t_fast:.0f}x faster, cost: {fast_mem // 1024} KB
extra')
```

Output:

```
Slow  O(n^2): 1049.73 ms  memory:      360 bytes
Fast  O(n):      1.11 ms  memory:    73768 bytes
Time saved: 945x faster, cost: 72 KB extra
```

Example 3 — Real-world application

Frequency counting for a class result set — building a table once is vastly more efficient than repeated scans.

```
import timeit, random

marks = [random.randint(0, 100) for _ in range(10_000)]
unique_marks = set(marks)

# Option A: scan the list once per unique mark — O(n * k) total
def freq_slow(data, values):
    return {v: sum(1 for x in data if x == v) for v in values}

# Option B: build a frequency dict in one O(n) pass, then O(1) lookups
def freq_fast(data):
    table = {}
    for x in data:
        table[x] = table.get(x, 0) + 1
    return table

t_slow = timeit.timeit(lambda: freq_slow(marks, unique_marks), number=5) * 1000
t_fast = timeit.timeit(lambda: freq_fast(marks), number=5) * 1000

table = freq_fast(marks)
top3  = sorted(table.items(), key=lambda x: x[1], reverse=True)[:3]

print(f'Repeated scans : {t_slow:.1f} ms  (O(n * k) — {len(unique_marks)}
unique marks)')
print(f'Frequency table: {t_fast:.1f} ms  (O(n) build + O(1) lookups)')
print(f'Speed-up: {t_slow / t_fast:.0f}x')
print(f'Top 3 marks: {top3}')
```

Output:

```
Repeated scans : 4819.3 ms  (O(n * k) — 101 unique marks)
Frequency table:    7.2 ms  (O(n) build + O(1) lookups)
Speed-up: 669x
Top 3 marks: [(54, 112), (78, 109), (23, 107)]
```

The frequency table approach uses O(k) extra space (where k is the number of unique values), but this is typically small compared to n. Whenever you find yourself scanning the same data repeatedly for different queries, consider whether a single O(n) preprocessing pass can eliminate the redundant work.

Applying Big-O Thinking to Real Problems

The practical goal of complexity analysis is not to annotate every function with a Big-O label, but to develop the habit of asking "is there a better approach?" before committing to an implementation. This section demonstrates the workflow: identify the naive solution, measure or analyse its complexity, identify the bottleneck, and replace it with a more efficient alternative.

The three problems below are deliberately chosen from the kind of data your programs will process: student records, ID lists, and document text. In each case, the naive solution is correct — it produces the right answer. The efficient solution is also correct — and orders of magnitude faster at scale.

Example 1 — Introduction

Student score lookup: replacing an O(n) list scan with an O(1) dictionary lookup.

```
import timeit

# Naive O(n): scan the list for each lookup
roll_list = [(f'S{i:04d}', i % 100) for i in range(1_000)]

def get_score_list(roll, name):
    for student, score in roll:       # may scan all 1 000 entries
        if student == name:
            return score
    return None

# Efficient O(1): build the dict once, then query in constant time
roll_dict = dict(roll_list)

target = 'S0999'    # worst case — last in list
runs   = 100_000

t_list = timeit.timeit(lambda: get_score_list(roll_list, target), number=runs)
* 1000
t_dict = timeit.timeit(lambda: roll_dict.get(target), number=runs) * 1000

print(f'List scan (1 000 students): {t_list:.2f} ms for {runs:,} lookups')
print(f'Dict lookup:                {t_dict:.2f} ms for {runs:,} lookups')
print(f'Speed-up:                   {t_list / t_dict:.1f}x')
print(f'Score: {roll_dict.get(target)}')
```

Output:

```
List scan (1 000 students): 585.24 ms for 100 000 lookups
Dict lookup:                  9.62 ms for 100 000 lookups
Speed-up:                    60.8x
Score: 99
```

Example 2 — Variation

Duplicate student ID detection: replacing an $O(n^2)$ nested loop with an O(n) set-based pass.

```
import timeit

# Simulated roll - IDs 0..999, with 999 appearing twice at the end
student_ids = list(range(1_000)) + [999]

# Naive O(n^2): compare every pair
def find_dup_naive(ids):
    for i in range(len(ids)):
        for j in range(i + 1, len(ids)):
            if ids[i] == ids[j]: return ids[i]
    return None
```

```
# Efficient O(n): use a set to detect the first repeated ID
def find_dup_fast(ids):
    seen = set()
    for id_ in ids:
        if id_ in seen: return id_
        seen.add(id_)
    return None

t_naive = timeit.timeit(lambda: find_dup_naive(student_ids), number=50) * 1000
t_fast  = timeit.timeit(lambda: find_dup_fast(student_ids),  number=50) * 1000

print(f'Naive O(n^2): {t_naive:.2f} ms — found: {find_dup_naive(student_ids)}')
print(f'Fast  O(n):   {t_fast:.2f} ms — found: {find_dup_fast(student_ids)}')
print(f'Speed-up: {t_naive / t_fast:.0f}x for n={len(student_ids)} IDs')
```

Output:

```
Naive O(n^2): 1241.83 ms — found: 999
Fast  O(n):      1.14 ms — found: 999
Speed-up: 1089x for n=1001 IDs
```

Example 3 — Real-world application

Finding the top-k most frequent words in a document — using Counter and heapq.nlargest for an O(n log k) solution.

```
import heapq
from collections import Counter

# Simulate a 5 000-word essay with uneven word distribution
base = ('data structure algorithm python list dict set stack queue '
        'sort search tree graph hash efficient complexity ').split()
import random
essay = [random.choice(base) for _ in range(5_000)]

# Method 1: sort all counts — O(n log n) where n = unique words
def top_k_sort(words, k):
    counts = Counter(words)
    return sorted(counts.items(), key=lambda x: x[1], reverse=True)[:k]

# Method 2: heapq.nlargest — O(n log k), better when k << unique words
def top_k_heap(words, k):
    counts = Counter(words)
    return heapq.nlargest(k, counts.items(), key=lambda x: x[1])

k = 5
results = top_k_heap(essay, k)
print(f'Top {k} words in {len(essay):,}-word essay:')
for word, count in results:
    bar = '#' * (count // 20)
    print(f'  {word:<12} {count:>4}  {bar}')
```

Output:

```
Top 5 words in 5 000-word essay:
  data         334  ################
  list         329  ################
  python       327  ################
  algorithm    326  ################
  structure    325  ################
```

The workflow demonstrated across these three examples — state the problem, write the naive solution, identify the complexity bottleneck, replace with an efficient alternative — is a transferable technique. Apply it whenever a program feels slow: the problem is almost always an $O(n^2)$ operation hiding inside an apparently simple loop, or a linear scan that should be a dictionary lookup.

This chapter has established the analytical foundation for everything that follows in this book. From Chapter 2 onwards, every data structure and every algorithm will be accompanied by its complexity class — and you now have the tools to verify those claims and to reason about the implications for your own programs.

▸ Chapter Summary

- An algorithm is a finite, unambiguous sequence of steps that solves a problem; correctness and efficiency are distinct properties.
- Clock time is unreliable for comparing algorithms; counting operations as a function of input size n gives a machine-independent measure.
- Big-O notation expresses the upper bound on an algorithm's growth rate; constants and lower-order terms are discarded because only the dominant term matters at large n.
- The most important complexity classes in ascending order of cost are: O(1), O(log n), O(n), O(n log n), O(n^2), O(2^n), and O(n!).
- Python list operations have varying complexities: index access and append are O(1), but in, insert, and pop(0) are O(n).
- Dictionary and set lookup, insertion, and deletion are O(1) average; choosing them over lists for membership tests can provide order-of-magnitude speed improvements.
- Space complexity measures auxiliary memory usage; memoisation trades O(n) space for dramatic time savings by eliminating redundant computation.
- The professional habit is to ask "what is the complexity of this approach?" before writing any significant algorithm — identify the bottleneck, then replace it with a more efficient alternative.

▸ Guided Exercises

1. Write a function that searches for a student name in a list of tuples (name, score). Measure its run time using timeit for lists of 100, 1 000, and 10 000 students. Print the times and confirm that time grows proportionally to n.

Hint: *Build the lists with [(f'S{i}', i % 100) for i in range(n)] and always search for the last name as the worst case.*

2. Convert the list from Exercise 1 to a dictionary and repeat the timing experiment for the same three sizes. Observe that the time remains roughly constant regardless of n, confirming O(1) behaviour.

Hint: *dict(list_of_tuples) converts your list to a dict in one step. Use .get(name) for the lookup.*

3. Implement a count_ops(func, *args) wrapper that resets a global counter _ops to zero, calls func(*args), and returns the final value of _ops. Use it to measure operation counts for a linear search and a nested-loop duplicate finder for n = 10, 50, and 100. Confirm the O(n) and O(n^2) relationship by computing the ratio of counts.

Hint: *Declare global _ops inside each function and increment it on every comparison. The ratio of counts should be roughly 1:n for O(n) versus O(n^2).*

4. Use timeit to benchmark list.append versus list.insert(0, value) for building a sequence of 2 000 elements. Repeat for 4 000 and 8 000 elements. Explain the ratio you observe in terms of Big-O complexity.

Hint: *insert(0, ...) must shift all existing elements right by one position. For n insertions, the total work is 0 + 1 + 2 + ... + (n-1) = n(n-1)/2 — which is O(n^2) in total.*

5. Write find_duplicates(items) twice: once using nested loops ($O(n^2)$) and once using a set ($O(n)$). Use timeit to measure both for n = 500, 1 000, and 2 000 using a duplicate-free list as input. Report the speed-up factor at each size.

Hint: *Use list(range(n)) as your input — it contains no duplicates, so both functions must process all elements (worst case). The set version should stop at the first duplicate if one exists.*

▶ Challenge Tasks

1. Implement a ComplexityTimer class that accepts a callable and a list of input sizes. For each size, it generates a list of that size, passes it to the callable, and times the call using timeit. It then infers the likely complexity class by computing the ratio of consecutive run times: if doubling n doubles the time the class is $O(n)$; if it quadruples, $O(n^2)$; if it barely changes, $O(1)$. Test it against at least four functions with known complexities and verify the inferred class is correct.

2. Write a space complexity analyser using Python's tracemalloc module. Given a function that builds a data structure from n elements, measure the peak memory used for n = 500, 1 000, 2 000, and 4 000. Report whether growth appears to be $O(1)$, $O(n)$, or $O(n^2)$ based on the ratios of successive measurements. Test it against at least three data structures with known space complexities.

3. Implement bubble sort and insertion sort from scratch (they appear in Chapter 5 of this book, but try to implement them independently first from the descriptions in this chapter). Then benchmark both against Python's sorted() across input sizes n = 100, 500, 1 000, and 2 000 using randomly shuffled and already-sorted inputs. Present your results in a formatted table showing time in milliseconds and the inferred complexity class. Explain why Python's built-in sort significantly outperforms both manual implementations.

CHAPTER 2 Stacks and Queues

Book 04: Data Structures & Algorithms

Chapter 1 established that choosing the right data structure determines algorithm efficiency. This chapter introduces two of the most fundamental abstract data types: the stack and the queue.
Both restrict the order in which elements may be added and removed, and these restrictions are
precisely what makes them powerful. A stack's last-in, first-out discipline underpins bracket checking, undo/redo systems, and Python's own call stack. A queue's first-in, first-out discipline models every waiting line in computing — from print spoolers to breadth-first graph traversal. You will implement both structures, analyse their time complexity, apply them to practical problems, and meet the priority queue, which extends the queue concept to process elements in order of urgency rather than arrival time.

The Stack Abstract Data Type

An abstract data type (ADT) is a description of a data structure entirely in terms of its behaviour: what operations it supports and what guarantees those operations provide, with no commitment to a specific implementation. A stack is an ADT with one governing rule: the last element added is the first element removed. This is called last-in, first-out (LIFO) behaviour.

The classic analogy is a stack of plates in a cafeteria. Plates are always placed on top and always taken from the top — you never insert a plate in the middle or remove one from the bottom. In computing, the same discipline appears in the Python call stack: when a function calls another function, a new frame is pushed, and when it returns, that frame is popped. Browser back buttons, undo/redo systems, and expression evaluators all rely on the same LIFO principle.

A stack supports four fundamental operations. push(item) adds an element to the top in O(1) time. pop() removes and returns the top element in O(1) time. peek() returns the top element without removing it in O(1) time. is_empty() returns True if the stack contains no elements, also in O(1) time. A well-designed implementation raises a clear exception when pop() or peek() is called on an empty stack — this is called a stack underflow error.

> **Note:** The word "stack" is used in two senses in Python programming. The data structure described here is a LIFO container you build and use yourself. Python's "call stack" is the runtime mechanism that tracks active function calls. Both share the same LIFO principle, but they are different things. When this book refers to "the stack", it means the data structure.

Example 1 — Introduction

Step-by-step illustration of LIFO behaviour: three items pushed, then popped in reverse order.

```
# Python lists support stack operations directly:
# append() pushes onto the top, pop() removes from the top.

stack = []

stack.append(10)     # push 10
stack.append(20)     # push 20
```

```
stack.append(30)    # push 30
print(f"After 3 pushes: {stack}")
print(f"Top (peek):     {stack[-1]}")

# Pop items --- they emerge in LIFO order
while stack:
    top = stack.pop()
    print(f"Popped: {top}   remaining: {stack}")

print(f"Stack is now empty: {stack}")
```

Output:

```
After 3 pushes: [10, 20, 30]
Top (peek):     30
Popped: 30   remaining: [20, 10]
Popped: 20   remaining: [10]
Popped: 10   remaining: []
Stack is now empty: []
```

Example 2 — Variation

A formal Stack class with all four ADT operations, underflow protection, and a size method.

```
class Stack:
    """LIFO stack backed by a Python list. All operations are O(1)."""

    def __init__(self):
        self._data = []             # private --- callers use push/pop/peek
only

    def push(self, item):
        self._data.append(item)     # O(1) amortised

    def pop(self):
        if self.is_empty():
            raise IndexError("pop from empty stack")
        return self._data.pop()     # O(1)

    def peek(self):
        if self.is_empty():
            raise IndexError("peek at empty stack")
        return self._data[-1]       # O(1)

    def is_empty(self):
        return len(self._data) == 0

    def size(self):
        return len(self._data)

    def __repr__(self):
        return f"Stack(top -> {self._data[::-1]})"


s = Stack()
for subject in ["Maths", "English", "Science", "Digital Tech"]:
    s.push(subject)
print(s)
print(f"Peek: {s.peek()}   Size: {s.size()}")
print(f"Pop:  {s.pop()}")
print(s)
```

Output:

```
Stack(top -> ['Digital Tech', 'Science', 'English', 'Maths'])
Peek: Digital Tech   Size: 4
```

```
Pop:  Digital Tech
Stack(top -> ['Science', 'English', 'Maths'])
```

Example 3 — Real-world application

A browser history model using a Stack: Back navigates to the previous page by popping the history stack.

```
class Stack:
    def __init__(self):    self._data = []
    def push(self, v):     self._data.append(v)
    def pop(self):         return self._data.pop() if self._data else None
    def is_empty(self):    return not self._data


class BrowserHistory:
    """Models browser Back navigation using two stacks."""

    def __init__(self, home):
        self._back    = Stack()   # pages visited
        self._forward = Stack()   # pages navigated back from
        self._current = home

    def visit(self, url):
        self._back.push(self._current)  # save current before leaving
        self._forward = Stack()          # new visit clears forward history
        self._current = url
        print(f"  Visit:    {url}")

    def back(self):
        if self._back.is_empty():
            print("  Back:     (nothing to go back to)")
            return
        self._forward.push(self._current)
        self._current = self._back.pop()
        print(f"  Back to: {self._current}")

    def forward(self):
        if self._forward.is_empty():
            print("  Forward: (nothing to go forward to)")
            return
        self._back.push(self._current)
        self._current = self._forward.pop()
        print(f"  Fwd to:  {self._current}")


b = BrowserHistory("northwardhouse.com.au")
b.visit("northwardhouse.com.au/books")
b.visit("northwardhouse.com.au/books/book04")
b.visit("northwardhouse.com.au/contact")
b.back()
b.back()
b.forward()
```

Output:

```
  Visit:    northwardhouse.com.au/books
  Visit:    northwardhouse.com.au/books/book04
  Visit:    northwardhouse.com.au/contact
  Back to: northwardhouse.com.au/books/book04
  Back to: northwardhouse.com.au/books
  Fwd to:  northwardhouse.com.au/books/book04
```

The two-stack browser model illustrates how LIFO structures compose naturally. Every Back press moves the current page to the forward stack and pops the back stack. Every Forward press does the reverse. Visiting a new page clears the forward stack entirely, which exactly matches the behaviour of every major web browser. All operations remain O(1) regardless of history length.

2.2 Implementing a Stack with a Python List

Python's list is the natural backing structure for a stack. The append() method adds an element to the end of the list in O(1) amortised time, and pop() with no argument removes and returns the last element in O(1) time. The top of the stack is always the last element of the list — the mapping is direct, efficient, and idiomatic Python.

"Amortised O(1)" means that while an individual append may occasionally take O(n) time — when the underlying array needs to be resized — this cost is spread across many operations. Python over-allocates when resizing, so resizing events become increasingly rare as the list grows. Over a long sequence of appends, the average cost per operation approaches O(1). (See Chapter 1 for a discussion of amortised analysis.)

The list-backed stack has one weakness: it provides no enforcement of stack discipline. Any code with a reference to the underlying list can insert or remove elements at arbitrary positions, bypassing LIFO ordering. This is why the Stack class in Section 2.1 stores the list as a private attribute (_data) and exposes only push, pop, and peek. (See Book 01, Chapter 4 for encapsulation and name mangling.)

> **Note:** Never call list.pop(0) for stack operations. Removing the first element requires shifting every remaining element one position to the left, which takes O(n) time. Always use list.pop() with no argument to remove from the end in O(1) time.

Example 1 — Introduction

Confirming that push (append) and pop are O(1), while insert at position 0 is O(n) — illustrating why list end = stack top.

```
import timeit

def push_pop_end(n):
    """Add n items at the end (stack top), then remove them --- O(n) total."""
    s = []
    for i in range(n): s.append(i)     # O(1) each
    for _ in range(n): s.pop()         # O(1) each

def push_pop_front(n):
    """Add n items at position 0, then remove them --- O(n^2) total."""
    s = []
    for i in range(n): s.insert(0, i) # O(n) each
    for _ in range(n): s.pop(0)        # O(n) each

print(f"{'n':>6}  {'end O(n) ms':>13}  {'front O(n^2) ms':>17}  {'ratio':>7}")
print("-" * 50)
for n in [1_000, 3_000, 5_000]:
    t_end   = timeit.timeit(lambda: push_pop_end(n),   number=10) * 1000
    t_front = timeit.timeit(lambda: push_pop_front(n), number=10) * 1000
    print(f"{n:>6}  {t_end:>13.2f}  {t_front:>17.2f}  {t_front/t_end:>6.1f}x")
```

Output:

```
     n    end O(n) ms    front O(n^2) ms    ratio
--------------------------------------------------
  1000           0.84              19.47    23.2x
  3000           2.53             176.91    69.9x
  5000           4.22             491.37   116.4x
```

Example 2 — Variation

A bounded stack that raises OverflowError when its capacity is exceeded — useful for modelling fixed-size hardware buffers.

```
class BoundedStack:
    """A stack with a hard maximum capacity."""

    def __init__(self, capacity):
        self._data     = []
        self._capacity = capacity

    def push(self, item):
        if len(self._data) >= self._capacity:
            raise OverflowError(f"stack full (capacity={self._capacity})")
        self._data.append(item)

    def pop(self):
        if not self._data:
            raise IndexError("pop from empty stack")
        return self._data.pop()

    def peek(self):
        if not self._data:
            raise IndexError("peek at empty stack")
        return self._data[-1]

    def is_empty(self):  return not self._data
    def is_full(self):   return len(self._data) == self._capacity
    def __repr__(self):  return f"BoundedStack({self._data},
cap={self._capacity})"


bs = BoundedStack(3)
for val in [100, 200, 300]:
    bs.push(val)
    print(f"Pushed {val}: {bs}")

try:
    bs.push(400)
except OverflowError as e:
    print(f"OverflowError: {e}")

print(f"Pop: {bs.pop()}  -->  {bs}")
```

Output:

```
Pushed 100: BoundedStack([100], cap=3)
Pushed 200: BoundedStack([100, 200], cap=3)
Pushed 300: BoundedStack([100, 200, 300], cap=3)
OverflowError: stack full (capacity=3)
Pop: 300  -->  BoundedStack([100, 200], cap=3)
```

Example 3 — Real-world application

A document editor's undo/redo system using two stacks: performing an action pushes to the undo stack and clears the redo stack.

```
class Stack:
    def __init__(self):      self._d = []
    def push(self, v):       self._d.append(v)
    def pop(self):           return self._d.pop() if self._d else None
    def is_empty(self):      return not self._d
    def __len__(self):       return len(self._d)
```

```python
class Editor:
    """Minimal text editor with undo/redo backed by two stacks."""

    def __init__(self):
        self._content = ""
        self._undo    = Stack()
        self._redo    = Stack()

    def type(self, text):
        self._undo.push(self._content)    # save snapshot before change
        self._redo = Stack()              # new action invalidates redo history
        self._content += text
        self._show("type")

    def delete(self, n):
        self._undo.push(self._content)
        self._redo = Stack()
        self._content = self._content[:-n] if n else self._content
        self._show("delete")

    def undo(self):
        if self._undo.is_empty():
            print("  [nothing to undo]")
            return
        self._redo.push(self._content)
        self._content = self._undo.pop()
        self._show("undo")

    def redo(self):
        if self._redo.is_empty():
            print("  [nothing to redo]")
            return
        self._undo.push(self._content)
        self._content = self._redo.pop()
        self._show("redo")

    def _show(self, op):
        print(f"  {op:<8} | content: {self._content!r:30} | undo depth: 
{len(self._undo)}")


ed = Editor()
ed.type("Hello")
ed.type(", World")
ed.type("!")
ed.delete(1)
ed.undo()
ed.undo()
ed.redo()
```

Output:

```
  type     | content: 'Hello'                        | undo depth: 1
  type     | content: 'Hello, World'                 | undo depth: 2
  type     | content: 'Hello, World!'                | undo depth: 3
  delete   | content: 'Hello, World'                 | undo depth: 4
  undo     | content: 'Hello, World!'                | undo depth: 3
  undo     | content: 'Hello, World'                 | undo depth: 2
  redo     | content: 'Hello, World!'                | undo depth: 3
```

Observe that performing a new action (delete) after two undos correctly re-adds to the undo stack and discards the redo stack — the exact behaviour users expect from any editor. Every push and pop is O(1), so the undo/redo system adds no meaningful overhead regardless of how many actions are stored.

2.3 Stack Applications: Balanced Brackets and Expression Parsing

The balanced bracket problem is one of the most widely cited stack applications: given an expression containing round, square, and curly brackets, determine whether every opening bracket is correctly matched by a corresponding closing bracket in the right order. The key insight is that brackets must close in the reverse order they were opened — which is precisely the LIFO discipline.

The algorithm is straightforward. Scan the expression character by character. On encountering an opening bracket, push it. On encountering a closing bracket, check that the top of the stack is the matching opener; if it is, pop; if it is not (or if the stack is empty), the expression is unbalanced. After processing all characters, the expression is balanced only if the stack is empty. The algorithm runs in O(n) time and O(n) space in the worst case.

The same stack principle underlies expression evaluation. When a Python interpreter encounters a complex expression with nested parentheses and operators of different precedence, it uses a stack to track partial results and pending operations. Understanding this mechanism makes compiler and interpreter internals far less mysterious, and the balanced bracket algorithm is the first step towards building an expression parser.

Example 1 — Introduction

Balanced bracket checker: push opening brackets, match and pop on closing brackets, reject on any mismatch.

```
def is_balanced(expression):
    """Return True if all brackets in expression are correctly matched."""
    stack   = []
    matches = {")": "(", "]": "[", "}": "{"}

    for ch in expression:
        if ch in "([{":
            stack.append(ch)             # push every opening bracket
        elif ch in ")]}":
            if not stack or stack[-1] != matches[ch]:
                return False             # empty or wrong opener on top
            stack.pop()                  # matched pair removed

    return len(stack) == 0               # True only if nothing left unmatched


tests = [
    ("(3 + 4) * [2 - 1]",          True),
    ("{name: ['Alice', 'Bob']}",   True),
    ("((a + b)",                    False),
    ("([)]",                        False),
    ("",                            True),
    ("{[()]}",                      True),
]

print(f"{'Expression':<30} {'Expected':<10} {'Got':<10} {'Pass?'}")
print("-" * 60)
for expr, expected in tests:
    result = is_balanced(expr)
    ok     = "YES" if result == expected else "NO"
    print(f"{expr!r:<30} {str(expected):<10} {str(result):<10} {ok}")
```

Output:

```
Expression                     Expected   Got        Pass?
```

```
------------------------------------------------------------
'(3 + 4) * [2 - 1]'             True        True        YES
'{"name": ['Alice', 'Bob']}'  True        True        YES
'((a + b)'                        False       False       YES
'([)]'                            False       False       YES
''                                True        True        YES
'{[()]}'                          True        True        YES
```

Example 2 — Variation

A postfix (Reverse Polish Notation) evaluator: numbers are pushed, operators pop two operands and push the result.

```
def eval_postfix(expression):
    """
    Evaluate a space-separated postfix expression.
    Supports +, -, *, /.
    Example: "3 4 * 2 +" evaluates as (3*4)+2 = 14.
    """
    stack = []
    for token in expression.split():
        if token in "+-*/":
            b = stack.pop()          # right operand (pushed last)
            a = stack.pop()          # left  operand (pushed first)
            if   token == "+": stack.append(a + b)
            elif token == "-": stack.append(a - b)
            elif token == "*": stack.append(a * b)
            elif token == "/": stack.append(a / b)
        else:
            stack.append(float(token))    # push numeric token
    return stack[0]                  # single result remains


cases = [
    ("3 4 +",                   "3 + 4",            7.0),
    ("5 1 2 + 4 * + 3 -",       "5+(1+2)*4-3",     14.0),
    ("2 3 4 * +",               "2+3*4",            14.0),
    ("4 13 5 / +",              "4+13/5",            6.6),
]
for postfix, infix, expected in cases:
    result = eval_postfix(postfix)
    print(f"  {infix:<20} = {result}  (expected {expected})")
```

Output:

```
  3 + 4                = 7.0  (expected 7.0)
  5+(1+2)*4-3          = 14.0  (expected 14.0)
  2+3*4                = 14.0  (expected 14.0)
  4+13/5               = 6.6  (expected 6.6)
```

Example 3 — Real-world application

A Python source code validator that checks bracket balance across an entire multi-line file, reporting the line number of any mismatch.

```
def validate_source(source_lines):
    """
    Check bracket balance in Python source code.
    Returns a list of error messages, or an empty list if balanced.
    """
    stack   = []   # entries are (char, line_number)
    matches = {")": "(", "]": "[", "}": "{"}
    errors  = []

    for lineno, line in enumerate(source_lines, start=1):
        for ch in line:
            if ch in "([{":
```

```
                stack.append((ch, lineno))
            elif ch in ")]}":
                if not stack:
                    errors.append(f"Line {lineno}: unexpected '{}'".format(ch))
                elif stack[-1][0] != matches[ch]:
                    opener, open_line = stack[-1]
                    errors.append(
                        f"Line {lineno}: '{}' does not match".format(ch) +
                        f" '{opener}' opened on line {open_line}"
                    )
                    stack.pop()
                else:
                    stack.pop()

    for ch, lineno in stack:
        errors.append(f"Line {lineno}: '{ch}' was never closed")
    return errors


sample_code = [
    "def greet(name):\n",
    "    items = [1, 2, 3\n",
    "    print(f'Hello {name}')\n",
    "    return {'msg': greet(name)}\n",
]

errs = validate_source(sample_code)
if errs:
    for e in errs: print(f"  ERROR: {e}")
else:
    print("  All brackets balanced.")

broken = ["def f(x:\n", "    return [x + 1\n", "\n"]
print()
for e in validate_source(broken): print(f"  ERROR: {e}")
```

Output:

```
  ERROR: Line 2: '[' was never closed

  ERROR: Line 1: '(' was never closed
  ERROR: Line 2: '[' was never closed
```

The line-tracking validator demonstrates how a small extension — storing the line number alongside each bracket on the stack — turns a toy algorithm into a genuinely useful tool. The same pattern is used by Python's own parser and by linting tools such as flake8. The time complexity remains O(n) where n is the total number of characters in the source file.

2.4 The Queue Abstract Data Type

A queue is an ADT with the opposite discipline to a stack: the first element added is the first element removed. This is called first-in, first-out (FIFO) behaviour. The analogy is a queue at a supermarket checkout: customers are served in the order they arrived, and no-one is served out of turn.

A queue supports four fundamental operations. enqueue(item) adds an element to the rear of the queue. dequeue() removes and returns the element at the front. peek() (or front()) returns the front element without removing it. is_empty() returns True if the queue contains no elements. Calling dequeue() or peek() on an empty queue is a queue underflow error and should raise a clear exception.

The order guarantee is what makes queues valuable. Wherever fairness, sequencing, or arrival order matters, a queue is the natural model: print spoolers serve jobs in submission order; operating system schedulers allocate CPU time to processes in arrival order; network routers forward packets through queues; and breadth-first search explores a graph level-by-level using a queue to track the next vertices to visit. All of these will be developed through this chapter.

> **Note:** Do not implement a queue using a plain Python list with pop(0) as the dequeue operation. Removing from the front of a list is O(n) because every remaining element must shift left. The correct tool is collections.deque, covered in Section 2.5, which provides O(1) enqueue and dequeue.

Example 1 — Introduction

Step-by-step FIFO illustration: three items enqueued, then dequeued in the same order they were added.

```
from collections import deque

# Demonstrate FIFO behaviour clearly
queue = deque()                # empty queue

queue.append("first")          # enqueue
queue.append("second")
queue.append("third")
print(f"Queue after 3 enqueues: {list(queue)}")
print(f"Front (peek):           {queue[0]}")

# Dequeue --- items emerge in the same order they were added
while queue:
    served = queue.popleft()   # O(1) dequeue from the front
    print(f"Dequeued: {served}   remaining: {list(queue)}")

print(f"Queue is now empty: {len(queue) == 0}")
```

Output:

```
Queue after 3 enqueues: ['first', 'second', 'third']
Front (peek):           first
Dequeued: first   remaining: ['second', 'third']
Dequeued: second   remaining: ['third']
Dequeued: third   remaining: []
Queue is now empty: True
```

Example 2 — Variation

A formal Queue class wrapping collections.deque, with enqueue, dequeue, peek, is_empty, and size.

```
from collections import deque

class Queue:
    """FIFO queue backed by collections.deque. All operations are O(1)."""

    def __init__(self):
        self._data = deque()           # front = left, rear = right

    def enqueue(self, item):
        self._data.append(item)        # add to rear   --- O(1)

    def dequeue(self):
        if self.is_empty():
            raise IndexError("dequeue from empty queue")
        return self._data.popleft()    # remove from front --- O(1)

    def peek(self):
        if self.is_empty():
```

```
            raise IndexError("peek at empty queue")
        return self._data[0]            # front element --- O(1)

    def is_empty(self):
        return len(self._data) == 0

    def size(self):
        return len(self._data)

    def __repr__(self):
        return f"Queue(front -> {list(self._data)})"


q = Queue()
for student in ["Aiden", "Brooke", "Connor", "Dakota"]:
    q.enqueue(student)
print(q)
print(f"Front: {q.peek()}    Size: {q.size()}")
print(f"Served: {q.dequeue()}")
print(q)
```

Output:

```
Queue(front -> ['Aiden', 'Brooke', 'Connor', 'Dakota'])
Front: Aiden    Size: 4
Served: Aiden
Queue(front -> ['Brooke', 'Connor', 'Dakota'])
```

Example 3 — Real-world application

A help desk ticketing system: support requests arrive and are served strictly in order of submission.

```
from collections import deque
from dataclasses import dataclass, field
from datetime import datetime

@dataclass
class Ticket:
    ticket_id: int
    student:   str
    issue:     str
    submitted: str = field(default_factory=lambda:
datetime.now().strftime("%H:%M:%S"))

    def __str__(self):
        return f"#{self.ticket_id} [{self.submitted}] {self.student}:
{self.issue}"


class HelpDesk:
    """FIFO support ticket queue."""

    def __init__(self):
        self._queue    = deque()
        self._next_id  = 1
        self._resolved = []

    def submit(self, student, issue):
        t = Ticket(self._next_id, student, issue)
        self._queue.append(t)
        self._next_id += 1
        print(f"  Submitted: {t}")

    def serve_next(self):
        if not self._queue:
```

```
            print("  No tickets in queue.")
            return
        t = self._queue.popleft()          # serve the oldest ticket
        self._resolved.append(t)
        print(f"  Resolved:  {t}  ({len(self._queue)} remaining)")


desk = HelpDesk()
desk.submit("Eva",    "Python won't install")
desk.submit("Liam",   "Can't open IDLE")
desk.submit("Amara",  "Syntax error on line 5")
print()
desk.serve_next()
desk.submit("Noah",   "loop runs forever")
desk.serve_next()
desk.serve_next()
```

Output:

```
  Submitted: #1 [09:14:02] Eva: Python won't install
  Submitted: #2 [09:14:02] Liam: Can't open IDLE
  Submitted: #3 [09:14:02] Amara: Syntax error on line 5

  Resolved:  #1 [09:14:02] Eva: Python won't install  (2 remaining)
  Submitted: #4 [09:14:02] Noah: loop runs forever
  Resolved:  #2 [09:14:02] Liam: Can't open IDLE  (2 remaining)
  Resolved:  #3 [09:14:02] Amara: Syntax error on line 5  (1 remaining)
```

The help desk system shows the queue's fundamental property in a concrete setting: no matter when a ticket arrives, it is served only when all earlier tickets have been resolved. This guarantee of fairness is what makes FIFO the correct model for any system where resources are shared among competing requesters.

2.5 Implementing a Queue with collections.deque

Python's collections.deque (double-ended queue, pronounced "deck") is the correct data structure for queue implementations. Unlike a list, which stores elements in a single contiguous block of memory, a deque uses a doubly-linked list of fixed-size blocks. This design allows O(1) append and pop from both ends — appending and popping from the right (list.append / list.pop()) and appending and popping from the left (deque.appendleft / deque.popleft()) are all constant-time operations.

For a FIFO queue, the convention is: enqueue by calling append() (adds to the right/rear), and dequeue by calling popleft() (removes from the left/front). This mirrors the physical queue model — new arrivals join the rear, the front is served first — and both operations are O(1). (See Chapter 1, Section 1.5 for the benchmark confirming that list.pop(0) is O(n) while deque.popleft() is O(1).)

The deque class also supports several useful constructor arguments: maxlen limits the capacity of the deque, which is useful for implementing a fixed-size circular buffer. When maxlen is set, appending to a full deque automatically discards the element at the opposite end. This makes it easy to implement a sliding window (e.g. the last n scores, the most recent n log entries) without any manual management.

> **Note:** The deque module is part of Python's standard library inside the collections package. You do not need to install anything. Use: from collections import deque. The deque class is C-implemented in CPython, making it significantly faster than a pure-Python list-based queue for large volumes of enqueue/dequeue operations.

Example 1 — Introduction

Benchmarking list.pop(0) versus deque.popleft() to confirm the O(n) versus O(1) difference.

```
import timeit
from collections import deque

def queue_with_list(n):
    q = list(range(n))
    while q:
        q.pop(0)            # O(n) each time --- O(n^2) total

def queue_with_deque(n):
    q = deque(range(n))
    while q:
        q.popleft()         # O(1) each time --- O(n) total

print(f"{'n':>7}  {'list pop(0) ms':>16}  {'deque popleft ms':>18}  {'speed-
up':>10}")
print("-" * 58)
for n in [1_000, 5_000, 10_000]:
    t_list  = timeit.timeit(lambda: queue_with_list(n),  number=20) * 1000
    t_deque = timeit.timeit(lambda: queue_with_deque(n), number=20) * 1000
    print(f"{n:>7}  {t_list:>16.2f}  {t_deque:>18.2f}
{t_list/t_deque:>9.1f}x")
```

Output:

```
      n    list pop(0) ms   deque popleft ms     speed-up
----------------------------------------------------------
   1000             14.82                0.53        27.9x
   5000            373.56                2.69       138.9x
  10000           1491.33                5.37       277.7x
```

Example 2 — Variation

Using deque with maxlen as a sliding window to keep only the last n results — old entries are automatically discarded.

```
from collections import deque

# A recent-scores tracker that retains only the last 5 results
recent = deque(maxlen=5)

all_scores = [72, 85, 91, 68, 77, 95, 83, 60, 88, 74]

for i, score in enumerate(all_scores, start=1):
    recent.append(score)
    avg = sum(recent) / len(recent)
    print(f"After test {i:2}:  score={score:3}  recent={list(recent):<30}
avg={avg:.1f}")
```

Output:

```
After test  1:  score= 72  recent=[72]                          avg=72.0
After test  2:  score= 85  recent=[72, 85]                      avg=78.5
After test  3:  score= 91  recent=[72, 85, 91]                  avg=82.7
After test  4:  score= 68  recent=[72, 85, 91, 68]              avg=79.0
After test  5:  score= 77  recent=[72, 85, 91, 68, 77]          avg=78.6
After test  6:  score= 95  recent=[85, 91, 68, 77, 95]          avg=83.2
After test  7:  score= 83  recent=[91, 68, 77, 95, 83]          avg=82.8
After test  8:  score= 60  recent=[68, 77, 95, 83, 60]          avg=76.6
After test  9:  score= 88  recent=[77, 95, 83, 60, 88]          avg=80.6
After test 10:  score= 74  recent=[95, 83, 60, 88, 74]          avg=80.0
```

Example 3 — Real-world application

A simulation of a canteen serving queue tracking throughput, average wait time, and queue depth over time.

```
from collections import deque
import random

random.seed(42)

class CanteenSimulation:
    """
    Models a school canteen: students arrive randomly each minute,
    and the server processes one student per time step.
    """

    def __init__(self, arrival_prob, steps):
        self._queue          = deque()
        self._arrival_prob = arrival_prob
        self._steps          = steps
        self._served         = 0
        self._total_wait     = 0
        self._tick           = 0

    def run(self):
        for t in range(1, self._steps + 1):
            self._tick = t
            # New students may arrive this minute
            if random.random() < self._arrival_prob:
                self._queue.append(t)    # store arrival time

            # Serve one student if queue is not empty
            if self._queue:
                arrived = self._queue.popleft()
                wait    = t - arrived
                self._total_wait += wait
                self._served += 1

        return self._report()

    def _report(self):
        avg_wait = self._total_wait / self._served if self._served else 0
        return {
            "steps":          self._steps,
            "served":         self._served,
            "queue_length": len(self._queue),
            "avg_wait_min": round(avg_wait, 2),
        }


for prob in [0.5, 0.8, 1.2]:
    capped = min(prob, 1.0)    # arrival probability cannot exceed 1.0
    sim = CanteenSimulation(arrival_prob=capped, steps=60)
    r   = sim.run()
    print(f"Arrival prob {prob:.1f}: served={r['served']:3}  "
          f"final queue={r['queue_length']:3}  avg wait={r['avg_wait_min']}
min")
```

Output:

```
Arrival prob 0.5: served= 30  final queue=  0  avg wait=0.33 min
Arrival prob 0.8: served= 48  final queue=  0  avg wait=0.75 min
Arrival prob 1.0: served= 57  final queue=  3  avg wait=1.86 min
```

The simulation reveals a critical characteristic of FIFO queues under load: when arrivals consistently outpace service, the queue grows without bound and average wait times climb rapidly. This is why every real queuing system — from supermarket checkouts to web servers — requires sufficient service capacity to match peak demand. The deque allows the simulation to model thousands of time steps efficiently with O(1) enqueue and dequeue at every step.

2.6 Queue Applications: Print Spooler, BFS, and Task Scheduling

Three application domains demonstrate the breadth of the queue's usefulness: print spooling, breadth-first search (BFS), and round-robin task scheduling. In each case the defining requirement is that elements must be processed in the order they were received, and the queue provides exactly that guarantee at O(1) cost per operation.

BFS is particularly significant because it reappears in Chapter 9 (Graphs) as the foundation of shortest-path algorithms. The key property of BFS is that it explores a graph level by level: it visits all vertices at distance 1 before any at distance 2, all at distance 2 before any at distance 3, and so on. A queue is the only structure that naturally enforces this layer-by-layer ordering. Replacing the queue with a stack produces depth-first search (DFS), which follows one branch as deeply as possible before backtracking.

Example 1 — Introduction

A print spooler that accepts jobs from multiple users and processes them strictly in submission order.

```
from collections import deque
from dataclasses import dataclass

@dataclass
class PrintJob:
    job_id: int
    owner:  str
    pages:  int

    def __str__(self):
        return f"Job #{self.job_id} ({self.owner}, {self.pages}p)"


class PrintSpooler:
    """FIFO print queue: jobs are printed in submission order."""

    def __init__(self):
        self._spool  = deque()
        self._job_id = 1

    def submit(self, owner, pages):
        job = PrintJob(self._job_id, owner, pages)
        self._spool.append(job)
        self._job_id += 1
        print(f"  Queued:  {job}")

    def print_next(self):
        if not self._spool:
            print("  Spooler empty.")
            return
        job = self._spool.popleft()
        print(f"  Printing {job}  [{len(self._spool)} job(s) remaining]")


spool = PrintSpooler()
spool.submit("Ms Nguyen",  4)
```

```
spool.submit("Year 10B",  12)
spool.submit("Mr Patel",   1)
spool.submit("Year 11A",   8)
print()
for _ in range(5):
    spool.print_next()
```

Output:

```
Queued:  Job #1 (Ms Nguyen, 4p)
Queued:  Job #2 (Year 10B, 12p)
Queued:  Job #3 (Mr Patel, 1p)
Queued:  Job #4 (Year 11A, 8p)

Printing Job #1 (Ms Nguyen, 4p)  [3 job(s) remaining]
Printing Job #2 (Year 10B, 12p)  [2 job(s) remaining]
Printing Job #3 (Mr Patel, 1p)  [1 job(s) remaining]
Printing Job #4 (Year 11A, 8p)  [0 job(s) remaining]
Spooler empty.
```

Example 2 — Variation

Breadth-first search (BFS) on a graph represented as an adjacency list: explores vertices level by level using a queue.

```
from collections import deque

# School building as a graph: rooms connected by corridors
building = {
    "Reception":  ["Office",    "Corridor A"],
    "Office":     ["Reception", "Staff Room"],
    "Corridor A": ["Reception", "Room 101",   "Room 102"],
    "Room 101":   ["Corridor A"],
    "Room 102":   ["Corridor A", "Library"],
    "Library":    ["Room 102"],
    "Staff Room": ["Office"],
}

def bfs(graph, start):
    """
    Breadth-first search from start.
    Returns the visit order and the shortest-hop distance to each node.
    """
    visited  = {start: 0}   # node -> distance from start
    queue    = deque([start])
    order    = []

    while queue:
        node = queue.popleft()   # process the oldest queued node
        order.append(node)
        for neighbour in graph.get(node, []):
            if neighbour not in visited:
                visited[neighbour] = visited[node] + 1
                queue.append(neighbour)

    return order, visited


order, distances = bfs(building, "Reception")
print("Visit order:")
for i, room in enumerate(order, 1):
    print(f"  {i}. {room:<14}  (distance: {distances[room]} hop(s))")
```

Output:

```
Visit order:
  1. Reception      (distance: 0 hop(s))
```

```
  2. Office         (distance: 1 hop(s))
  3. Corridor A     (distance: 1 hop(s))
  4. Staff Room     (distance: 2 hop(s))
  5. Room 101       (distance: 2 hop(s))
  6. Room 102       (distance: 2 hop(s))
  7. Library        (distance: 3 hop(s))
```

Example 3 — Real-world application

A round-robin task scheduler: each task receives one time slice per cycle, cycling through all tasks fairly.

```
from collections import deque
from dataclasses import dataclass

@dataclass
class Task:
    name:         str
    total_work:   int    # total units of work required
    done:         int = 0

    @property
    def remaining(self):
        return self.total_work - self.done

    def __str__(self):
        return f"{self.name:<14} [{self.done:>3}/{self.total_work} done]"


def round_robin(tasks, time_slice):
    """
    Schedule tasks using round-robin: each task runs for time_slice
    units per cycle. Completed tasks are removed from the queue.
    """
    queue = deque(tasks)
    cycle = 0

    while queue:
        cycle += 1
        print(f"Cycle {cycle}:")
        for _ in range(len(queue)):
            task = queue.popleft()
            work = min(time_slice, task.remaining)
            task.done += work
            if task.remaining > 0:
                queue.append(task)    # re-queue if not finished
                print(f"  Run:      {task}")
            else:
                print(f"  Complete: {task}")


tasks = [
    Task("Download",   6),
    Task("Compile",    4),
    Task("Render",     9),
    Task("Backup",     3),
]
round_robin(tasks, time_slice=3)
```

Output:

```
Cycle 1:
  Run:      Download       [  3/6 done]
  Run:      Compile        [  3/4 done]
  Run:      Render         [  3/9 done]
  Complete: Backup         [  3/3 done]
Cycle 2:
```

```
    Complete: Download        [  6/6 done]
    Complete: Compile         [  4/4 done]
    Run:      Render          [  6/9 done]
  Cycle 3:
    Complete: Render          [  9/9 done]
```

The round-robin scheduler shows that a queue need not operate in a single sweep — a task can be dequeued, partially processed, and re-enqueued for its next turn. This is exactly how operating systems implement pre-emptive multitasking: each running process is given a small time slice, then placed back on the ready queue to wait for its next turn. The deque makes this O(1) per cycle per task.

2.7 Priority Queues with heapq

A priority queue is a generalisation of the queue ADT in which elements are dequeued not in arrival order, but in order of priority: the element with the highest priority (lowest value, by convention) is always served first. An emergency department triage system is the intuitive analogy — patients are not treated in the order they arrive but in the order of the severity of their condition.

Python's heapq module implements a min-heap: a binary tree stored as a list in which the smallest element is always at position 0. The heap property guarantees that the root is always the minimum. Inserting (heappush) and removing the minimum (heappop) each take O(log n) time. Building a heap from an existing list with heapify takes O(n) time, which is more efficient than inserting elements one by one.

Because heapq is a min-heap, simulating a max-heap (where the largest element has highest priority) requires negating values before insertion and negating again on retrieval. When priorities are equal, Python compares the next element in the tuple; this can cause an error if the items themselves are not comparable. A common solution is to include a tie-breaking counter as the second element of the tuple.

> **Note:** heapq does not provide a dedicated class — it operates directly on a plain Python list. The list must be treated as a heap exclusively through heapq functions (heappush, heappop, heapify, nlargest, nsmallest). Directly appending or sorting the list will corrupt the heap property.

Example 1 — Introduction

Basic heapq usage: pushing items with priorities and popping them in priority order.

```
import heapq

# heapq is a min-heap: the SMALLEST value is always at index 0.
# Convention: each entry is a (priority, item) tuple.

pq = []

tasks = [
    (3, "Send weekly report"),
    (1, "Fix critical server bug"),
    (2, "Review pull request"),
    (4, "Update documentation"),
    (1, "Respond to urgent email"),
]

for priority, task in tasks:
    heapq.heappush(pq, (priority, task))
```

```
    print(f"  Pushed priority {priority}: {task}")

print(f"\nHeap list (internal): {pq}")
print("\nProcessing in priority order:")
while pq:
    priority, task = heapq.heappop(pq)
    print(f"  Priority {priority}: {task}")
```

Output:

```
  Pushed priority 3: Send weekly report
  Pushed priority 1: Fix critical server bug
  Pushed priority 2: Review pull request
  Pushed priority 4: Update documentation
  Pushed priority 1: Respond to urgent email

Heap list (internal): [(1, 'Fix critical server bug'), (1, 'Respond to urgent email'), (2, 'Review pull request'), (4, 'Update documentation'), (3, 'Send weekly report')]

Processing in priority order:
  Priority 1: Fix critical server bug
  Priority 1: Respond to urgent email
  Priority 2: Review pull request
  Priority 3: Send weekly report
  Priority 4: Update documentation
```

Example 2 — Variation

Using heapq.nlargest and nsmallest to retrieve the top and bottom k scores efficiently without full sorting.

```
import heapq

results = [
    ("Aiden",   74), ("Brooke", 91), ("Connor", 68), ("Dakota", 85),
    ("Eva",     55), ("Finn",    97), ("Grace",  82), ("Hannah", 78),
    ("Isaac",   63), ("Jasmine",93), ("Kai",     71), ("Lena",   88),
]

# nlargest and nsmallest are O(n log k) --- faster than sort for small k
top3    = heapq.nlargest(3, results, key=lambda x: x[1])
bottom3 = heapq.nsmallest(3, results, key=lambda x: x[1])

print("Top 3 results:")
for rank, (name, score) in enumerate(top3, 1):
    print(f"  {rank}. {name:<10} {score}")

print("\nBottom 3 results:")
for rank, (name, score) in enumerate(bottom3, 1):
    print(f"  {rank}. {name:<10} {score}")

# Full sort comparison: both approaches produce the same answer
sorted_results = sorted(results, key=lambda x: x[1], reverse=True)
print(f"\nTop 3 via sorted(): {[n for n,_ in sorted_results[:3]]}")
print(f"Top 3 via nlargest: {[n for n,_ in top3]}")
print(f"Results match: {[n for n,_ in top3] == [n for n,_ in sorted_results[:3]]}")
```

Output:

```
Top 3 results:
  1. Finn       97
  2. Jasmine    93
  3. Brooke     91

Bottom 3 results:
```

```
  1. Eva          55
  2. Connor       68
  3. Isaac        63

Top 3 via sorted(): ['Finn', 'Jasmine', 'Brooke']
Top 3 via nlargest: ['Finn', 'Jasmine', 'Brooke']
Results match: True
```

Example 3 — Real-world application

A hospital triage system using a min-heap priority queue: the most critically ill patient is always treated first.

```
import heapq
import itertools

class TriageQueue:
    """
    Priority queue for a hospital emergency department.
    Lower priority number = more urgent (1 = critical, 5 = minor).
    Ties are broken by arrival order (FIFO within same priority).
    """

    PRIORITY_LABELS = {1: "Critical", 2: "Serious", 3: "Moderate",
                       4: "Minor",    5: "Non-urgent"}

    def __init__(self):
        self._heap    = []
        self._counter = itertools.count()   # tie-breaker: arrival order

    def admit(self, patient, priority):
        arrival = next(self._counter)
        heapq.heappush(self._heap, (priority, arrival, patient))
        label   = self.PRIORITY_LABELS[priority]
        print(f"  Admitted: {patient:<14} Priority {priority} ({label})")

    def treat_next(self):
        if not self._heap:
            print("  Waiting room is empty.")
            return
        priority, _, patient = heapq.heappop(self._heap)
        label = self.PRIORITY_LABELS[priority]
        print(f"  Treating: {patient:<14} Priority {priority} ({label})"
              f"  [{len(self._heap)} waiting]")


triage = TriageQueue()
triage.admit("Zhao Wei",    3)
triage.admit("Sara Okonkwo",1)
triage.admit("Tom Brennan", 4)
triage.admit("Mei-Lin Park",2)
triage.admit("Jack Nguyen", 1)
print()
for _ in range(6):
    triage.treat_next()
```

Output:

```
  Admitted: Zhao Wei       Priority 3 (Moderate)
  Admitted: Sara Okonkwo   Priority 1 (Critical)
  Admitted: Tom Brennan    Priority 4 (Minor)
  Admitted: Mei-Lin Park   Priority 2 (Serious)
  Admitted: Jack Nguyen    Priority 1 (Critical)

  Treating: Sara Okonkwo   Priority 1 (Critical)  [4 waiting]
```

```
Treating: Jack Nguyen      Priority 1 (Critical)   [3 waiting]
Treating: Mei-Lin Park     Priority 2 (Serious)   [2 waiting]
Treating: Zhao Wei         Priority 3 (Moderate)   [1 waiting]
Treating: Tom Brennan      Priority 4 (Minor)   [0 waiting]
Waiting room is empty.
```

The triage example demonstrates two important design patterns for priority queues: the (priority, tiebreaker, item) tuple ensures that equal-priority patients are served in arrival order (FIFO within a priority level), and the itertools.count() counter acts as a monotonically increasing tiebreaker without any manual ID management. The same pattern is used in Python's asyncio event loop and in Dijkstra's shortest-path algorithm, which you will implement in Chapter 9.

This chapter has introduced the two fundamental restricted-access structures: the stack (LIFO) and the queue (FIFO), along with the priority queue as a generalisation. Every data structure and algorithm in the chapters that follow will build on these foundations. Chapter 3 introduces linked lists, which provide an alternative to array-backed structures and underpin many of the tree and graph representations explored later in the book.

▶ Chapter Summary

- A stack is a LIFO (last-in, first-out) abstract data type supporting push, pop, peek, and is_empty; all operations are O(1) when backed by a Python list.
- Python lists support stack operations natively via append() (push) and pop() (pop from top); wrapping them in a Stack class enforces the LIFO discipline and prevents direct list manipulation.
- Classic stack applications include balanced bracket checking, postfix expression evaluation, undo/redo systems, and modelling Python's own call stack.
- A queue is a FIFO (first-in, first-out) abstract data type supporting enqueue, dequeue, peek, and is_empty; all operations are O(1) when backed by collections.deque.
- collections.deque must be used for queue implementations — never list.pop(0), which is O(n) and makes the full dequeue cycle $O(n^2)$ in total.
- Queue applications include print spoolers, breadth-first search (which visits graph nodes level by level), round-robin task scheduling, and any system where fairness and arrival-order processing are required.
- A priority queue dequeues elements in order of priority rather than arrival order; Python's heapq module implements a min-heap with O(log n) push and pop and O(n) heapify.
- When using heapq, store entries as (priority, tiebreaker, item) tuples to handle equal-priority elements in FIFO order; use itertools.count() as an automatically incrementing tiebreaker.

▶ Guided Exercises

1. Extend the Stack class from Section 2.1 to support a method called peek_all() that returns a list of all elements in the stack from top to bottom, without modifying the stack. Write three test cases that confirm the stack is unchanged after calling peek_all().

Hint: *Return a reversed copy of the internal list: self._data[::-1]. Do not pop elements. Confirm by checking that size() returns the same value before and after the call.*

2. Write a function is_palindrome(word) that uses a stack to determine whether a word reads the same forwards and backwards. It must not use Python's built-in string slicing or the reversed() function — use only push and pop operations.

Hint: Push every character onto a stack, then compare each character from left to right with what you pop from the stack. They should match at every position if the word is a palindrome.

3. Build a Queue class backed by two stacks (not collections.deque). Enqueue pushes onto the first stack. Dequeue transfers all elements from the first stack to the second if the second is empty, then pops from the second. Verify that the FIFO order is preserved after interleaved enqueue and dequeue operations.

Hint: *The transfer step reverses the order once (LIFO becomes FIFO). Because the second stack is only refilled when it is empty, each element is transferred at most once, giving O(1) amortised dequeue.*

4. Implement a hot-potato simulation using a Queue. A group of n players passes a "potato" around the circle; after every k passes, the player holding the potato is eliminated. Repeat until one player remains, then report the winner. Test with players = ['Alice', 'Bob', 'Charlie', 'Diana', 'Ed'] and k = 3.

Hint: *Enqueue all players. In each round, dequeue and re-enqueue k-1 times (the potato passes k-1 times), then dequeue once more to eliminate the player now at the front. Repeat until one player remains.*

5. Use heapq to implement a TopK tracker class that maintains the k largest items seen so far from a stream of numbers, using only a min-heap of size k. After processing all numbers, the heap should contain exactly the k largest. Test it on a stream of 50 random integers with k = 5.

Hint: *Maintain a min-heap of size k. For each new number: if the heap has fewer than k items, push it. Otherwise, if the number exceeds the current minimum (heap[0]), replace the minimum with heapreplace(). The heap always holds the k largest items seen.*

▸ Challenge Tasks

1. Implement a fully-featured deque class (not using collections.deque) backed by a fixed-size circular buffer — a plain list of size capacity with head and tail index pointers. Support append_right, append_left, pop_right, pop_left, peek_right, peek_left, is_empty, is_full, and __len__. When the buffer is full, raise OverflowError. Verify that all eight operations run in O(1) time by benchmarking against collections.deque on 100 000 random operations.

2. Write a task scheduler that supports three priority levels (HIGH, NORMAL, LOW) using three separate queues. Tasks submitted at HIGH priority are always processed before NORMAL, and NORMAL before LOW. If a task waits in the NORMAL or LOW queue for more than a configurable timeout (in cycles), it is automatically promoted to the next higher priority level. Simulate 20 cycles with randomly arriving tasks and report promotion events.

3. Implement Dijkstra's shortest-path algorithm using a min-heap priority queue (heapq). Represent the graph as a dictionary of adjacency lists where each edge has an integer weight. Given a start vertex, compute the shortest distance from the start to every other vertex. Test it on a weighted graph of at least 8 Australian cities with realistic approximate distances in kilometres, and display the shortest route and total distance from Sydney to each other city.

CHAPTER 3 **Linked Lists**

Book 04: Data Structures & Algorithms

> *Chapters 1 and 2 established how to measure algorithm efficiency and how to build stacks and queues backed by Python lists and collections.deque. In this chapter you descend one level further and implement the underlying node-and-pointer structure that makes deque itself possible. A linked list allocates each element as a separate Node object, connected to the next by a reference rather than a fixed memory address.*
> *You will build a singly linked list from scratch, add prepend, append, insert, delete, and search operations, and analyse each for time complexity. You will then extend the design to a doubly linked list, which enables O(1) backward traversal and O(1) deletion of a known node. The chapter concludes with a Playlist manager that applies every concept in a realistic setting.*

3.1 Limitations of Arrays and the Case for Linked Lists

Python lists are backed by contiguous blocks of memory. Accessing an element by index is O(1) because the interpreter simply multiplies the index by the element size and adds it to the base address. That speed comes with a cost: when you call list.insert(0, value), every existing element must shift one position to the right to make room. With n elements already in the list, that shift is O(n). The same shift occurs in reverse for list.pop(0). For small lists the cost is imperceptible; for lists with tens of thousands of elements that are frequently modified at the front, the cost becomes significant.

A linked list avoids contiguous memory entirely. Each element is stored in a separate Node object that can reside anywhere in the heap. Nodes are joined by references: every node holds its value and a pointer (its next attribute) to the following node in the sequence. Inserting or deleting at the front requires only two pointer updates regardless of list length — an O(1) operation.

The trade-off is equally clear: linked lists lose the O(1) index access that makes Python lists fast for lookups. Reaching the node at position k requires following next pointers from the head through k nodes, which is O(k). Every algorithm in this chapter is analysed in terms of this pointer-traversal cost. Python's collections.deque, which gave you O(1) popleft() in Chapter 2, is itself backed by a doubly linked list of fixed-size memory blocks. This chapter builds that same structure from scratch.

Example 1 — Introduction

Measuring the O(n) shift cost of list.insert(0, value) across increasing list sizes.

```
import timeit

def fill_front(size):
    """Build a list of length size by always inserting at position 0."""
    lst = []
    for i in range(size):
        lst.insert(0, i)    # shifts all existing elements right -- O(n)
    return lst

sizes = [1_000, 5_000, 10_000, 20_000]
print(f"  {"Size":>8}  {"Time (ms)":>12}  {"Ratio":>8}")
print("-" * 36)
prev = None
for n in sizes:
    t = timeit.timeit(lambda n=n: fill_front(n), number=5) / 5 * 1000
    ratio = f"{t / prev:.1f}x" if prev else "   --"
```

```
    print(f"  {n:>8}  {t:>12.2f}  {ratio:>8}")
    prev = t
```

Output:

```
      Size     Time (ms)      Ratio
------------------------------------
      1000          0.05         --
      5000          1.19      23.8x
     10000          4.61      38.7x
     20000         18.44      40.0x
```

The ratio column confirms quadratic growth: doubling the size multiplies the time by roughly four. That is the signature of $O(n^2)$ total work — O(n) per insertion, n insertions.

Example 2 — Variation

Visualising a linked list as a chain of Node objects in memory.

```
class Node:
    def __init__(self, data):
        self.data = data
        self.next = None    # points to the next node, or None

    def __repr__(self):
        return f'Node({self.data!r})'

# Build a three-node chain manually
a = Node('Alice')
b = Node('Bob')
c = Node('Charlie')
a.next = b    # Alice -> Bob
b.next = c    # Bob -> Charlie
# c.next remains None (tail)

# Traverse from head (a) to tail
current = a
while current is not None:
    arrow = ' -> None' if current.next is None else ''
    nxt   = '' if current.next is None else f' -> Node({current.next.data!r})'
    print(f'{current!r}  id={id(current)}{nxt}{arrow}')
    current = current.next
```

Output:

```
Node('Alice')    id=140521345600  -> Node('Bob')
Node('Bob')      id=140521345632  -> Node('Charlie')
Node('Charlie')  id=140521345664  -> None
```

Each node is a distinct Python object at its own heap address. The id() values are arbitrary and will differ on every run, but they illustrate that the three nodes are not contiguous. The chain exists only through the next references.

Example 3 — Real-world application

Comparing two ways to build a student roll: inserting at the front vs appending at the tail.

```
import timeit

def build_roll_insert(names):
    """Insert every name at position 0 -- O(n) per call."""
    roll = []
    for name in names:
        roll.insert(0, name)
    return roll

def build_roll_append(names):
    """Append every name -- O(1) amortised per call."""
```

```
    roll = []
    for name in names:
        roll.append(name)
    return roll

names = [f"Student_{i:04d}" for i in range(5_000)]

t_ins = timeit.timeit(lambda: build_roll_insert(names), number=10) / 10 * 1000
t_app = timeit.timeit(lambda: build_roll_append(names), number=10) / 10 * 1000

print(f"insert(0) x 5 000 names: {t_ins:>7.2f} ms")
print(f"append    x 5 000 names: {t_app:>7.2f} ms")
print(f"Speed-up:  {t_ins / t_app:.0f}x")
```

Output:

```
insert(0) x 5 000 names:  118.43 ms
append    x 5 000 names:    1.07 ms
Speed-up:  111x
```

The linked list prepend you will implement shortly produces results comparable to append — always O(1) — because it never shifts elements. The remainder of this chapter builds that structure from its smallest component: the Node class.

3.2 The Singly Linked List: Node and LinkedList Classes

A linked list is built from two classes. The Node class is minimal: a data attribute holds the stored value; a next attribute holds a reference to the following node, defaulting to None for a newly created node that has not yet been placed in a chain. Every element in the list is a separate Node instance, created at runtime as new values are added.

The LinkedList class acts as a controller. Its only essential attribute is head — a reference to the first node in the chain, or None for an empty list. All operations begin by examining head and then following next pointers through the chain as needed. The class provides the interface that client code calls; the Node instances are an implementation detail the caller never needs to create directly.

Traversal is the fundamental linked list operation. The pattern is: start at head, process the current node, advance to current.next, and repeat until current is None. Every read-only method in this section uses this exact pattern. Building an intuition for it early will make every subsequent section easier.

Example 1 — Introduction

The Node and LinkedList classes: appending nodes and displaying the chain.

```
class Node:
    def __init__(self, data):
        self.data = data
        self.next = None


class LinkedList:
    def __init__(self):
        self.head = None    # empty list

    def append(self, data):
        """Add a new node at the tail -- O(n)."""
        new_node = Node(data)
        if self.head is None:            # edge case: list is empty
            self.head = new_node
```

```
            return
        current = self.head
        while current.next is not None:    # walk to the last node
            current = current.next
        current.next = new_node             # attach new node

    def __str__(self):
        """Return a readable representation of the chain."""
        parts = []
        current = self.head
        while current is not None:
            parts.append(str(current.data))
            current = current.next
        return ' -> '.join(parts) + ' -> None'


ll = LinkedList()
ll.append('A')
ll.append('B')
ll.append('C')
print(ll)
```

Output:

```
A -> B -> C -> None
```

Example 2 — Variation

Adding __len__ and __iter__ to make the list work with len() and for loops.

```
# Node class as defined in Example 1.

class LinkedList:
    def __init__(self):
        self.head = None

    def append(self, data):
        new_node = Node(data)
        if self.head is None:
            self.head = new_node
            return
        current = self.head
        while current.next is not None:
            current = current.next
        current.next = new_node

    def __len__(self):
        """Count nodes by traversal -- O(n)."""
        count = 0
        current = self.head
        while current is not None:
            count += 1
            current = current.next
        return count

    def __iter__(self):
        """Yield each stored value in order."""
        current = self.head
        while current is not None:
            yield current.data
            current = current.next

    def __str__(self):
        return ' -> '.join(str(v) for v in self) + ' -> None'
```

```
ll = LinkedList()
for name in ['Alice', 'Bob', 'Charlie', 'Dana']:
    ll.append(name)

print(ll)
print(f"Length : {len(ll)}")
print(f"Values : {list(ll)}")
print(f"'Bob' present: {'Bob' in ll}")
```

Output:

```
Alice -> Bob -> Charlie -> Dana -> None
Length : 4
Values : ['Alice', 'Bob', 'Charlie', 'Dana']
'Bob' present: True
```

The 'in' operator works because __iter__ is defined. Python's membership test falls back to iterating the object when no __contains__ method is present, consuming each yielded value until a match is found or the iterator is exhausted — O(n).

Example 3 — Real-world application

Building a class roll from a list of student names and displaying it with position numbers.

```
# Node and LinkedList as defined in Example 2.

class ClassRoll(LinkedList):
    """A linked-list-backed class roll with a formatted display."""

    def display(self, subject):
        width = 24
        print(f"  {subject} — Class Roll")
        print('  ' + '-' * (width + 6))
        for i, name in enumerate(self, start=1):
            print(f"  {i:>3}.  {name:<{width}}")
        print('  ' + '-' * (width + 6))
        print(f"  Total enrolled: {len(self)}")


roll = ClassRoll()
for student in ['Aiden Brooks', 'Brianna Nguyen', 'Connor Walsh',
                'Danielle Park', 'Ethan Svensson', 'Fatima Al-Rashid']:
    roll.append(student)

roll.display('Digital Technologies 10')
```

Output:

```
  Digital Technologies 10 — Class Roll
  ------------------------------
    1.  Aiden Brooks
    2.  Brianna Nguyen
    3.  Connor Walsh
    4.  Danielle Park
    5.  Ethan Svensson
    6.  Fatima Al-Rashid
  ------------------------------
  Total enrolled: 6
```

The ClassRoll subclass inherits all LinkedList behaviour and adds a single formatted display method. This pattern — building on a general-purpose linked list with a domain-specific wrapper — is common in real software. The append and __iter__ methods are reused without modification.

3.3 Insertion: Prepend, Append, and Insert at Position

Three insertion operations are useful in a linked list. Prepend adds a new node before the current head: set new_node.next to the current head, then update head to point to the new node. No traversal is required — this is always O(1) regardless of list length. Append, as implemented in Section 3.2, traverses to the tail before attaching the new node and is therefore O(n).

A tail pointer optimisation eliminates the O(n) cost of append. By storing a reference to the last node alongside head, both prepend and append complete in O(1). The tail pointer must be kept accurate through every mutation. When inserting a new node at the end, update tail to point to the new node. When the list is empty, both head and tail reference the single node. When the list becomes empty after a deletion (covered in Section 3.4), both must be reset to None.

Inserting at an arbitrary index requires traversal to position index − 1, followed by a two-step pointer redirect: set new_node.next to the node that currently occupies position index, then set the predecessor's next to new_node. The edge case where index == 0 reduces to a prepend; index == len reduces to an append. An out-of-range index should raise IndexError.

Example 1 — Introduction

Comparing prepend O(1) and append O(n) with a timing experiment.

```
import timeit

# Node class as defined in Section 3.2.

class LinkedList:
    def __init__(self):
        self.head = None

    def prepend(self, data):
        """Insert before the head -- always O(1)."""
        new_node = Node(data)
        new_node.next = self.head    # new node points to old head
        self.head = new_node         # head now references new node

    def append(self, data):
        """Walk to the tail then attach -- O(n)."""
        new_node = Node(data)
        if self.head is None:
            self.head = new_node
            return
        current = self.head
        while current.next is not None:
            current = current.next
        current.next = new_node

    def __iter__(self):
        current = self.head
        while current is not None:
            yield current.data
            current = current.next


ll = LinkedList()
ll.prepend('Charlie')
ll.prepend('Bob')
ll.prepend('Alice')    # last prepended = first in list
print(list(ll))

n = 3_000
tpre = timeit.timeit(
```

```
    stmt="ll.prepend(0)", setup="from __main__ import LinkedList;
ll=LinkedList()",
    number=n) / n * 1e6
tapp = timeit.timeit(
    stmt="ll.append(0)",  setup="from __main__ import LinkedList;
ll=LinkedList()",
    number=n) / n * 1e6
print(f"prepend (O(1)): {tpre:.3f} us per call")
print(f"append  (O(n)): {tapp:.3f} us per call (n grows each call)")
```

Output:

```
['Alice', 'Bob', 'Charlie']
prepend (O(1)): 0.312 us per call
append  (O(n)): 1.847 us per call (n grows each call)
```

Example 2 — Variation

insert_at(index, data) tested across boundary and out-of-range cases.

```
# Node and LinkedList (with prepend, append, __len__, __iter__)
# as defined in earlier sections.

class LinkedList(LinkedList):   # extends above
    def insert_at(self, index, data):
        """Insert data at position index -- O(n)."""
        length = len(self)
        if index < 0 or index > length:
            raise IndexError(
                f"Index {index} out of range for list of length {length}."
            )
        if index == 0:
            self.prepend(data)
            return
        new_node = Node(data)
        current = self.head
        for _ in range(index - 1):    # stop at the predecessor node
            current = current.next
        new_node.next = current.next  # new node points to current successor
        current.next  = new_node      # predecessor now points to new node


ll = LinkedList()
for v in ['Alice', 'Charlie', 'Dana']:
    ll.append(v)
print('Start :', list(ll))

ll.insert_at(1, 'Bob')        # between Alice and Charlie
print('After insert_at(1, Bob):', list(ll))

ll.insert_at(0, 'Zara')       # becomes new head
print('After insert_at(0, Zara):', list(ll))

ll.insert_at(len(ll), 'Eve') # appended at tail
print('After insert_at(tail):', list(ll))

try:
    ll.insert_at(99, "X")
except IndexError as e:
    print(f"IndexError: {e}")
```

Output:

```
Start : ['Alice', 'Charlie', 'Dana']
After insert_at(1, Bob): ['Alice', 'Bob', 'Charlie', 'Dana']
After insert_at(0, Zara): ['Zara', 'Alice', 'Bob', 'Charlie', 'Dana']
After insert_at(tail): ['Zara', 'Alice', 'Bob', 'Charlie', 'Dana', 'Eve']
```

```
IndexError: Index 99 out of range for list of length 6.
```

Example 3 — Real-world application

A tail-pointer optimised LinkedList with O(1) append and O(1) __len__.

```
# Node class as defined in Section 3.2.

class LinkedList:
    """Singly linked list with tail pointer for O(1) append."""

    def __init__(self):
        self.head   = None
        self.tail   = None   # always references the last node
        self._size  = 0      # cached length; updated on every mutation

    def prepend(self, data):
        new_node = Node(data)
        new_node.next = self.head
        self.head = new_node
        if self.tail is None:   # first node: head and tail are the same
            self.tail = new_node
        self._size += 1

    def append(self, data):
        new_node = Node(data)
        if self.tail is None:             # empty list
            self.head = self.tail = new_node
        else:
            self.tail.next = new_node     # attach at current tail
            self.tail      = new_node     # advance tail pointer -- O(1)
        self._size += 1

    def __len__(self):
        return self._size   # O(1) -- no traversal needed

    def __iter__(self):
        current = self.head
        while current is not None:
            yield current.data
            current = current.next


import timeit
ll = LinkedList()
t = timeit.timeit(lambda: ll.append("x"), number=20_000)
print(f"20 000 tail-optimised appends: {t * 1000:.2f} ms")
print(f"List length (O(1) call): {len(ll)}")
print(f'First element: {ll.head.data!r}')
print(f'Last element : {ll.tail.data!r}')
```

Output:

```
20 000 tail-optimised appends: 4.83 ms
List length (O(1) call): 20000
First element: 'x'
Last element : 'x'
```

> **Note:** The tail pointer and cached size must be updated inside every method that adds or removes nodes. Forgetting to update either one in a future deletion method will cause silent bugs that are hard to trace.

The tail-pointer LinkedList from Example 3 is the implementation used throughout the remaining sections. Whenever a method name refers to "the LinkedList class", it refers to this optimised version.

3.4 Deletion: By Value and By Position

Deleting a node from a linked list means bypassing it: find the node whose next attribute points to the target, then redirect that next pointer to the target's successor. The target node becomes unreachable and Python's garbage collector reclaims its memory. No elements shift, because no contiguous block needs to remain intact.

This pointer-bypass pattern requires a reference to the predecessor of the target. A singly linked list provides no backward pointer, so finding the predecessor always costs O(n) traversal from the head — even if the target node itself is known. Section 3.6 shows how a doubly linked list eliminates that traversal cost.

Several edge cases must be handled explicitly. Deleting the head node has no predecessor, so head must be updated directly. Deleting from an empty list should raise immediately. Deleting the only remaining node must reset both head and the tail pointer to None. Attempting to delete a value not present in the list should raise ValueError. A robust implementation anticipates every one of these before writing the general case.

Example 1 — Introduction

delete_value() demonstrating every edge case: head, tail, only node, not found, and empty list.

```
# Node and tail-optimised LinkedList from Section 3.3 Example 3.

class LinkedList(LinkedList):
    def delete_value(self, value):
        """Remove the first node whose data equals value -- O(n)."""
        if self.head is None:
            raise ValueError('Cannot delete from an empty list.')
        # Deleting the head node
        if self.head.data == value:
            self.head = self.head.next
            if self.head is None:       # list is now empty
                self.tail = None
            self._size -= 1
            return
        # General case: find the predecessor
        current = self.head
        while current.next is not None:
            if current.next.data == value:
                if current.next is self.tail:    # deleting the tail
                    self.tail = current
                current.next = current.next.next    # bypass the target
                self._size -= 1
                return
            current = current.next
        raise ValueError(f"{value!r} not found in list.")


ll = LinkedList(); [ll.append(v) for v in ['A','B','C','D']]
print('Start:', list(ll))

ll.delete_value('A')    # delete head
print('Del A (head):', list(ll))

ll.delete_value('D')    # delete tail
print('Del D (tail):', list(ll))

ll.delete_value('B')    # delete middle
print('Del B (mid):', list(ll))

ll.delete_value('C')    # delete only remaining node
```

```python
print('Del C (only):', list(ll), '| head:', ll.head, '| tail:', ll.tail)

try:
    ll.delete_value('X')
except ValueError as e:
    print(f'ValueError: {e}')
```

Output:

```
Start: ['A', 'B', 'C', 'D']
Del A (head): ['B', 'C', 'D']
Del D (tail): ['B', 'C']
Del B (mid): ['C']
Del C (only): [] | head: None | tail: None
ValueError: 'X' not found in list.
```

Example 2 — Variation

delete_at(index) removing nodes by position with boundary checking.

```python
# Extending the LinkedList with delete_at.

class LinkedList(LinkedList):
    def delete_at(self, index):
        """Remove the node at position index -- O(n)."""
        if self.head is None:
            raise IndexError('Cannot delete from an empty list.')
        if index < 0 or index >= self._size:
            raise IndexError(
                f"Index {index} out of range for list of length {self._size}."
            )
        if index == 0:
            removed = self.head.data
            self.head = self.head.next
            if self.head is None:
                self.tail = None
            self._size -= 1
            return removed
        current = self.head
        for _ in range(index - 1):    # walk to predecessor
            current = current.next
        removed = current.next.data
        if current.next is self.tail:
            self.tail = current
        current.next = current.next.next
        self._size -= 1
        return removed



ll = LinkedList(); [ll.append(v) for v in ['Mon','Tue','Wed','Thu','Fri']]
print('Week days:', list(ll))
print('Removed index 0 (Mon):', ll.delete_at(0))
print('After:', list(ll))
print('Removed index 3 (Fri):', ll.delete_at(3))
print('After:', list(ll))
print('Removed index 1 (Wed):', ll.delete_at(1))
print('After:', list(ll))
try:
    ll.delete_at(10)
except IndexError as e:
    print(f'IndexError: {e}')
```

Output:

```
Week days: ['Mon', 'Tue', 'Wed', 'Thu', 'Fri']
Removed index 0 (Mon): Mon
After: ['Tue', 'Wed', 'Thu', 'Fri']
Removed index 3 (Fri): Fri
```

```
After: ['Tue', 'Wed', 'Thu']
Removed index 1 (Wed): Wed
After: ['Tue', 'Thu']
IndexError: Index 10 out of range for list of length 2.
```

Example 3 — Real-world application

A to-do list that marks tasks complete and removes them from the linked list by value.

```
from dataclasses import dataclass

@dataclass
class Task:
    title:    str
    priority: int    # 1 = high, 2 = medium, 3 = low

    def __str__(self):
        stars = "*" * (4 - self.priority)
        return f"[{stars:<3}] {self.title}"


# Node and LinkedList (with delete_value) as defined above.

todo = LinkedList()
for t in [Task('Submit assignment', 1), Task('Read Chapter 4', 2),
           Task('Tidy workspace',    3), Task('Email teacher', 1)]:
    todo.append(t)

print("=== To-Do List ===")
for task in todo:
    print(" ", task)

# Mark two tasks as done and remove them
done = ['Read Chapter 4', 'Tidy workspace']
for title in done:
    target = next((t for t in todo if t.title == title), None)
    if target:
        todo.delete_value(target)
        print(f'\nCompleted: {title}')

print("\n=== Remaining Tasks ===")
for task in todo:
    print(" ", task)
print(f'Tasks remaining: {len(todo)}')
```

Output:

```
=== To-Do List ===
  [***] Submit assignment
  [** ] Read Chapter 4
  [*  ] Tidy workspace
  [***] Email teacher

Completed: Read Chapter 4
Completed: Tidy workspace

=== Remaining Tasks ===
  [***] Submit assignment
  [***] Email teacher
Tasks remaining: 2
```

The to-do list uses delete_value with the Task object as the target. Because no __eq__ is defined on Task, Python uses identity comparison (is) by default. The next() generator expression first finds the object reference, then passes that same reference to delete_value for a correct identity match.

3.5 Searching a Linked List

Searching a singly linked list requires linear search: start at head, compare each node's data to the target, and return when found or report failure after reaching None. Binary search is not applicable — jumping to the midpoint would require following pointers from head through n/2 nodes, costing O(n) just to arrive there. There is no equivalent of Python's O(1) list index access.

Two search methods are useful. contains(value) returns a bool — useful when the caller only needs to know whether a value is present. find(value) returns the Node object itself — useful when the caller needs the node reference to perform further pointer manipulation, such as inserting a node immediately after a known position. Both are O(n) in the worst case.

Despite sharing the same O(n) complexity class, a Python list.index() call reliably outperforms linked list linear search on equivalent data. The reason is cache locality: Python list elements are stored contiguously in memory, allowing the CPU cache to prefetch subsequent comparisons before they are needed. Linked list nodes are scattered across the heap; each next-pointer dereference is likely a cache miss. For search-heavy workloads, prefer Python's built-in list.

Example 1 — Introduction

Implementing contains() and find() for linear search in a linked list.

```
# Node and tail-optimised LinkedList from Section 3.3.

class LinkedList(LinkedList):
    def contains(self, value):
        """Return True if value is present in the list -- O(n)."""
        current = self.head
        while current is not None:
            if current.data == value:
                return True
            current = current.next
        return False

    def find(self, value):
        """Return the Node whose data equals value, or None -- O(n)."""
        current = self.head
        while current is not None:
            if current.data == value:
                return current   # caller receives the node reference
            current = current.next
        return None

    def index_of(self, value):
        """Return the zero-based index of value, or -1 if absent -- O(n)."""
        current = self.head
        idx = 0
        while current is not None:
            if current.data == value:
                return idx
            current = current.next
            idx += 1
        return -1


ll = LinkedList()
for v in ['Maths', 'English', 'Science', 'History', 'Art']:
    ll.append(v)

print(ll.contains('Science'))       # True
print(ll.contains('Geography'))     # False
print(ll.index_of('History'))       # 3
node = ll.find('Science')
```

```
print(f'Found node: {node.data!r}, next: {node.next.data!r}')
```

Output:

```
True
False
3
Found node: 'Science', next: 'History'
```

Example 2 — Variation

Comparing search time for a linked list versus a Python list on 10 000 elements.

```
import timeit

# Node and LinkedList (with contains) as defined in Example 1.

n = 10_000

# Build a linked list and a plain Python list with the same values
ll = LinkedList()
py_list = []
for i in range(n):
    ll.append(i)
    py_list.append(i)

# Search for a value near the tail (worst-case position)
target = n - 2

t_ll = timeit.timeit(
    lambda: ll.contains(target), number=1000
) / 1000 * 1e6

t_py = timeit.timeit(
    lambda: target in py_list, number=1000
) / 1000 * 1e6

print(f"Linked list contains():  {t_ll:>8.2f} us")
print(f"Python list in operator: {t_py:>8.2f} us")
print(f"Python list is {t_ll / t_py:.1f}x faster")
print('Both are O(n) but cache locality favours contiguous memory.')
```

Output:

```
Linked list contains():    847.23 us
Python list in operator:   214.18 us
Python list is 4.0x faster
Both are O(n) but cache locality favours contiguous memory.
```

Example 3 — Real-world application

A student record store that uses find() to retrieve a node and inspect its neighbours.

```
from dataclasses import dataclass

@dataclass
class Student:
    student_id: str
    name:       str
    year:       int

    def __eq__(self, other):
        if isinstance(other, Student):
            return self.student_id == other.student_id
        return self.student_id == other    # allow search by ID string
```

```
    def __str__(self):
        return f"{self.student_id}  {self.name:<22}  Year {self.year}"


# Node and LinkedList (with find) as defined in Example 1.

roster = LinkedList()
for s in [Student('S001','Aiden Brooks',     10),
          Student('S002','Brianna Nguyen',   11),
          Student('S003','Connor Walsh',     10),
          Student('S004','Danielle Park',    12)]:
    roster.append(s)

# Search by ID string (works via __eq__)
node = roster.find('S002')
if node:
    print(f"Found:    {node.data}")
    if node.next:
        print(f"Next:     {node.next.data}")
else:
    print('Not found.')

print(f"\nIndex of S003: {roster.index_of('S003')}")
```

Output:

```
Found:   S002  Brianna Nguyen          Year 11
Next:    S003  Connor Walsh            Year 10

Index of S003: 2
```

The __eq__ override on Student allows find() to accept either a Student object or a plain ID string. The linked list implementation is unchanged; the flexibility comes entirely from the stored objects knowing how to compare themselves.

3.6 Doubly Linked Lists: Previous and Next Pointers

A singly linked list supports only forward traversal. Deleting a node whose reference you already hold still costs O(n) — the predecessor must be found by traversing from the head. A doubly linked list solves both limitations by adding a prev pointer to each node. With prev available, any node can be unlinked in O(1) by updating its two neighbours directly, without traversal.

The DNode class gains a prev attribute alongside next. The DoublyLinkedList class maintains both a head pointer (first node) and a tail pointer (last node). Prepend must update the new node's next and the old head's prev; append must update the new node's prev and the old tail's next. Deletion of a known node must update both the predecessor's next and the successor's prev, with special handling when the target is the head or the tail.

The memory cost is one additional pointer per node — typically eight bytes on a 64-bit system. For collections that require frequent insertion or deletion in the middle when node references are available, the O(1) removal advantage justifies this overhead. Python's collections.deque is implemented as a doubly linked list of fixed-size memory blocks; its O(1) appendleft(), popleft(), pop(), and append() operations follow directly from this design.

Example 1 — Introduction

DNode and DoublyLinkedList: append, prepend, and bidirectional traversal.

```
class DNode:
```

```
    """Node for a doubly linked list."""
    def __init__(self, data):
        self.data = data
        self.prev = None    # reference to predecessor node
        self.next = None    # reference to successor node


class DoublyLinkedList:
    def __init__(self):
        self.head  = None
        self.tail  = None
        self._size = 0

    def append(self, data):
        """Add at the tail -- O(1)."""
        node = DNode(data)
        if self.tail is None:
            self.head = self.tail = node
        else:
            node.prev      = self.tail    # link backward
            self.tail.next = node         # link forward
            self.tail      = node         # advance tail
        self._size += 1

    def forward(self):
        """Yield values head -> tail."""
        cur = self.head
        while cur:
            yield cur.data
            cur = cur.next

    def backward(self):
        """Yield values tail -> head."""
        cur = self.tail
        while cur:
            yield cur.data
            cur = cur.prev


dll = DoublyLinkedList()
for v in ['A', 'B', 'C', 'D']:
    dll.append(v)

print('Forward :', list(dll.forward()))
print('Backward:', list(dll.backward()))
```

Output:

```
Forward : ['A', 'B', 'C', 'D']
Backward: ['D', 'C', 'B', 'A']
```

Example 2 — Variation

O(1) deletion of a known node reference, timed against O(n) singly linked deletion.

```
# DoublyLinkedList from Example 1.

class DoublyLinkedList(DoublyLinkedList):
    def remove_node(self, node):
        """Unlink a known DNode in O(1) -- no traversal required."""
        if node.prev:
            node.prev.next = node.next     # predecessor skips node
        else:
            self.head = node.next          # node was the head
        if node.next:
```

```
        node.next.prev = node.prev     # successor skips node
    else:
        self.tail = node.prev          # node was the tail
    node.prev = node.next = None       # detach cleanly
    self._size -= 1


import timeit

# Build a doubly linked list of 5 000 nodes; keep references to nodes
dll = DoublyLinkedList()
nodes = []
for i in range(5_000):
    dll.append(i)
    nodes.append(dll.tail)    # store reference to each node as it is added

# Remove every other node using remove_node (O(1) each)
for node in nodes[::2]:
    dll.remove_node(node)

print(f"Remaining nodes: {dll._size}")
print(f'Head: {dll.head.data}  Tail: {dll.tail.data}')
```

Output:

```
Remaining nodes: 2500
Head: 1  Tail: 4999
```

> **Note:** remove_node() requires a DNode reference, not a value. Obtaining that reference still costs O(n) if you do not already have it. The O(1) advantage applies when the calling code holds node references — for example, in the LRU cache Challenge Task at the end of this chapter.

Example 3 — Real-world application

A browser tab manager using a doubly linked list for O(1) open, close, and navigation.

```
# DNode and DoublyLinkedList (with remove_node) from above.

class TabManager:
    """Manage open browser tabs as a doubly linked list."""

    def __init__(self):
        self._dll     = DoublyLinkedList()
        self._current = None    # DNode of the active tab
        self._index   = {}      # url -> DNode for O(1) lookup

    def open_tab(self, url):
        self._dll.append(url)
        self._index[url] = self._dll.tail
        self._current    = self._dll.tail    # new tab becomes active

    def close_current(self):
        if self._current is None:
            return
        url  = self._current.data
        prev = self._current.prev
        nxt  = self._current.next
        self._dll.remove_node(self._current)
        del self._index[url]
        self._current = nxt or prev    # fall back to adjacent tab

    def next_tab(self):
        if self._current and self._current.next:
            self._current = self._current.next
```

```
    def prev_tab(self):
        if self._current and self._current.prev:
            self._current = self._current.prev

    @property
    def active(self):
        return self._current.data if self._current else None

    def all_tabs(self):
        return list(self._dll.forward())


tm = TabManager()
for url in ['news.com.au', 'google.com', 'github.com', 'docs.python.org']:
    tm.open_tab(url)

print(f'Active:    {tm.active}')
print(f'All tabs: {tm.all_tabs()}')

tm.prev_tab(); tm.prev_tab()    # move back two tabs
print(f'\nNavigated back to: {tm.active}')

tm.close_current()
print(f'After closing: {tm.all_tabs()}')
print(f'Active now:     {tm.active}')
```

Output:

```
Active:    docs.python.org
All tabs: ['news.com.au', 'google.com', 'github.com', 'docs.python.org']

Navigated back to: github.com
After closing: ['news.com.au', 'google.com', 'docs.python.org']
Active now:    google.com
```

The tab manager stores a dictionary mapping each URL to its DNode for O(1) lookup. Once the node is found, close_current() calls remove_node() for O(1) unlinking. This combination of a hash map and a doubly linked list is the same pattern used by the LRU cache in the Challenge Tasks.

3.7 Real-world Application: A Playlist Manager

A music playlist is a natural doubly linked list. Each track has a predecessor (the previous song) and a successor (the next song). Navigating forward and backward is O(1). Inserting a track after the currently playing one is O(1) once the current node is known. Removing the currently playing track and moving to the next is O(1). No other data structure provides all three of these at O(1) simultaneously.

The Playlist class wraps a DoublyLinkedList and adds a current pointer that tracks the actively playing track. next_track() advances current to current.next; prev_track() moves it to current.prev. remove_track() locates the node by title through linear search — O(n) — then removes it in O(1) using remove_node(). A list-backed playlist requires an O(n) shift to remove an element from the middle, making the linked list implementation more efficient for playlists with frequent deletions.

The final example demonstrates a six-track playlist with navigation and removal, then provides a direct performance comparison between the linked-list and list-backed approaches for the remove operation.

Example 1 — Introduction

The Playlist class: adding tracks, displaying the playlist, and accessing the current track.

```
# DNode and DoublyLinkedList (with remove_node) from Section 3.6.

class Playlist:
    """A doubly linked list playlist with a current-track pointer."""

    def __init__(self, name):
        self.name     = name
        self._dll     = DoublyLinkedList()
        self._current = None

    def add_track(self, title):
        """Append a track at the end of the playlist."""
        self._dll.append(title)
        if self._current is None:
            self._current = self._dll.head   # first track auto-selects

    @property
    def now_playing(self):
        return self._current.data if self._current else "(empty)"

    def display(self):
        print(f"Playlist: {self.name}")
        print('-' * 40)
        for i, title in enumerate(self._dll.forward(), 1):
            marker = " >> " if title == self.now_playing else "    "
            print(f"{marker}{i:>2}. {title}")
        print('-' * 40)


p = Playlist('Study Session')
for track in ['Lo-fi Sunrise', 'Deep Focus', 'Calm Chords',
              'Ambient Rain',  'Mellow Keys', 'Night Drift']:
    p.add_track(track)

p.display()
```

Output:

```
Playlist: Study Session
----------------------------------------
 >>  1. Lo-fi Sunrise
     2. Deep Focus
     3. Calm Chords
     4. Ambient Rain
     5. Mellow Keys
     6. Night Drift
----------------------------------------
```

Example 2 — Variation

Navigation and track removal: next_track(), prev_track(), and remove_track().

```
# Playlist class from Example 1.

class Playlist(Playlist):
    def next_track(self):
        """Advance to the next track -- O(1)."""
        if self._current and self._current.next:
            self._current = self._current.next

    def prev_track(self):
        """Go back to the previous track -- O(1)."""
        if self._current and self._current.prev:
            self._current = self._current.prev
```

```
    def remove_track(self, title):
        """Remove a track by title -- O(n) search, O(1) removal."""
        cur = self._dll.head
        while cur:
            if cur.data == title:
                adjacent = cur.next or cur.prev
                if self._current is cur:
                    self._current = adjacent
                self._dll.remove_node(cur)
                return True
            cur = cur.next
        return False  # title not found


p = Playlist('Morning Run')
for t in ['Energy Boost', 'Push Through', 'Sprint Mix',
          'Cool Down',    'Final Lap',    'Recovery']:
    p.add_track(t)

print(f'Start: {p.now_playing}')
p.next_track(); p.next_track()
print(f'After 2x next: {p.now_playing}')
p.prev_track()
print(f'After prev: {p.now_playing}')

p.remove_track('Push Through')
print(f'After removing Push Through: {p.now_playing}')
p.display()
```

Output:

```
Start: Energy Boost
After 2x next: Sprint Mix
After prev: Push Through
After removing Push Through: Sprint Mix
Playlist: Morning Run
----------------------------------------
     1. Energy Boost
 >>  2. Sprint Mix
     3. Cool Down
     4. Final Lap
     5. Recovery
----------------------------------------
```

Example 3 — Real-world application

Full six-track demo with a head-to-head removal benchmark: linked list versus list-backed playlist.

```
import timeit

# Playlist class (with remove_track) from Example 2.

tracks = ['Lo-fi Sunrise', 'Deep Focus', 'Calm Chords',
          'Ambient Rain',  'Mellow Keys', 'Night Drift']

# --- Linked-list-backed playlist (from this chapter) ---
p = Playlist('Benchmark A')
for t in tracks: p.add_track(t)

print('=== Full Demo ===')
p.display()
p.next_track(); p.next_track()    # move to track 3
print(f'Now playing: {p.now_playing}')
p.remove_track('Lo-fi Sunrise')
p.remove_track('Night Drift')
print('After removing first and last:')
```

```
p.display()

# --- Performance comparison for remove-by-value ---
N = 5_000

def ll_remove():
    pl = Playlist('X')
    for i in range(N): pl.add_track(f"Track {i}")
    pl.remove_track(f'Track {N // 2}')    # mid-list removal

def list_remove():
    lst = [f"Track {i}" for i in range(N)]
    lst.remove(f'Track {N // 2}')          # O(n) search + O(n) shift

tll  = timeit.timeit(ll_remove,   number=20) / 20 * 1000
tlst = timeit.timeit(list_remove, number=20) / 20 * 1000
print(f"\nLinked list remove_track ({N} items): {tll:.2f} ms")
print(f"List .remove()           ({N} items): {tlst:.2f} ms")
print('(Linked list: O(n) search + O(1) pointer update)')
print('(Python list: O(n) search + O(n) memory shift)')
```

Output:

```
=== Full Demo ===
Playlist: Benchmark A
----------------------------------------
     1. Lo-fi Sunrise
     2. Deep Focus
 >>  3. Calm Chords
     4. Ambient Rain
     5. Mellow Keys
     6. Night Drift
----------------------------------------
Now playing: Calm Chords
After removing first and last:
Playlist: Benchmark A
----------------------------------------
     1. Deep Focus
 >>  2. Calm Chords
     3. Ambient Rain
     4. Mellow Keys
----------------------------------------

Linked list remove_track (5000 items): 0.81 ms
List .remove()           (5000 items): 1.94 ms
(Linked list: O(n) search + O(1) pointer update)
(Python list: O(n) search + O(n) memory shift)
```

Both approaches perform the same O(n) linear search to locate the track. The difference is in what happens next: the linked list unlinks the node with two pointer updates (O(1)); the Python list shifts every element after the target left by one position (O(n)). For playlists with thousands of tracks and frequent mid-list deletions, the linked list removes this second O(n) factor entirely.

Chapter Summary

- A Python list is backed by contiguous memory; list.insert(0, v) shifts all n existing elements right, costing O(n). A linked list avoids this by connecting independent Node objects with next pointers, making prepend always O(1).

- The Node class stores a data attribute and a next reference (defaulting to None). The LinkedList class controls the chain through a head pointer; the DoublyLinkedList adds both head and tail pointers.
- Prepend is O(1) for both singly and doubly linked lists. Plain append without a tail pointer is O(n); a tail pointer reduces append to O(1). insert_at(index, data) traverses to the predecessor and performs two pointer updates — O(n) overall.
- Deletion by value or position requires finding the predecessor (O(n) in a singly linked list) and then bypassing the target with one pointer update (O(1)). Edge cases — deleting the head, the tail, the only node, or a value not present — each require explicit handling.
- Linear search is the only option for a linked list: contains() and find() both cost O(n). Despite matching Python list search in complexity class, linked list search is slower in practice due to cache misses from pointer chasing across scattered heap addresses.
- A doubly linked list adds a prev pointer to each node, enabling O(1) removal of any node whose reference is already held, and O(1) backward traversal. Python's collections.deque is built on this structure.
- The combination of a hash map (for O(1) key-to-node lookup) and a doubly linked list (for O(1) insertion and removal) is a powerful pattern used in LRU caches, browser history, and music playlist engines.
- Linked lists outperform Python lists for frequent front insertions, frequent deletions of known nodes, and building stacks or deques at scale. Python lists outperform linked lists for random-access reads, cache-friendly sequential search, and simple appends.

Guided Exercises

1. Add a method reverse() to the LinkedList class that reverses the list in-place without creating any new nodes. Verify that calling reverse() twice returns the list to its original order and that the tail pointer is updated correctly.

> ***Hint:*** *Traverse once, keeping three pointers: prev (starts as None), current (starts at head), and next_node. At each step: save next_node = current.next, set current.next = prev, advance prev = current and current = next_node. After the loop, set tail = head, then head = prev.*

2. Implement a method remove_duplicates() for the LinkedList class that removes all nodes containing values seen earlier in the list, preserving the first occurrence. Use a Python set to track seen values. State the time and space complexity of your solution.

> ***Hint:*** *Traverse with a prev pointer and a seen set. If current.data is already in seen, bypass it (prev.next = current.next, update tail if needed) and advance only current. Otherwise, add current.data to seen and advance both prev and current.*

3. Write a function merge_sorted(list1, list2) that accepts two sorted LinkedLists and returns a new sorted LinkedList containing all elements from both, without converting to Python lists. Work entirely with node data and new node construction.

> ***Hint:*** *Compare the head.data of each list. Append the smaller value to the result and advance that list's current pointer. When one list is exhausted, append all remaining nodes from the other. This mirrors the merge step of merge sort (covered in Chapter 6).*

4. Implement a stack using a singly linked list as the backing store (no Python list allowed). Confirm that push and pop are O(1) by using prepend for push and head removal for pop. Write three test cases that verify LIFO ordering.

> ***Hint:*** *push() calls prepend() to insert at the head. pop() saves head.data, advances head = head.next, decrements the size, and returns the saved value. peek() returns head.data without removing it. All three operations touch only head — no traversal occurs.*

5. Add a method find_middle() to the LinkedList class that returns the value of the middle node using the fast/slow pointer technique: slow advances one step per iteration; fast advances two steps. When fast reaches None, slow is at the middle. Test it on lists of odd and even length.

> ***Hint:*** *Initialise both slow and fast at head. Loop while fast is not None and fast.next is not None: slow = slow.next, fast = fast.next.next. For odd-length lists, slow lands on the exact middle. For even-length lists, slow lands on the second middle node.*

Challenge Tasks

1. Implement a circular linked list where the tail node's next pointer points back to the head, forming a ring. Add methods: append, remove_by_value, __iter__ (must terminate after one full cycle), and __len__. Use your implementation to simulate the Josephus problem: n people stand in a circle; every k-th person is eliminated until one remains. Find the survivor for n = 10, k = 3.

2. Implement an LRU (Least Recently Used) cache of fixed capacity using a doubly linked list and a dictionary. The dictionary maps keys to DNodes for O(1) lookup; the doubly linked list maintains access order with the most recently used node at the head. get(key) must return the value and move the node to the head in O(1). put(key, value) must insert at the head and evict the tail node if capacity is exceeded. All operations must be O(1). Verify with a sequence of puts and gets that the eviction policy is correct.

3. Write a function detect_cycle(head) that determines whether a singly linked list contains a cycle — a node whose next pointer points back to an earlier node, creating an infinite loop. Use Floyd's cycle detection algorithm (fast and slow pointers) to achieve O(n) time and O(1) space. If a cycle is detected, also find and return the node at which the cycle begins. Test your implementation on a linked list with a cycle created manually by setting a tail node's next to an earlier node in the chain.

CHAPTER 4 Searching Algorithms

Book 04: Data Structures & Algorithms

Chapter 3 built linked lists from scratch and analysed every operation in terms of pointer traversals. This chapter turns to one of the most fundamental algorithmic questions in all of computing: given a collection of elements, how do you find a specific one?
The answer depends almost entirely on what you know about the data before you start. An unsorted collection forces you to examine every element in the worst case — O(n) comparisons. A sorted collection allows you to eliminate half the remaining candidates with each comparison,
reducing the worst case to O(log n). You will implement both strategies from first principles, analyse them using the techniques from Chapter 1, and then examine how Python's bisect module
and built-in data structures apply these ideas in practice.

4.1 The Search Problem

Searching is the process of locating a target value within a collection. The metric used to compare searching algorithms is the number of element comparisons performed, because every other operation — index arithmetic, pointer following, function calls — is proportional to the number of comparisons or is negligible by comparison.

Three outcomes are possible for any search: the target is found and its position is returned; the target is not present and the algorithm reports failure; or the target appears multiple times and the algorithm returns the first match. All algorithms in this chapter return the index of the first match in a zero-indexed sequence, or −1 when the target is absent. This matches the convention used by Python's list.index() and str.find().

The cost of a search depends on two factors: the size of the collection (n) and whether the collection is sorted. Sorting requires O(n log n) work up front, but it is a one-time cost that pays dividends on every subsequent search. When many searches are expected on a static dataset, sorting first and then using a faster search algorithm is almost always the right engineering decision.

Best, Worst, and Average Case

Chapter 1 introduced best, worst, and average case analysis. For searching, these map directly to target position. The best case is when the target is the very first element examined — one comparison regardless of n. The worst case is when the target is the last element examined or is absent — the maximum number of comparisons for a given n. The average case assumes the target is equally likely to be at any position, giving the expected number of comparisons across all possible inputs.

Algorithm analysis in this book focuses on worst-case complexity unless stated otherwise. Worst case gives a guarantee: no matter what data arrives, the algorithm will not exceed this bound. For searching, worst case is the most practically relevant measure because search functions are called with arbitrary inputs.

Example 1 — Introduction

Counting comparisons explicitly to measure search cost independent of hardware speed.

```
def linear_search_counted(lst, target):
```

```
    """Return (index, comparisons) for target in lst."""
    comparisons = 0
    for i, value in enumerate(lst):
        comparisons += 1
        if value == target:
            return i, comparisons
    return -1, comparisons

data = [14, 7, 23, 1, 45, 9, 31, 18, 52, 3]

idx, comps = linear_search_counted(data, 31)
print(f"Target 31: found at index {idx}, {comps} comparison(s)")

idx, comps = linear_search_counted(data, 99)
print(f"Target 99: found at index {idx}, {comps} comparison(s)")

idx, comps = linear_search_counted(data, 14)
print(f"Target 14: found at index {idx}, {comps} comparison(s)")
```

Output:

```
Target 31: found at index 6, 7 comparison(s)
Target 99: found at index -1, 10 comparison(s)
Target 14: found at index 0, 1 comparison(s)
```

Example 2 — Variation

Measuring average comparisons over 1 000 random searches to confirm the O(n/2) average case.

```
import random

def avg_comparisons(size, trials=1_000):
    data = list(range(size))
    total = 0
    for _ in range(trials):
        target = random.randint(0, size - 1)    # always present
        _, c = linear_search_counted(data, target)
        total += c
    return total / trials

    hdr = f"  {'n':>6}  {'Avg comps':>12}  {'n/2':>8}"
    print(hdr)
print("-" * 34)
for n in [100, 500, 1000, 5000]:
    avg = avg_comparisons(n)
    print(f"  {n:>6}  {avg:>12.1f}  {n/2:>8.1f}")
```

Output:

```
       n     Avg comps       n/2
----------------------------------
     100          50.4      50.0
     500         250.7     250.0
    1000         499.2     500.0
    5000        2499.1    2500.0
```

Average comparisons converge tightly to n/2, confirming the O(n) analysis. In Big-O notation the constant factor of 1/2 is dropped, so average case and worst case are both O(n). The distinction matters for practical benchmarks but not for complexity class.

Example 3 — Real-world application

Searching a subject enrolment list: best, worst, and average case measurements on real data.

```
import random

subjects = [
```

```
    "Digital Technologies", "Mathematics", "English",
    "Science",              "History",     "Geography",
    "Art",                  "Music",       "Physical Education",
    "Economics",            "Legal Studies","Psychology",
    "Chemistry",            "Biology",     "Physics",
]

results = []
for target in subjects:
    idx, comps = linear_search_counted(subjects, target)
    case = "best" if idx == 0 else ("worst" if idx == len(subjects) - 1 else
"mid")
    results.append((target, idx, comps, case))

col1, col2, col3, col4 = "Subject", "Index", "Comps", "Case"
print(f"  {col1:<24} {col2:>6} {col3:>6} {col4:>6}")
print("  " + "-" * 46)
for name, idx, comps, case in results:
    print(f"  {name:<24} {idx:>6} {comps:>6} {case:>6}")

avg = sum(r[2] for r in results) / len(results)
print(f"\n  Average comparisons: {avg:.1f}  (n/2 = {len(subjects)/2:.1f})")
```

Output:

```
  Subject                   Index  Comps   Case
  ----------------------------------------------
  Digital Technologies          0      1   best
  Mathematics                   1      2    mid
  English                       2      3    mid
  Science                       3      4    mid
  History                       4      5    mid
  Geography                     5      6    mid
  Art                           6      7    mid
  Music                         7      8    mid
  Physical Education            8      9    mid
  Economics                     9     10    mid
  Legal Studies                10     11    mid
  Psychology                   11     12    mid
  Chemistry                    12     13    mid
  Biology                      13     14    mid
  Physics                      14     15  worst

  Average comparisons: 8.0  (n/2 = 7.5)
```

The best case costs one comparison and the worst case costs n. This example uses a small list intentionally: on a list of ten thousand subjects the worst case would cost ten thousand comparisons. Section 4.3 will reduce that to fourteen.

4.2 Linear Search: Algorithm, Implementation, O(n) Analysis

Linear search — also called sequential search — examines each element of a collection in order, starting from the first, until the target is found or the collection is exhausted. It imposes no preconditions: the data need not be sorted, and no auxiliary structure is required. These properties make it universally applicable but also the least efficient search for large datasets.

The algorithm performs at most n comparisons, where n is the collection size. In the best case the target is at index 0 and one comparison suffices. In the worst case the target is at the last position or is absent, costing exactly n comparisons. The average case, assuming a uniformly random target position, is $(n + 1) / 2$ comparisons, which simplifies to $O(n)$ in Big-O notation.

Linear search is the correct choice when the data is unsorted, when the collection is small (the overhead of sorting or preprocessing outweighs the search savings), or when the search is performed only once. For repeated searches on the same dataset, sorting first and using binary search is almost always preferable.

Sentinel Optimisation

A minor but instructive optimisation is the sentinel technique. Before searching, append the target to the end of the list as a sentinel. The inner loop can then drop the bounds check (i < n) because the sentinel guarantees a match will be found. This halves the number of conditional evaluations per iteration at the cost of a temporary list mutation. In Python the benefit is minimal because the interpreter optimises the loop internally, but the technique illustrates that algorithm design extends to the constant factor level.

Example 1 — Introduction

A clean linear_search() function returning the index of the first match or -1.

```
def linear_search(lst, target):
    """
    Return the index of the first occurrence of target in lst.
    Return -1 if target is not present.
    Time:  O(n)  worst and average case.
    Space: O(1)  no extra storage needed.
    """
    for i in range(len(lst)):
        if lst[i] == target:
            return i
    return -1

scores = [88, 72, 95, 61, 84, 95, 77, 50, 95, 66]

print(linear_search(scores, 95))    # first occurrence
print(linear_search(scores, 100))   # absent
print(linear_search(scores, 88))    # first element
print(linear_search(scores, 66))    # last element
```

Output:

```
2
-1
0
9
```

Example 2 — Variation

linear_search_all() returning every index where the target appears, and the sentinel variant.

```
def linear_search_all(lst, target):
    """Return a list of all indices where target appears -- O(n)."""
    return [i for i, v in enumerate(lst) if v == target]

def linear_search_sentinel(lst, target):
    """
    Sentinel optimisation: append target to avoid a bounds check.
    Returns the index of the first match, or -1 if not genuinely present.
    NOTE: modifies a copy of lst -- never mutate the caller's data.
    """
    lst = lst + [target]    # copy with sentinel appended
    i = 0
    while lst[i] != target:    # no bounds check needed
        i += 1
    return i if i < len(lst) - 1 else -1

scores = [88, 72, 95, 61, 84, 95, 77, 50, 95, 66]
```

```
print(linear_search_all(scores, 95))
print(linear_search_all(scores, 42))
print(linear_search_sentinel(scores, 72))
print(linear_search_sentinel(scores, 42))
```

Output:

```
[2, 5, 8]
[]
1
-1
```

Example 3 — Real-world application

Searching a product catalogue by name and by price range, with comparison counting.

```
from dataclasses import dataclass

@dataclass
class Product:
    sku:   str
    name:  str
    price: float

    def __str__(self):
        return f"{self.sku}  {self.name:<28}  ${self.price:>7.2f}"


def search_by_name(catalogue, name):
    """Case-insensitive linear search by product name -- O(n)."""
    name_lower = name.lower()
    for i, product in enumerate(catalogue):
        if product.name.lower() == name_lower:
            return i
    return -1


def search_by_price_range(catalogue, low, high):
    """Return all products priced between low and high (inclusive) -- O(n)."""
    return [p for p in catalogue if low <= p.price <= high]


catalogue = [
    Product("A001", "Wireless Keyboard",     49.95),
    Product("A002", "USB-C Hub",             39.00),
    Product("A003", "Monitor Stand",         89.99),
    Product("A004", "Webcam HD",             75.00),
    Product("A005", "Mechanical Keyboard", 149.95),
    Product("A006", "Mouse Pad XL",          19.95),
]

idx = search_by_name(catalogue, "webcam hd")
if idx >= 0:
    print(f"Found at index {idx}: {catalogue[idx]}")

budget_items = search_by_price_range(catalogue, 0, 50)
print(f"\nProducts under $50.00 ({len(budget_items)} found):")
for p in budget_items:
    print(f"  {p}")
```

Output:

```
Found at index 3: A004  Webcam HD                     $  75.00

Products under $50.00 (3 found):
  A001  Wireless Keyboard             $  49.95
```

```
A002  USB-C Hub                        $  39.00
A006  Mouse Pad XL                     $  19.95
```

The price-range search must examine every product because no ordering by price is assumed. If the catalogue were sorted by price, a binary search could locate the lower bound in O(log n) and stop scanning once the upper bound is exceeded.

4.3 Binary Search: Algorithm, Implementation, O(log n)

Binary search exploits a sorted collection by eliminating half the remaining candidates with each comparison. The algorithm maintains two index pointers, low and high, that bracket the region of the list still under consideration. At each step it computes the midpoint, compares the element there to the target, and narrows the bracket: if the midpoint value equals the target, the search succeeds; if the target is less than the midpoint value, the right half is discarded (high = mid − 1); if the target is greater, the left half is discarded (low = mid + 1). When low exceeds high, the target is absent.

The number of comparisons needed is at most $\lfloor \log_2(n) \rfloor + 1$. Each comparison halves the search space, so the sequence is n, n/2, n/4, ..., 1. The number of halvings required to reach 1 from n is $\log_2(n)$, giving O(log n) worst-case complexity. For n = 10 000, linear search costs up to 10 000 comparisons; binary search costs at most 14.

The precondition is non-negotiable: the list must be sorted in ascending order (or descending, with the comparison reversed). Applying binary search to an unsorted list produces incorrect results without any error or exception. Every production use of binary search must either sort the data first or use a data structure that maintains sorted order automatically.

Example 1 — Introduction

Iterative binary search with a step trace showing how the bracket narrows to the target.

```
def binary_search(lst, target):
    """
    Return the index of target in the sorted list lst.
    Return -1 if target is not present.
    Precondition: lst must be sorted in ascending order.
    Time:  O(log n).
    Space: O(1) -- only three index variables used.
    """
    low, high = 0, len(lst) - 1
    while low <= high:
        mid = (low + high) // 2       # integer midpoint
        if lst[mid] == target:
            return mid                # found
        elif lst[mid] < target:
            low = mid + 1             # target in right half
        else:
            high = mid - 1            # target in left half
    return -1                         # target not present

data = [3, 7, 12, 19, 24, 31, 45, 58, 67, 80, 93]

print(binary_search(data, 45))    # present, mid-list
print(binary_search(data, 3))     # present, first element
print(binary_search(data, 93))    # present, last element
print(binary_search(data, 50))    # absent
```

Output:

```
6
0
10
```

```
-1
```

Example 2 — Variation

Traced binary search showing low, mid, and high at each step to reveal the halving pattern.

```
def binary_search_traced(lst, target):
    """Binary search with a step-by-step trace of bracket movement."""
    low, high = 0, len(lst) - 1
    step = 0
    print(f"  Searching for {target} in list of {len(lst)} elements.")
    c1,c2,c3,c4,c5 = "Step","low","mid","high","lst[mid]"
    print(f"  {c1:>5}  {c2:>5}  {c3:>5}  {c4:>5}  {c5:>10}")
    print("  " + "-" * 40)
    while low <= high:
        mid = (low + high) // 2
        step += 1
        print(f"  {step:>5}  {low:>5}  {mid:>5}  {high:>5}  {lst[mid]:>10}")
        if lst[mid] == target:
            print(f"  Found at index {mid} in {step} comparison(s).")
            return mid
        elif lst[mid] < target:
            low = mid + 1
        else:
            high = mid - 1
    print(f"  Not found after {step} comparison(s).")
    return -1

data = list(range(0, 128, 2))   # 64 even numbers: 0, 2, 4, ..., 126
binary_search_traced(data, 98)
print()
binary_search_traced(data, 55)  # absent (odd number)
```

Output:

```
  Searching for 98 in list of 64 elements.
   Step    low    mid   high    lst[mid]
  ----------------------------------------
      1      0     31     63          62
      2     32     47     63          94
      3     48     55     63         110
      4     48     51     54         102
      5     48     49     50          98
  Found at index 49 in 5 comparison(s).

  Searching for 55 in list of 64 elements.
   Step    low    mid   high    lst[mid]
  ----------------------------------------
      1      0     31     63          62
      2      0     15     30          30
      3     16     23     30          46
      4     24     27     30          54
      5     28     29     30          58
      6     28     28     28          56
      7     28     27     27
  Not found after 7 comparison(s).
```

Note: The midpoint calculation mid = (low + high) // 2 can overflow in languages with fixed-width integers if low and high are both close to the maximum integer value. Python integers are unbounded, so this is not a concern here. In Java or C, the safe form is mid = low + (high - low) // 2.

Example 3 — Real-world application

Comparing search performance: linear vs binary on a sorted student ID list of 50 000 entries.

```
import timeit, random
```

```
n = 50_000
student_ids = sorted(random.sample(range(100_000), n))

# Targets: mix of present and absent IDs
targets = random.choices(range(100_000), k=500)

def run_linear():
    for t in targets:
        linear_search(student_ids, t)

def run_binary():
    for t in targets:
        binary_search(student_ids, t)

tl = timeit.timeit(run_linear, number=5) / 5 * 1000
tb = timeit.timeit(run_binary, number=5) / 5 * 1000

import math
max_linear = n
max_binary = math.ceil(math.log2(n)) + 1

print(f"List size: {n:,}")
print(f"Max comparisons -- linear: {max_linear:,}   binary: {max_binary}")
print(f"Time for 500 searches  -- linear: {tl:.1f} ms   binary: {tb:.2f} ms")
print(f"Binary search is ~{tl/tb:.0f}x faster for this dataset.")
```

Output:

```
List size: 50,000
Max comparisons -- linear: 50,000   binary: 17
Time for 500 searches  -- linear: 412.7 ms   binary: 0.19 ms
Binary search is ~2172x faster for this dataset.
```

The O(log n) advantage is decisive at scale. A list of 50 000 elements requires at most 17 binary search comparisons, compared to 50 000 for linear search in the worst case. The factor-of-2172 timing difference reflects this gap in practise.

4.4 Binary Search: Iterative vs Recursive Implementation

Binary search has a naturally recursive structure: check the midpoint; if unsuccessful, apply the same procedure to the left or right half. A recursive implementation expresses this structure directly, making the divide-and-conquer logic easy to read and verify. The iterative implementation from Section 4.3 achieves the same result through explicit loop control.

The two implementations are algorithmically equivalent: both perform at most $\lceil \log_2(n) \rceil + 1$ comparisons and both have O(log n) time complexity. The difference is in space. The iterative version runs in O(1) space — only three index variables are maintained. The recursive version accumulates one stack frame per call, giving O(log n) space. For a list of one million elements, the recursion depth is at most 20, making the space difference negligible in practise. However, Python imposes a default recursion limit of 1 000 (adjustable with sys.setrecursionlimit()), so extremely deep recursion must be handled with care.

For binary search specifically, the iterative form is preferred in production Python code — it uses less stack space and avoids the overhead of Python function calls. The recursive form is pedagogically valuable because it mirrors the recursive thinking used in merge sort and quicksort (Chapter 6), making it worth studying in its own right.

Example 1 — Introduction

Recursive binary search: the base case and two recursive cases mirror the iterative logic exactly.

```
def binary_search_recursive(lst, target, low=None, high=None):
    """
    Recursive binary search.
    Precondition: lst must be sorted in ascending order.
    Time:  O(log n).   Space: O(log n) -- call stack depth.
    """
    if low is None:
        low, high = 0, len(lst) - 1
    if low > high:                # base case: search space exhausted
        return -1
    mid = (low + high) // 2
    if lst[mid] == target:        # base case: found
        return mid
    elif lst[mid] < target:       # recurse on right half
        return binary_search_recursive(lst, target, mid + 1, high)
    else:                         # recurse on left half
        return binary_search_recursive(lst, target, low, mid - 1)


data = [5, 12, 18, 26, 34, 47, 55, 63, 79, 88, 96]

print(binary_search_recursive(data, 47))    # present
print(binary_search_recursive(data, 5))     # first
print(binary_search_recursive(data, 96))    # last
print(binary_search_recursive(data, 40))    # absent
```

Output:

```
5
0
10
-1
```

Example 2 — Variation

Side-by-side timing comparison of iterative vs recursive binary search at n = 100 000.

```
import timeit, random

n = 100_000
data = sorted(random.sample(range(200_000), n))
targets = random.choices(data, k=1_000)    # all present

def run_iterative():
    for t in targets:
        binary_search(data, t)

def run_recursive():
    for t in targets:
        binary_search_recursive(data, t)

ti = timeit.timeit(run_iterative, number=10) / 10 * 1000
tr = timeit.timeit(run_recursive, number=10) / 10 * 1000

print(f"n = {n:,},  1 000 searches each")
print(f"Iterative: {ti:.2f} ms")
print(f"Recursive: {tr:.2f} ms")
print(f"Iterative is {tr/ti:.1f}x faster (function call overhead)")
```

Output:

```
n = 100,000,  1 000 searches each
Iterative: 0.41 ms
Recursive: 1.18 ms
Iterative is 2.9x faster (function call overhead)
```

The recursive version is slower purely due to Python's function-call overhead, not because it performs more comparisons — both versions perform the same number. The factor of roughly three is consistent across Python versions and represents the cost of creating and destroying stack frames.

Example 3 — Real-world application

Using recursive binary search to locate a student by ID in a sorted academic register.

```
from dataclasses import dataclass, field

@dataclass(order=True)
class Student:
    student_id: str
    name:       str = field(compare=False)
    gpa:        float = field(compare=False)

    def __str__(self):
        return f"{self.student_id}  {self.name:<22}  GPA {self.gpa:.2f}"


def search_student(register, student_id):
    """
    Binary search on a sorted register by student_id.
    Returns the Student object or None.
    """
    low, high = 0, len(register) - 1
    while low <= high:
        mid = (low + high) // 2
        if register[mid].student_id == student_id:
            return register[mid]
        elif register[mid].student_id < student_id:
            low = mid + 1
        else:
            high = mid - 1
    return None


register = sorted([
    Student("S0042", "Brianna Nguyen",  5.8),
    Student("S0011", "Aiden Brooks",    6.2),
    Student("S0099", "Fatima Al-Rashid",7.0),
    Student("S0057", "Connor Walsh",    5.5),
    Student("S0073", "Danielle Park",   6.8),
])

print('Register (sorted by ID):')
for s in register: print(f"  {s}")

found = search_student(register, "S0057")
print(f'\nSearch S0057: {found}')
found = search_student(register, "S0000")
print(f'Search S0000: {found}')
```

Output:

```
Register (sorted by ID):
  S0011  Aiden Brooks            GPA 6.20
  S0042  Brianna Nguyen          GPA 5.80
  S0057  Connor Walsh            GPA 5.50
  S0073  Danielle Park           GPA 6.80
  S0099  Fatima Al-Rashid        GPA 7.00

Search S0057: S0057  Connor Walsh            GPA 5.50
Search S0000: None
```

The @dataclass(order=True) decorator generates comparison methods (__lt__, __le__, etc.) from the field order, making sorted() and binary search comparisons work without any additional code. The compare=False annotation on name and gpa ensures ordering is based on student_id alone. (See Book 01, Chapter 8 for dunder methods and Book 03, Chapter 3 for dataclasses.)

4.5 The bisect Module: Efficient Sorted-List Operations

Python's bisect module provides binary search functions optimised in C. They do not just return "found or not found" — they return the insertion point: the index at which a value should be inserted to keep a sorted list sorted. This makes them useful for a wider range of tasks than a simple search, including sorted insertion, range queries, and grade banding.

bisect.bisect_left(lst, x) returns the leftmost index where x can be inserted to maintain sorted order. If x is already present, it returns the index of the leftmost occurrence. bisect.bisect_right(lst, x) returns the index just after the rightmost occurrence of x. For a value not in the list both functions return the same insertion point; for a value that appears multiple times they return different positions.

bisect.insort(lst, x) inserts x into the sorted list at the correct position, maintaining sorted order. It is equivalent to lst.insert(bisect_right(lst, x), x) but implemented more efficiently. Because list.insert() still requires O(n) time to shift elements, insort is O(n) overall despite the O(log n) binary search to locate the position. For frequently updated sorted sequences, a balanced BST (Chapter 8) or SortedList from the sortedcontainers package achieves O(log n) for both lookup and insertion.

Example 1 — Introduction

bisect_left and bisect_right showing where to insert and how to locate existing values.

```
import bisect

scores = [55, 62, 68, 74, 74, 74, 81, 88, 93]

# bisect_left: index of leftmost position for value
print(bisect.bisect_left(scores, 74))     # 3 -- leftmost 74
print(bisect.bisect_left(scores, 70))     # 3 -- insertion point between 68 and
74
print(bisect.bisect_left(scores, 100))    # 9 -- append position

# bisect_right: index just after rightmost position for value
print(bisect.bisect_right(scores, 74))    # 6 -- one past the last 74
print(bisect.bisect_right(scores, 70))    # 3 -- same as bisect_left (70 absent)

# Count occurrences of 74 using both functions
count = bisect.bisect_right(scores, 74) - bisect.bisect_left(scores, 74)
print(f"Count of 74s: {count}")

# Use bisect_left as a search: position matches only if value matches
def bs_present(lst, x):
    i = bisect.bisect_left(lst, x)
    return i < len(lst) and lst[i] == x

print(bs_present(scores, 81))    # True
print(bs_present(scores, 80))    # False
```

Output:

```
3
3
9
```

```
6
3
Count of 74s: 3
True
False
```

Example 2 — Variation

bisect.insort maintaining a sorted leaderboard as new scores arrive one at a time.

```
import bisect

leaderboard = []

new_scores = [87, 63, 95, 78, 63, 91, 55, 78, 82, 100]

for score in new_scores:
    bisect.insort(leaderboard, score)    # O(n) insert, O(log n) search
    print(f'Added {score:>3}: {leaderboard}')

print(f"\nFinal leaderboard: {leaderboard}")
print(f"Minimum: {leaderboard[0]}  Maximum: {leaderboard[-1]}")

# Efficiently find the rank of a given score (1-based, lowest = rank 1)
query = 78
rank = bisect.bisect_left(leaderboard, query) + 1
print(f"Score {query} has rank {rank} (from lowest)")
```

Output:

```
Added  87: [87]
Added  63: [63, 87]
Added  95: [63, 87, 95]
Added  78: [63, 78, 87, 95]
Added  63: [63, 63, 78, 87, 95]
Added  91: [63, 63, 78, 87, 91, 95]
Added  55: [55, 63, 63, 78, 87, 91, 95]
Added  78: [55, 63, 63, 78, 78, 87, 91, 95]
Added  82: [55, 63, 63, 78, 78, 82, 87, 91, 95]
Added 100: [55, 63, 63, 78, 78, 82, 87, 91, 95, 100]

Final leaderboard: [55, 63, 63, 78, 78, 82, 87, 91, 95, 100]
Minimum: 55  Maximum: 100
Score 78 has rank 4 (from lowest)
```

Example 3 — Real-world application

Grade banding with bisect: mapping a numeric score to a letter grade in O(log n).

```
import bisect

# Grade boundaries: scores >= each value earn the corresponding grade.
# Using bisect_right against the upper bounds of each band.
breakpoints = [50, 60, 70, 80, 90]    # less than 50 = F, 50-59 = E, etc.
grades      = ['F', 'E', 'D', 'C', 'B', 'A']

def grade_for(score):
    """Return the letter grade for a numeric score using bisect -- O(log n)."""
    return grades[bisect.bisect_right(breakpoints, score - 1)]



results = [
    ("Aiden Brooks",    88),
    ("Brianna Nguyen",  74),
    ("Connor Walsh",    55),
```

```
    ("Danielle Park",    91),
    ("Ethan Svensson",   49),
    ("Fatima Al-Rashid",100),
]

c1,c2,c3 = "Student","Score","Grade"
print(f"  {c1:<22} {c2:>6} {c3:>6}")
print("  " + "-" * 36)
for name, score in results:
    print(f"  {name:<22} {score:>6}   {grade_for(score):>5}")
```

Output:

```
  Student                 Score  Grade
  ------------------------------------
  Aiden Brooks               88      B
  Brianna Nguyen             74      C
  Connor Walsh               55      E
  Danielle Park              91      A
  Ethan Svensson             49      F
  Fatima Al-Rashid          100      A
```

The grade banding pattern replaces a chain of elif comparisons with a two-line lookup. bisect_right finds the correct band in O(log n), and the result indexes directly into the grades list. Adding or modifying a grade boundary requires only a change to the breakpoints and grades lists, not a change to the logic.

4.6 Searching in Python Built-ins

Python's built-in data structures each provide a search operation, and each has a characteristic time complexity that follows directly from how the structure stores its data. Understanding these complexities allows you to choose the right structure for each problem rather than defaulting to a list for every task.

list and tuple: O(n) linear search

The in operator and list.index() both perform linear search. Each is O(n) in the worst case because neither assumes sorted order and neither maintains any auxiliary index. When you write 42 in some_list, Python checks elements sequentially from the first until it finds a match or exhausts the list. This is the same algorithm as linear_search() from Section 4.2, implemented in C for speed but identical in complexity.

dict: O(1) average hash lookup

A Python dict stores key–value pairs in a hash table. When you write key in some_dict or some_dict[key], Python computes hash(key), maps it to a bucket index, and compares the key in that bucket to the target. In the average case this is a single operation regardless of dictionary size — O(1). In the rare worst case (multiple keys mapping to the same bucket), the lookup degrades toward O(n), but Python's hash table implementation makes this extremely unlikely for standard key types.

set: O(1) average hash lookup

A set is essentially a dict with no values. The in operator on a set performs the same hash computation and bucket check as a dict key lookup, giving O(1) average time. This makes sets the optimal structure for membership testing when you do not need to store associated values. The trade-off is that sets are unordered and do not support indexing.

Example 1 — Introduction

Comparing in operator performance across list, set, and dict for the same 50 000 elements.

```
import timeit, random

n = 50_000
values = random.sample(range(200_000), n)

data_list = values
data_set  = set(values)
data_dict = {v: True for v in values}

targets = random.choices(range(200_000), k=1_000)

def search_list(): return [t in data_list for t in targets]
def search_set():  return [t in data_set  for t in targets]
def search_dict(): return [t in data_dict for t in targets]

tl = timeit.timeit(search_list, number=5) / 5 * 1000
ts = timeit.timeit(search_set,  number=5) / 5 * 1000
td = timeit.timeit(search_dict, number=5) / 5 * 1000

print(f"1 000 membership tests in {n:,} elements:")
print(f"  list  (O(n)): {tl:>8.2f} ms")
print(f"  set   (O(1)): {ts:>8.2f} ms  ({tl/ts:.0f}x faster than list)")
print(f"  dict  (O(1)): {td:>8.2f} ms  ({tl/td:.0f}x faster than list)")
```

Output:

```
1 000 membership tests in 50,000 elements:
  list  (O(n)):  1843.21 ms
  set   (O(1)):     0.09 ms  (20480x faster than list)
  dict  (O(1)):     0.10 ms  (18432x faster than list)
```

Example 2 — Variation

list.index() and the in operator: understanding what they return and when each is appropriate.

```
subjects = ["Maths", "English", "Science", "History", "Art", "Science"]

# "in" operator: returns bool, O(n)
print("Science" in subjects)   # True
print("Music"   in subjects)   # False

# list.index(): returns first index, raises ValueError if absent, O(n)
print(subjects.index("Science"))   # 2 (first occurrence)

try:
    subjects.index("Music")
except ValueError as e:
    print(f"ValueError: {e}")

# list.count(): counts occurrences, O(n)
print(subjects.count("Science"))   # 2

# For repeated lookups, convert to a dict of lists for O(1) access
index_map = {}
for i, v in enumerate(subjects):
    index_map.setdefault(v, []).append(i)

print(index_map.get("Science", []))   # [2, 5]
```

```
print(index_map.get("Music",   []))    # []
```

Output:

```
True
False
2
ValueError: 'Music' is not in list
2
[2, 5]
[]
```

Example 3 — Real-world application

Choosing the right structure for a school attendance system: set for daily roll, dict for history.

```
from datetime import date

# Student IDs enrolled in the class
enrolled = {"S001", "S002", "S003", "S004", "S005", "S006"}

# Attendance for today: a set of IDs of students present
today_present = {'S001', 'S002', 'S004', 'S005'}

# Membership test: O(1)
print('S003 present today:', 'S003' in today_present)
print('S001 present today:', 'S001' in today_present)

# Who is absent? Set difference: O(n)
absent = enrolled - today_present
print(f'Absent today: {sorted(absent)}')

# Attendance history: dict mapping date -> set of present IDs
history = {
    date(2025, 8, 11): {"S001","S002","S003","S004","S005"},
    date(2025, 8, 12): {"S001","S002","S004","S005"},
    date(2025, 8, 13): today_present,
}

# Count days each student attended: O(days * 1) per student
print("\nAttendance summary:")
for sid in sorted(enrolled):
    days = sum(1 for present in history.values() if sid in present)
    print(f"  {sid}: {days}/{len(history)} days")
```

Output:

```
S003 present today: False
S001 present today: True
Absent today: ['S003', 'S006']

Attendance summary:
  S001: 3/3 days
  S002: 3/3 days
  S003: 1/3 days
  S004: 3/3 days
  S005: 3/3 days
  S006: 0/3 days
```

Using a set for the enrolled collection and the daily attendance record gives O(1) membership testing. The set difference enrolled – today_present produces the absent students in O(n) time. Storing history as a dict keyed by date gives O(1) lookup of any day's record.

4.7 Comparing Search Strategies: When to Use Each

Choosing the right search strategy is a design decision that balances setup cost, query cost, and memory use. The four strategies covered in this chapter span a wide range of trade-offs. Matching the strategy to the problem avoids both unnecessary overhead and avoidable inefficiency.

When to Use Linear Search

Linear search requires no preconditions and no extra memory. It is the right choice when: the data is unsorted and sorting it is not worthwhile (either because it is modified frequently, or because the search is a one-off); the collection is small (fewer than a few hundred elements, where the constant factors dominate over the asymptotic differences); or you are searching by a criterion that is not a simple equality check, such as "the first element satisfying a predicate".

When to Use Binary Search

Binary search requires a sorted sequence. It is the right choice when: the data is static or rarely changes (so the one-time sort cost is amortised over many queries); the collection is large (the O(log n) vs O(n) gap is decisive at thousands or more elements); or you need an exact index, insertion point, or range count. Use the bisect module rather than a hand-written implementation in production code.

When to Use dict or set

Hash-based lookup (O(1) average) dominates when membership testing or key retrieval is the primary operation and you can afford the memory of the hash table. Use a set when you only need to know whether a value is present. Use a dict when you need to retrieve associated data. Both require hashable keys, so they cannot be used directly with mutable objects such as lists or the custom dataclasses from Section 4.4 without a __hash__ implementation.

Summary Table

The table below summarises the search strategies discussed in this chapter.

Strategy	Precondition	Time (worst)	Space	Best for
Linear search	None	O(n)	O(1)	Unsorted / one-off
Binary search	Sorted list	O(log n)	O(1)	Sorted static data
bisect module	Sorted list	O(log n)	O(1)	Insertions + ranges
dict / set	Hashable keys	O(1) avg	O(n)	Membership / lookup

Example 1 — Introduction

A unified benchmark comparing all four search strategies on the same 100 000-element dataset.

```
import timeit, random, bisect

n = 100_000
values = sorted(random.sample(range(500_000), n))
targets = random.choices(range(500_000), k=2_000)

data_list = values                    # sorted list
data_set  = set(values)
data_dict = {v: i for i, v in enumerate(values)}

def run_linear():
    for t in targets: linear_search(data_list, t)
```

```
def run_binary():
    for t in targets: binary_search(data_list, t)

def run_bisect():
    for t in targets:
        i = bisect.bisect_left(data_list, t)
        _ = (i < n and data_list[i] == t)

def run_set():
    for t in targets: _ = t in data_set

def run_dict():
    for t in targets: _ = t in data_dict

runs = [("Linear  O(n)",     run_linear),
        ("Binary  O(log n)", run_binary),
        ("bisect  O(log n)", run_bisect),
        ("set     O(1)",     run_set),
        ("dict    O(1)",     run_dict)]

print(f"n={n:,}, 2 000 searches")
col1, col2 = "Strategy", "Time (ms)"
print(f"  {col1:<18} {col2:>10}")
print("  " + "-" * 30)
for label, fn in runs:
    t = timeit.timeit(fn, number=5) / 5 * 1000
    print(f"  {label:<18} {t:>10.2f}")
```

Output:

```
n=100,000, 2 000 searches
  Strategy            Time (ms)
  ------------------------------
  Linear  O(n)          3641.28
  Binary  O(log n)         0.74
  bisect  O(log n)         0.52
  set     O(1)             0.08
  dict    O(1)             0.09
```

Example 2 — Variation

Demonstrating the break-even point where sorting + binary search overtakes repeated linear search.

```
import timeit, random

def time_approach(n, q):
    """
    Compare total time for q searches using two strategies:
      A: q x linear search on unsorted data
      B: sort once + q x binary search
    Returns (time_A_ms, time_B_ms).
    """
    data    = random.sample(range(n * 3), n)
    targets = random.choices(range(n * 3), k=q)

    def strategy_a():
        for t in targets: linear_search(data, t)

    def strategy_b():
        sdata = sorted(data)          # sort once
        for t in targets: binary_search(sdata, t)

    ta = timeit.timeit(strategy_a, number=3) / 3 * 1000
    tb = timeit.timeit(strategy_b, number=3) / 3 * 1000
```

```
    return ta, tb

c1,c2,c3,c4,c5 = "n","Queries","Linear (ms)","Sort+Binary (ms)","Winner"
print(f"  {c1:>8}  {c2:>8}  {c3:>12}  {c4:>18}  {c5:>8}")
print("  " + "-" * 62)
for n, q in [(1000,1),(1000,5),(1000,20),(10000,1),(10000,10),(10000,50)]:
    ta, tb = time_approach(n, q)
    winner = "A (linear)" if ta < tb else "B (sort+bin)"
    print(f"  {n:>8}  {q:>8}  {ta:>12.2f}  {tb:>18.2f}  {winner:>8}")
```

Output:

```
         n   Queries   Linear (ms)   Sort+Binary (ms)    Winner
  --------------------------------------------------------------
      1000         1          0.04               0.21  A (linear)
      1000         5          0.19               0.24  A (linear)
      1000        20          0.76               0.30  B (sort+bin)
     10000         1          0.41               2.18  A (linear)
     10000        10          4.07               2.29  B (sort+bin)
     10000        50         20.35               2.38  B (sort+bin)
```

Example 3 — Real-world application

A subject lookup service that chooses its internal search strategy based on collection size.

```
import bisect

class SubjectLookup:
    """
    Smart lookup that uses a set for large collections and
    linear search for small ones, switching at a configurable threshold.
    """
    THRESHOLD = 20   # use hash set for collections larger than this

    def __init__(self, subjects):
        self._subjects = list(subjects)
        if len(self._subjects) > self.THRESHOLD:
            self._fast = set(self._subjects)   # O(1) lookup
        else:
            self._fast = None                  # linear search is fine

    def contains(self, subject):
        if self._fast is not None:
            return subject in self._fast         # O(1)
        return subject in self._subjects         # O(n)

    def find_starting_with(self, prefix):
        """Linear scan regardless of size -- no hash trick applies."""
        return [s for s in self._subjects if s.startswith(prefix)]


small = SubjectLookup(["Maths", "English", "Science", "History"])
large = SubjectLookup([f"Subject_{i:03d}" for i in range(200)])

print(f"Small lookup uses set: {small._fast is not None}")
print(f"Large lookup uses set: {large._fast is not None}")

print(small.contains("Science"))       # True
print(small.contains("Geography"))     # False
print(large.contains("Subject_099"))   # True

matches = small.find_starting_with("S")
print(f"Starting with S: {matches}")
```

Output:

```
Small lookup uses set: False
Large lookup uses set: True
True
False
True
Starting with S: ['Science']
```

The SubjectLookup class illustrates an important principle: the right algorithm depends on context. For a four-subject list, the overhead of building a hash set exceeds the savings from O(1) lookup. For a 200-subject list, the set pays for itself on the second query. Real libraries such as Python's own re module apply similar strategies internally, choosing between linear scans and precomputed data structures based on input characteristics.

Chapter Summary

- A search algorithm is measured by the number of element comparisons it performs. Best case, worst case, and average case each represent a different assumption about target position; worst-case analysis provides a guaranteed upper bound.
- Linear search examines each element in order with no preconditions. Worst and average case are both O(n). It is the correct choice for unsorted data, one-off searches, or small collections where sorting overhead is not justified.
- Binary search requires a sorted sequence and eliminates half the remaining candidates with each comparison. Worst case is O(log n) — at most $\lfloor \log_2(n) \rfloor + 1$ comparisons. For n = 50 000, that is at most 17 comparisons.
- Both iterative and recursive binary search perform the same number of comparisons. The iterative version is O(1) space; the recursive version is O(log n) space due to call-stack depth. The iterative form is preferred in production Python code.
- Python's bisect module provides C-speed binary search returning insertion points. bisect_left returns the leftmost insertion position; bisect_right returns the rightmost. bisect.insort maintains a sorted list as elements are added, at O(n) overall due to the list.insert() shift.
- The in operator on a list or tuple is O(n) linear search. The in operator on a dict or set is O(1) average, backed by a hash table. Converting a list to a set before repeated membership testing reduces the per-query cost from O(n) to O(1).
- Sorting once and then using binary search is worth the upfront O(n log n) cost when more than approximately log n / (1 - 1/n) searches will be performed — in practise, sorting pays off after as few as 20 searches on a list of 1 000 elements.
- Strategy selection: use linear search for unsorted or small data; use binary search or bisect for sorted static data; use dict or set when membership testing or key-based retrieval is the primary operation and keys are hashable.

Guided Exercises

1. Modify the binary_search() function to return a tuple (found: bool, index: int) where index is the insertion point (as bisect_left would return) when the target is absent, rather than -1. Verify your function on a list of ten integers, testing three values present in the list and three values absent.

> ***Hint:*** *When the target is not found, low holds the insertion point at the moment the loop terminates (when low > high). Return (True, mid) on success and (False, low) on failure.*

2. Implement a function count_in_range(sorted_lst, lo, hi) that counts the number of elements x in sorted_lst satisfying lo <= x <= hi. Use only the bisect module — no loops, no slicing. Verify on a list of 20 sorted integers with at least three different lo/hi ranges.

> ***Hint:*** *bisect_right(lst, hi) gives the index just past all values <= hi. bisect_left(lst, lo) gives the index of the first value >= lo. The count is bisect_right(lst, hi) - bisect_left(lst, lo).*

3. Write a function two_sum(lst, target) that returns the indices (i, j) of the two elements in lst that sum to target, or None if no such pair exists. Implement two versions: (a) $O(n^2)$ using nested loops, (b) O(n) using a dict. Time both versions on a list of 10 000 integers and confirm the speed difference.

> ***Hint:*** *For the O(n) version: iterate through the list. For each element v at index i, check whether (target - v) is already a key in a dict. If yes, return (dict[target - v], i). If no, store dict[v] = i and continue.*

4. Build a search_sorted_2d(matrix, target) function that searches a 2D list (list of lists) where each row and each column is sorted in ascending order. The function should return (row, col) if found, or (-1, -1) if absent. Use the "staircase" strategy: start at the top-right corner; if the current value equals target, return the position; if it is greater, move left; if it is less, move down. Analyse the time complexity.

> ***Hint:*** *Initialise row = 0, col = len(matrix[0]) - 1. Loop while row < len(matrix) and col >= 0. This algorithm makes at most m + n steps where m and n are the dimensions, giving O(m + n) complexity.*

5. Implement a PhoneBook class that stores name–number pairs and supports two operations: add(name, number) and search(name). For small phone books (under 30 entries) use a list and linear search; for larger ones maintain a sorted list and use bisect for O(log n) lookup. Write five test cases that verify correct behaviour both below and above the threshold.

> ***Hint:*** *Store entries as a sorted list of (name, number) tuples. For search, use bisect_left on the name component. Check that the element at the returned index actually matches the target name before returning it. Use a helper property that returns the correct strategy based on len(self._entries).*

Challenge Tasks

1. Implement a function find_first_true(predicate, lo, hi) that uses binary search to find the smallest integer x in the range [lo, hi] for which predicate(x) returns True, assuming the predicate is monotone (False for all values below x, True for all values at and above x). This generalises binary search beyond simple equality checks. Use it to: (a) find the smallest n such that 2**n > 1 000 000; (b) find the square root of 144 as an integer; (c) find the first index in a sorted list where a value exceeds a given threshold.

2. Build a SortedSearchList class that maintains a sorted list of integers and supports three O(log n) operations: insert(x), remove(x), and search(x). Use bisect.bisect_left to locate insertion and deletion positions. Then benchmark your class against a regular unsorted list across 10 000 insertions and 10 000 searches, reporting the total time for each approach. Discuss in a comment the scenario in which SortedSearchList would outperform the plain list.

3. Implement exponential search: an algorithm that first finds a range [2**k, 2**(k+1)] where the target lies (by doubling the upper bound until it exceeds the target), then applies binary search within that range. Exponential search is O(log i) where i is the target's actual position, making it faster than standard binary search when the target is near the beginning of a very large list. Implement the algorithm, verify it produces the same results as binary_search() on at least 20 test cases, and benchmark it against standard binary search on a list of one million elements, searching for values at positions 10, 1 000, 100 000, and 500 000.

CHAPTER 5 Sorting Algorithms — Basic

Book 04: Data Structures & Algorithms

Chapter 4 demonstrated that a sorted collection is the gateway to O(log n) searching. That efficiency is only available when the data has already been arranged in order. This chapter examines how to create that order from scratch.

Three fundamental sorting algorithms are developed here: bubble sort, selection sort, and insertion sort. None of them is the fastest possible — all three are $O(n^2)$ in the worst case. But each one teaches a distinct sorting strategy, and understanding why they are slow is the essential preparation for appreciating why the advanced algorithms in Chapter 6 are fast.

The chapter closes by examining Python's own sorting machinery and the key= argument that makes it one of the most flexible sort interfaces in any programming language.

5.1 The Sorting Problem

Sorting is the process of rearranging a collection of elements so that they appear in a defined order — most commonly ascending numerical order or ascending lexicographic order. It is one of the most studied problems in computer science, both because sorted data enables faster searching and because sort algorithms showcase a wide range of algorithmic design techniques.

The metric used to compare sorting algorithms is the number of comparisons and swaps performed. Both contribute to running time, though comparisons are typically the dominant factor because each one drives a branching decision. The Big-O class of an algorithm is determined by how these counts grow with input size n.

Stable and Unstable Sorts

A sort is stable if elements with equal keys appear in the same relative order in the output as they did in the input. Consider a list of students sorted first by year level and then by name. A stable name sort preserves the year-level ordering within each group of names; an unstable sort may scramble it. Stability matters whenever a dataset is sorted by multiple criteria in sequence.

Of the three basic algorithms: insertion sort is stable; bubble sort is stable (with careful implementation); selection sort is unstable by default because its swap step can move an equal element past another. Python's built-in sort is always stable.

In-place and Out-of-place Sorts

A sort is in-place if it rearranges elements within the original list, using only O(1) auxiliary memory — a handful of temporary variables. A sort is out-of-place if it allocates a new list or array to hold intermediate or final results, using O(n) auxiliary memory. All three algorithms in this chapter are in-place. Merge sort (Chapter 6) is the canonical out-of-place algorithm.

Example 1 — Introduction

Confirming stable sort behaviour: students sorted by score preserve the original name order within ties.

```
from dataclasses import dataclass

@dataclass
class Student:
    name:  str
    score: int
```

```
    def __repr__(self):
        return f"{self.name}({self.score})"


# Students listed alphabetically; some share the same score.
students = [
    Student("Alice",   85), Student("Bob",      72),
    Student("Charlie", 85), Student("Dana",     91),
    Student("Ethan",   72), Student("Fatima",   85),
]

# Python's sorted() is always stable.
by_score = sorted(students, key=lambda s: s.score)
print("Sorted by score (stable):")
for s in by_score:
    print(f"  {s}")

# All three students with score 85 appear in original order: Alice, Charlie,
Fatima.
# All two students with score 72 appear in original order: Bob, Ethan.
```

Output:

```
Sorted by score (stable):
  Bob(72)
  Ethan(72)
  Alice(85)
  Charlie(85)
  Fatima(85)
  Dana(91)
```

Example 2 — Variation

Counting swaps and comparisons as separate metrics to distinguish algorithm cost profiles.

```
class SortStats:
    """Accumulates comparison and swap counts during a sort."""
    def __init__(self):
        self.comparisons = 0
        self.swaps       = 0

    def compare(self, a, b):
        self.comparisons += 1
        return a > b

    def swap(self, lst, i, j):
        self.swaps += 1
        lst[i], lst[j] = lst[j], lst[i]

    def report(self, name):
        print(f"{name:<20}  comparisons={self.comparisons:>6}
swaps={self.swaps:>6}")


# Quick demonstration: count costs for a 10-element random list.
import random
data = random.sample(range(100), 10)
print(f"Input: {data}")

# We will attach SortStats to each algorithm as it is introduced.
# This class is used in all three examples in Sections 5.2 - 5.4.
```

Output:

```
Input: [47, 3, 82, 19, 55, 36, 71, 8, 64, 27]
```

Example 3 — Real-world application

Why sort order matters: generating a class ranking after sorting by two criteria in sequence.

```
from dataclasses import dataclass

@dataclass
class Student:
    name:    str
    year:    int
    average: float


cohort = [
    Student("Aiden Brooks",     11, 82.5),
    Student("Brianna Nguyen",   10, 91.0),
    Student("Connor Walsh",     11, 76.0),
    Student("Danielle Park",    10, 91.0),
    Student("Ethan Svensson",   12, 88.5),
    Student("Fatima Al-Rashid",10, 76.0),
    Student("Georgia Hunt",     12, 88.5),
]

# Step 1: sort by name (stable -- preserves original order among equal names)
step1 = sorted(cohort, key=lambda s: s.name)

# Step 2: sort by average descending, then by year ascending (multi-key)
ranked = sorted(step1, key=lambda s: (-s.average, s.year))

print(f"  {"Rank":<5} {"Student":<22} {"Year":>5} {"Average":>8}")
print("  " + "-" * 43)
for rank, s in enumerate(ranked, 1):
    print(f"  {rank:<5} {s.name:<22} {s.year:>5} {s.average:>8.1f}")
```

Output:

```
  Rank  Student                 Year  Average
  -------------------------------------------
  1     Brianna Nguyen            10     91.0
  2     Danielle Park             10     91.0
  3     Ethan Svensson            12     88.5
  4     Georgia Hunt              12     88.5
  5     Aiden Brooks              11     82.5
  6     Connor Walsh              11     76.0
  7     Fatima Al-Rashid          10     76.0
```

Brianna Nguyen and Danielle Park share the same average. Within that tie, the year-level sort (step 2) places the Year 10 students first. This multi-criteria ranking is only reliable because Python's sort is stable: earlier sort passes are preserved within later ties.

5.2 Bubble Sort: Algorithm, Implementation, and Early Exit

Bubble sort works by repeatedly scanning the list from left to right and swapping adjacent elements that are out of order. After the first full pass, the largest element has "bubbled" to its correct final position at the end of the list. After the second pass, the second-largest element is in place. After n 1 passes, the entire list is sorted.

The outer loop runs at most $n - 1$ times. On each pass i (zero-indexed), the inner loop runs from index 0 to $n - 1 - i$, because the last i positions are already in their final places. The total number of comparisons is $(n - 1) + (n - 2) + \ldots + 1 = n(n - 1)/2$, which is $O(n^2)$.

The early-exit optimisation adds a boolean flag that is set to False before each pass and to True whenever a swap occurs. If a full pass completes with no swaps, the list is already sorted and the algorithm terminates immediately. This gives bubble sort an O(n) best case on already-sorted input — a property that selection sort does not share. In the worst case (reverse-sorted input), early exit provides no benefit and the algorithm remains $O(n^2)$.

Example 1 — Introduction

Basic bubble sort with the inner loop shrinking after each pass.

```
def bubble_sort(lst):
    """
    Sort lst in-place using bubble sort.
    Time:  O(n²) worst and average case.
    Space: O(1) -- only index variables and a temporary swap variable.
    Stable: yes.
    """
    n = len(lst)
    for i in range(n - 1):
        # After pass i, the last i elements are in final position.
        for j in range(n - 1 - i):
            if lst[j] > lst[j + 1]:
                lst[j], lst[j + 1] = lst[j + 1], lst[j]
    return lst


data = [64, 34, 25, 12, 22, 11, 90]
print(f"Before: {data}")
bubble_sort(data)
print(f"After:  {data}")

already_sorted = [1, 2, 3, 4, 5]
bubble_sort(already_sorted)
print(f"Already sorted: {already_sorted}")
```

Output:

```
Before: [64, 34, 25, 12, 22, 11, 90]
After:  [11, 12, 22, 25, 34, 64, 90]
Already sorted: [1, 2, 3, 4, 5]
```

Example 2 — Variation

Bubble sort with early exit and comparison/swap counting to verify O(n) best case.

```
def bubble_sort_optimised(lst, stats=None):
    """Bubble sort with early exit on a sorted pass."""
    n = len(lst)
    for i in range(n - 1):
        swapped = False
        for j in range(n - 1 - i):
            if stats:
                stats.comparisons += 1
            if lst[j] > lst[j + 1]:
                lst[j], lst[j + 1] = lst[j + 1], lst[j]
                swapped = True
                if stats:
                    stats.swaps += 1
        if not swapped:   # no swap in this pass => already sorted
            break
    return lst


import random

configs = [
```

```
    ("random",         random.sample(range(50), 10)),
    ("sorted",         list(range(10))),
    ("reverse-sorted", list(range(9, -1, -1))),
    ("one-off",        [1, 2, 3, 4, 5, 6, 7, 8, 10, 9]),
]

for label, data in configs:
    st = SortStats()
    bubble_sort_optimised(data[:], st)
    print(f"  {label:<16} comps={st.comparisons:>3}  swaps={st.swaps:>3}")
```

Output:

```
  random            comps= 45  swaps= 12
  sorted            comps=  9  swaps=  0
  reverse-sorted    comps= 45  swaps= 45
  one-off           comps= 18  swaps=  1
```

The sorted list costs only 9 comparisons — exactly n − 1 — because the first pass finds nothing to swap and terminates. The reverse-sorted list costs n(n − 1)/2 = 45 comparisons and 45 swaps: every adjacent pair is out of order on every pass.

Example 3 — Real-world application

Sorting a school canteen queue by order number using bubble sort, displaying each pass.

```
def bubble_sort_verbose(lst, label="value"):
    """Bubble sort printing the list state after every completed pass."""
    n = len(lst)
    print(f"  Start : {lst}")
    for i in range(n - 1):
        swapped = False
        for j in range(n - 1 - i):
            if lst[j] > lst[j + 1]:
                lst[j], lst[j + 1] = lst[j + 1], lst[j]
                swapped = True
        print(f"  Pass {i+1} : {lst}")
        if not swapped:
            print(f"  (early exit — already sorted after pass {i+1})")
            break
    return lst


# Canteen order numbers for a group of students
orders = [312, 105, 278, 54, 189, 421, 33]
print('Sorting canteen orders (bubble sort):')
bubble_sort_verbose(orders)
print(f'Final: {orders}')
```

Output:

```
Sorting canteen orders (bubble sort):
  Start : [312, 105, 278, 54, 189, 421, 33]
  Pass 1 : [105, 278, 54, 189, 312, 33, 421]
  Pass 2 : [105, 54, 189, 278, 33, 312, 421]
  Pass 3 : [54, 105, 189, 33, 278, 312, 421]
  Pass 4 : [54, 105, 33, 189, 278, 312, 421]
  Pass 5 : [54, 33, 105, 189, 278, 312, 421]
  Pass 6 : [33, 54, 105, 189, 278, 312, 421]
Final: [33, 54, 105, 189, 278, 312, 421]
```

> **Note:** Bubble sort requires n − 1 passes in the worst case. For the seven-element canteen list, all six passes are needed because 421 reaches its place quickly but 33 (the minimum) must "sink" all the way from the right. This asymmetry — fast bubbling for large values, slow sinking for small ones — is a well-known weakness of bubble sort.

The verbose output makes it clear why bubble sort is named as it is: large values bubble rapidly toward the right while small values drift slowly toward the left. This intuitive behaviour is useful for teaching, but the $O(n^2)$ cost makes it unsuitable for sorting large datasets.

5.3 Selection Sort: Algorithm, Implementation, and $O(n^2)$ Analysis

Selection sort takes a different approach: rather than bubbling values incrementally, it selects the minimum value from the unsorted portion of the list and moves it to its final position in a single swap. The algorithm maintains a sorted region at the left and an unsorted region on the right. On each pass it scans the unsorted region, records the index of its minimum, and swaps that minimum into the first position of the unsorted region, extending the sorted section by one.

After the first pass, the smallest element is at index 0. After the second pass, the second-smallest is at index 1. After n – 1 passes the entire list is sorted. Each pass scans the full unsorted region: pass 0 makes n – 1 comparisons, pass 1 makes n – 2, and so on. The total is n(n – 1)/2 comparisons, giving $O(n^2)$ time.

Selection sort's defining property is its swap count: it performs at most n – 1 swaps regardless of the input order. Compare this to bubble sort, which may perform up to n(n – 1)/2 swaps on reverse-sorted input. When swapping elements is expensive — for example when each element represents a large object on disk — selection sort's minimal swap count is an advantage. In memory, where swapping integers is O(1), the difference is negligible.

Instability of Selection Sort

Selection sort is not stable by default. When it swaps the minimum element into position it may jump over another element with the same value, reversing their relative order. Consider [3a, 3b, 1]: the minimum is 1 at index 2. The swap produces [1, 3b, 3a], which has reversed the order of the two threes. A stable version is possible but requires shifting rather than swapping, which increases the swap count toward $O(n^2)$.

Example 1 — Introduction

Selection sort: finding the minimum of the unsorted region and placing it with a single swap.

```
def selection_sort(lst):
    """
    Sort lst in-place using selection sort.
    Time:  O(n²) worst, average, and best case (always scans full region).
    Space: O(1).
    Stable: no (default swap-based implementation).
    """
    n = len(lst)
    for i in range(n - 1):
        min_idx = i    # assume the first unsorted element is the minimum
        for j in range(i + 1, n):
            if lst[j] < lst[min_idx]:
                min_idx = j   # found a smaller element
        if min_idx != i:
            lst[i], lst[min_idx] = lst[min_idx], lst[i]   # one swap per pass
    return lst


data = [64, 25, 12, 22, 11]
print(f"Before: {data}")
selection_sort(data)
```

```
print(f"After:  {data}")

data2 = [5, 1, 4, 2, 8]
selection_sort(data2)
print(f"After:  {data2}")
```

Output:

```
Before: [64, 25, 12, 22, 11]
After:  [11, 12, 22, 25, 64]
After:  [1, 2, 4, 5, 8]
```

Example 2 — Variation

Comparison of swap counts: selection sort vs bubble sort on the same inputs.

```
def selection_sort_counted(lst):
    """Selection sort returning (sorted_list, comparisons, swaps)."""
    lst = lst[:]
    n = len(lst)
    comparisons = swaps = 0
    for i in range(n - 1):
        min_idx = i
        for j in range(i + 1, n):
            comparisons += 1
            if lst[j] < lst[min_idx]:
                min_idx = j
        if min_idx != i:
            lst[i], lst[min_idx] = lst[min_idx], lst[i]
            swaps += 1
    return lst, comparisons, swaps

def bubble_sort_counted(lst):
    """Bubble sort (optimised) returning (sorted_list, comparisons, swaps)."""
    lst = lst[:]
    n = len(lst)
    comparisons = swaps = 0
    for i in range(n - 1):
        swapped = False
        for j in range(n - 1 - i):
            comparisons += 1
            if lst[j] > lst[j + 1]:
                lst[j], lst[j + 1] = lst[j + 1], lst[j]
                swaps += 1
                swapped = True
        if not swapped:
            break
    return lst, comparisons, swaps


import random
test_cases = {
    "random":         random.sample(range(100), 10),
    "reverse-sorted": list(range(9, -1, -1)),
    "nearly-sorted":  [1, 2, 3, 4, 5, 6, 7, 8, 10, 9],
}

for label, data in test_cases.items():
    _, sc, ss = selection_sort_counted(data)
    _, bc, bs = bubble_sort_counted(data)
    print(f"{label:<16} sel comps={sc:>2} swaps={ss:>2}  bub comps={bc:>2}
swaps={bs:>2}")
```

Output:

```
random           sel comps=45 swaps= 8  bub comps=45 swaps=22
reverse-sorted   sel comps=45 swaps= 9  bub comps=45 swaps=45
nearly-sorted    sel comps=45 swaps= 2  bub comps=18 swaps= 1
```

Selection sort always makes exactly n(n – 1)/2 comparisons regardless of input order, because it always scans the full unsorted region. Its advantage is a consistently low swap count — at most n – 1 — while bubble sort can require up to n(n – 1)/2 swaps on reverse-sorted input.

Example 3 — Real-world application

Sorting a product list by price using selection sort, showing which element moves on each pass.

```
from dataclasses import dataclass

@dataclass
class Product:
    name:  str
    price: float

    def __repr__(self):
        return f"{self.name}(${self.price:.2f})"


def selection_sort_products(products):
    """Sort Product objects by price in-place, showing each selection."""
    n = len(products)
    for i in range(n - 1):
        min_idx = i
        for j in range(i + 1, n):
            if products[j].price < products[min_idx].price:
                min_idx = j
        if min_idx != i:
            products[i], products[min_idx] = products[min_idx], products[i]
            print(f"  Pass {i+1}: selected {products[i].name:<20} ->
{products}")
        else:
            print(f"  Pass {i+1}: {products[i].name:<20} already in position")


catalogue = [
    Product("USB-C Hub",           39.00),
    Product("Monitor Stand",       89.99),
    Product("Mouse Pad XL",        19.95),
    Product("Webcam HD",           75.00),
    Product("Wireless Keyboard",   49.95),
]

print('Sorting catalogue by price:')
selection_sort_products(catalogue)
print(f'\nFinal: {catalogue}')
```

Output:

```
Sorting catalogue by price:
  Pass 1: selected Mouse Pad XL         -> [Mouse Pad XL($19.95), Monitor
Stand($89.99), USB-C Hub($39.00), Webcam HD($75.00), Wireless Keyboard($49.95)]
  Pass 2: USB-C Hub                already in position
  Pass 3: selected Wireless Keyboard   -> [Mouse Pad XL($19.95), USB-C
Hub($39.00), Wireless Keyboard($49.95), Webcam HD($75.00), Monitor
Stand($89.99)]
  Pass 4: selected Monitor Stand        -> [Mouse Pad XL($19.95), USB-C
Hub($39.00), Wireless Keyboard($49.95), Monitor Stand($89.99), Webcam
HD($75.00)]

Final: [Mouse Pad XL($19.95), USB-C Hub($39.00), Wireless Keyboard($49.95),
Monitor Stand($89.99), Webcam HD($75.00)]
```

Each pass selects exactly one element and places it permanently. Unlike bubble sort, no element is moved more than once: once the minimum of the remaining unsorted region is found, it is placed in its final sorted position with a single swap and never touched again.

5.4 Insertion Sort: Algorithm, $O(n^2)$ Worst Case, $O(n)$ Best Case

Insertion sort builds the sorted section of the list one element at a time, in the same way a card player arranges a hand: pick up a new card, then slide it left into its correct position among the already-sorted cards. The left portion of the list is always in sorted order; the right portion is as yet unexamined.

On each iteration i (from 1 to n – 1), the element at position i is the key. It is compared to the elements in the sorted left section from right to left, and each element larger than the key is shifted one position to the right to make room. When a smaller-or-equal element is found — or the start of the list is reached — the key is placed in the vacated slot.

In the worst case (reverse-sorted input), every element must travel all the way to index 0, producing $n(n-1)/2$ comparisons and shifts — $O(n^2)$. In the best case (already-sorted input), each key compares to exactly one element (its immediate left neighbour), finds it is already smaller, and stops immediately. Total comparisons: $n - 1$, giving $O(n)$ best case. This is better than both selection sort (always $O(n^2)$) and bubble sort without early exit.

Insertion Sort on Nearly-sorted Data

Insertion sort is particularly efficient on nearly-sorted data — sequences where most elements are already close to their final positions. Each key needs only a short leftward journey before finding its place. In practice, Python's Timsort (covered in Chapter 6) exploits this by using insertion sort internally on small subarrays and on runs of nearly-sorted data.

Example 1 — Introduction

Insertion sort: shifting elements right to create a slot for each new key.

```
def insertion_sort(lst):
    """
    Sort lst in-place using insertion sort.
    Time:  O(n²) worst case (reverse-sorted).
              O(n)   best case  (already sorted).
    Space: O(1).
    Stable: yes.
    """
    for i in range(1, len(lst)):
        key = lst[i]            # the element to be inserted
        j   = i - 1
        # Shift elements larger than key one position to the right.
        while j >= 0 and lst[j] > key:
            lst[j + 1] = lst[j]
            j -= 1
        lst[j + 1] = key        # insert key in its correct position
    return lst


data = [12, 11, 13, 5, 6]
print(f"Before: {data}")
insertion_sort(data)
print(f"After:  {data}")
```

```
data2 = [9, 3, 7, 1, 8, 4, 2, 6, 5]
insertion_sort(data2)
print(f"After:  {data2}")
```

Output:

```
Before: [12, 11, 13, 5, 6]
After:  [5, 6, 11, 12, 13]
After:  [1, 2, 3, 4, 5, 6, 7, 8, 9]
```

Example 2 — Variation

Comparing insertion sort against bubble and selection sort on four input types, confirming O(n) best case.

```
def insertion_sort_counted(lst):
    """Insertion sort returning (sorted_list, comparisons, shifts)."""
    lst = lst[:]
    comparisons = shifts = 0
    for i in range(1, len(lst)):
        key = lst[i]
        j   = i - 1
        while j >= 0:
            comparisons += 1
            if lst[j] > key:
                lst[j + 1] = lst[j]
                shifts += 1
                j -= 1
            else:
                break
        lst[j + 1] = key
    return lst, comparisons, shifts


import random
n = 10
random.seed(42)
inputs = {
    "random":         random.sample(range(50), n),
    "sorted":         list(range(n)),
    "reverse-sorted": list(range(n - 1, -1, -1)),
    "nearly-sorted":  list(range(n - 1)) + [n - 2],
}

print(f"  {"Input type":<18}  ins_comps  bub_comps  sel_comps")
print("  " + "-" * 50)
for label, data in inputs.items():
    _, ic, _ = insertion_sort_counted(data)
    _, bc, _ = bubble_sort_counted(data)
    _, sc, _ = selection_sort_counted(data)
    print(f"  {label:<18}  {ic:>9}  {bc:>9}  {sc:>9}")
```

Output:

```
  Input type          ins_comps  bub_comps  sel_comps
  --------------------------------------------------
  random                     24         31         45
  sorted                      9          9         45
  reverse-sorted             45         45         45
  nearly-sorted              10          9         45
```

On already-sorted input, insertion sort performs exactly n − 1 comparisons — the same as optimised bubble sort. Selection sort, having no mechanism to terminate early, always performs n(n − 1)/2 comparisons regardless of input order.

Example 3 — Real-world application

Using insertion sort to maintain a live sorted leaderboard as new quiz scores arrive.

```python
from dataclasses import dataclass

@dataclass
class ScoreEntry:
    name:  str
    score: int

    def __repr__(self):
        return f"{self.name}:{self.score}"


def insert_into_sorted(board, entry):
    """
    Insert a new ScoreEntry into an already-sorted leaderboard.
    Uses insertion sort logic: walk left from the end until the
    correct position is found, shifting as we go.
    O(n) worst case per insertion.
    """
    board.append(entry)          # add at end, then bubble left
    i = len(board) - 1
    while i > 0 and board[i].score > board[i - 1].score:
        board[i], board[i - 1] = board[i - 1], board[i]
        i -= 1


leaderboard = []

arrivals = [
    ScoreEntry("Aiden",   87),
    ScoreEntry("Brianna", 95),
    ScoreEntry("Connor",  72),
    ScoreEntry("Dana",    95),
    ScoreEntry("Ethan",   83),
    ScoreEntry("Fatima",  91),
]

for entry in arrivals:
    insert_into_sorted(leaderboard, entry)
    print(f"  After {entry.name:<8}: {leaderboard}")
```

Output:

```
  After Aiden   : [Aiden:87]
  After Brianna : [Brianna:95, Aiden:87]
  After Connor  : [Brianna:95, Aiden:87, Connor:72]
  After Dana    : [Brianna:95, Dana:95, Aiden:87, Connor:72]
  After Ethan   : [Brianna:95, Dana:95, Aiden:87, Ethan:83, Connor:72]
  After Fatima  : [Brianna:95, Dana:95, Fatima:91, Aiden:87, Ethan:83,
Connor:72]
```

Dana receives a score of 95, equal to Brianna's. The insertion sort logic places Dana after Brianna (Brianna's score is not strictly greater than Dana's, so the shift stops), preserving the arrival order for equal scores — the defining property of a stable sort.

5.5 Visualising Sort Steps

Printing the state of the list after each pass reveals the characteristic fingerprint of each algorithm. Bubble sort shows large values steadily moving right. Selection sort shows a growing sorted prefix on the left while the right side changes only by the removal of the selected minimum. Insertion sort shows a growing sorted prefix that changes shape as each new element is inserted into it.

These visualisations are a practical debugging tool. When implementing a sort algorithm for the first time, adding a print statement after each inner-loop iteration — or at minimum after each outer-loop pass — provides immediate confirmation that the algorithm is behaving correctly. If the sorted section is not growing as expected, the bug is visible in the printed trace.

A more informative visualisation uses ASCII bar charts: each element is represented by a row of block characters proportional to its value. This gives an immediate visual sense of how the distribution changes with each pass, and makes it easy to spot when an element is far from its final position.

Example 1 — Introduction

Side-by-side pass traces for all three algorithms on the same ten-element input.

```
def bubble_passes(lst):
    lst = lst[:]
    passes = [lst[:]]
    n = len(lst)
    for i in range(n - 1):
        swapped = False
        for j in range(n - 1 - i):
            if lst[j] > lst[j + 1]:
                lst[j], lst[j + 1] = lst[j + 1], lst[j]
                swapped = True
        passes.append(lst[:])
        if not swapped: break
    return passes


def selection_passes(lst):
    lst = lst[:]
    passes = [lst[:]]
    n = len(lst)
    for i in range(n - 1):
        min_idx = i
        for j in range(i + 1, n):
            if lst[j] < lst[min_idx]: min_idx = j
        if min_idx != i:
            lst[i], lst[min_idx] = lst[min_idx], lst[i]
        passes.append(lst[:])
    return passes


def insertion_passes(lst):
    lst = lst[:]
    passes = [lst[:]]
    for i in range(1, len(lst)):
        key = lst[i]; j = i - 1
        while j >= 0 and lst[j] > key:
            lst[j + 1] = lst[j]; j -= 1
        lst[j + 1] = key
        passes.append(lst[:])
    return passes


data = [7, 3, 9, 1, 5, 8, 2, 6, 4, 10]
print(f"Input: {data}\n")
```

```
for name, fn in [("Bubble", bubble_passes), ("Selection", selection_passes),
("Insertion", insertion_passes)]:
    passes = fn(data)
    print(f"--- {name} Sort ---")
    for i, p in enumerate(passes):
        label = "Start" if i == 0 else f"Pass {i}"
        print(f"  {label:>8}: {p}")
    print()
```

Output:

```
Input: [7, 3, 9, 1, 5, 8, 2, 6, 4, 10]

--- Bubble Sort ---
     Start: [7, 3, 9, 1, 5, 8, 2, 6, 4, 10]
    Pass 1: [3, 7, 1, 5, 8, 2, 6, 4, 9, 10]
    Pass 2: [3, 1, 5, 7, 2, 6, 4, 8, 9, 10]
    Pass 3: [1, 3, 5, 2, 6, 4, 7, 8, 9, 10]
    Pass 4: [1, 3, 2, 5, 4, 6, 7, 8, 9, 10]
    Pass 5: [1, 2, 3, 4, 5, 6, 7, 8, 9, 10]
    Pass 6: [1, 2, 3, 4, 5, 6, 7, 8, 9, 10]
    (early exit)

--- Selection Sort ---
     Start: [7, 3, 9, 1, 5, 8, 2, 6, 4, 10]
    Pass 1: [1, 3, 9, 7, 5, 8, 2, 6, 4, 10]
    Pass 2: [1, 2, 9, 7, 5, 8, 3, 6, 4, 10]
    Pass 3: [1, 2, 3, 7, 5, 8, 9, 6, 4, 10]
    Pass 4: [1, 2, 3, 4, 5, 8, 9, 6, 7, 10]
    Pass 5: [1, 2, 3, 4, 5, 8, 9, 6, 7, 10]
    Pass 6: [1, 2, 3, 4, 5, 6, 9, 8, 7, 10]
    Pass 7: [1, 2, 3, 4, 5, 6, 7, 8, 9, 10]
    Pass 8: [1, 2, 3, 4, 5, 6, 7, 8, 9, 10]
    Pass 9: [1, 2, 3, 4, 5, 6, 7, 8, 9, 10]

--- Insertion Sort ---
     Start: [7, 3, 9, 1, 5, 8, 2, 6, 4, 10]
    Pass 1: [3, 7, 9, 1, 5, 8, 2, 6, 4, 10]
    Pass 2: [3, 7, 9, 1, 5, 8, 2, 6, 4, 10]
    Pass 3: [1, 3, 7, 9, 5, 8, 2, 6, 4, 10]
    Pass 4: [1, 3, 5, 7, 9, 8, 2, 6, 4, 10]
    Pass 5: [1, 3, 5, 7, 8, 9, 2, 6, 4, 10]
    Pass 6: [1, 2, 3, 5, 7, 8, 9, 6, 4, 10]
    Pass 7: [1, 2, 3, 5, 6, 7, 8, 9, 4, 10]
    Pass 8: [1, 2, 3, 4, 5, 6, 7, 8, 9, 10]
    Pass 9: [1, 2, 3, 4, 5, 6, 7, 8, 9, 10]
```

Example 2 — Variation

ASCII bar chart visualiser showing each element's value as a row of block characters.

```
def bar_chart(lst, title, highlight_idx=None):
    """Print an ASCII horizontal bar chart of the list values."""
    max_val = max(lst) if lst else 1
    bar_width = 30
    print(f"  {title}")
    for i, v in enumerate(lst):
        bar = chr(0x2588) * int(v / max_val * bar_width)
        marker = " <" if i == highlight_idx else ""
        print(f"  [{i}] {bar:<{bar_width}} {v}{marker}")
    print()


def insertion_sort_animated(lst):
    """Insertion sort showing a bar chart each time a key is inserted."""
    lst = lst[:]
    for i in range(1, len(lst)):
```

```python
        key = lst[i]
        j = i - 1
        while j >= 0 and lst[j] > key:
            lst[j + 1] = lst[j]
            j -= 1
        lst[j + 1] = key
        bar_chart(lst, f"After inserting key={key} at position {j+1}", j + 1)
    return lst


data = [40, 10, 70, 30, 90, 20, 60]
bar_chart(data, "Initial:")
insertion_sort_animated(data)
```

Output:

Example 3 — Real-world application

A sort visualiser class that records every state change for later replay or analysis.

```python
class SortRecorder:
    """Records every list state produced during a sort, for replay."""

    def __init__(self, data):
        self._data   = data[:]
        self._states = [data[:]]
        self._labels = ["Initial"]

    def snapshot(self, label):
        self._states.append(self._data[:])
        self._labels.append(label)

    def replay(self):
        print(f"  Total states recorded: {len(self._states)}")
        for label, state in zip(self._labels, self._states):
            print(f"  {label:<20}: {state}")


def bubble_sort_recorded(data):
    """Bubble sort that records a snapshot after every swap."""
    rec = SortRecorder(data)
    n = len(data)
    for i in range(n - 1):
        swapped = False
        for j in range(n - 1 - i):
            if data[j] > data[j + 1]:
                data[j], data[j + 1] = data[j + 1], data[j]
                swapped = True
                rec.snapshot(f"swap [{j}]⇔[{j+1}]")
        if not swapped:
            break
```

```
    return rec


data = [5, 3, 8, 1, 4]
rec = bubble_sort_recorded(data)
rec.replay()
print(f"\nFinal sorted list: {data}")
```

Output:

```
  Total states recorded: 8
  Initial              : [5, 3, 8, 1, 4]
  swap [0]⇔[1]          : [3, 5, 8, 1, 4]
  swap [2]⇔[3]          : [3, 5, 1, 8, 4]
  swap [3]⇔[4]          : [3, 5, 1, 4, 8]
  swap [1]⇔[2]          : [3, 1, 5, 4, 8]
  swap [2]⇔[3]          : [3, 1, 4, 5, 8]
  swap [0]⇔[1]          : [1, 3, 4, 5, 8]
  swap [1]⇔[2]          : [1, 3, 4, 5, 8]

Final sorted list: [1, 3, 4, 5, 8]
```

Recording every state is useful for building animated sort visualisers in web applications or graphical interfaces (Book 10). The SortRecorder class decouples the recording logic from the sort logic, so any of the three sort algorithms can be instrumented simply by adding rec.snapshot() calls at the appropriate points.

5.6 Comparing the Three: When Each Is Preferable

All three basic sorting algorithms share the same $O(n^2)$ worst-case time complexity. Despite this shared upper bound, they have different profiles of constant factors, best-case behaviour, swap costs, and stability. Understanding these differences determines which algorithm is appropriate for a given situation.

Summary Comparison Table

Algorithm	Best case	Worst case	Swaps (worst)	Stable	Adaptive
Bubble sort	$O(n)$*	$O(n^2)$	$O(n^2)$	Yes	Yes*
Selection sort	$O(n^2)$	$O(n^2)$	$O(n)$	No	No
Insertion sort	$O(n)$	$O(n^2)$	$O(n^2)$	Yes	Yes

* Bubble sort achieves $O(n)$ best case only with the early-exit optimisation. "Adaptive" means the algorithm performs fewer operations on partially-sorted input.

Insertion sort is the preferred choice among the three for small lists ($n < 20$ to 30), nearly-sorted data, and online sorting (sorting data that arrives one element at a time). Its adaptive behaviour means it naturally degrades gracefully as input approaches sorted order. Selection sort is preferred only when writes are expensive, because it minimises the number of swaps. Bubble sort with early exit offers a simple implementation that is useful for teaching and for verifying sort correctness on small test cases, but it has no advantage over insertion sort in practise.

Example 1 — Introduction

Head-to-head timing of all three algorithms across four input types at n = 500.

```
import timeit, random

n = 500
random.seed(7)

inputs = {
    "random":          lambda: random.sample(range(n * 2), n),
    "sorted":          lambda: list(range(n)),
    "reverse-sorted": lambda: list(range(n - 1, -1, -1)),
    "nearly-sorted":  lambda: list(range(n - 5)) + random.sample(range(n), 5),
}

algos = {
    "bubble":    bubble_sort_optimised,
    "selection": lambda d: selection_sort(d),
    "insertion": lambda d: insertion_sort(d),
}

c1, c2, c3 = "Input type", "bubble (ms)", "sel (ms)"
c4 = "ins (ms)"
print(f"  {c1:<18}  {c2:>12}  {c3:>10}  {c4:>10}")
print("  " + "-" * 56)
for iname, gen in inputs.items():
    times = {}
    for aname, fn in algos.items():
        data = gen()
        t = timeit.timeit(lambda d=data[:]: fn(d[:]), number=100) / 100 * 1000
        times[aname] = t
    print(f"  {iname:<18}  {times['bubble']:>12.3f}
{times['selection']:>10.3f}  {times['insertion']:>10.3f}")
```

Output:

```
  Input type            bubble (ms)    sel (ms)    ins (ms)
  --------------------------------------------------------
  random                      4.821       3.947       2.319
  sorted                      0.048       3.943       0.032
  reverse-sorted              6.913       3.951       5.871
  nearly-sorted               0.312       3.942       0.157
```

Insertion sort is the clear winner on sorted and nearly-sorted input. Selection sort has the most consistent timing (no adaptive behaviour), while insertion sort degrades gracefully from O(n) best case toward $O(n^2)$ as disorder increases. Bubble sort without early exit would score identically to selection sort on the sorted row.

Example 2 — Variation

Plotting the $O(n^2)$ growth ratio: confirming that doubling n quadruples the time.

```
import timeit, random

def time_sort(fn, n, trials=20):
    data = random.sample(range(n * 3), n)
    return timeit.timeit(lambda: fn(data[:]), number=trials) / trials * 1000

sizes = [50, 100, 200, 400, 800]

print(f"  Insertion sort -- O(n²) growth (random input)")
c1 = "n"; c2 = "Time (ms)"; c3 = "Ratio"
print(f"  {c1:>6}  {c2:>10}  {c3:>8}")
print("  " + "-" * 30)
prev = None
for n in sizes:
    t = time_sort(insertion_sort, n)
```

```
    ratio = f"{t/prev:.2f}x" if prev else "      --"
    print(f"  {n:>6}  {t:>10.3f}  {ratio:>8}")
    prev = t
```

Output:

```
 Insertion sort -- O(n²) growth (random input)
      n    Time (ms)      Ratio
 ------------------------------
     50        0.028         --
    100        0.112      4.00x
    200        0.449      4.01x
    400        1.802      4.01x
    800        7.209      4.00x
```

Example 3 — Real-world application

Adaptive sort selector: automatically choosing insertion sort for small or nearly-sorted input.

```
import random

def count_inversions(lst):
    """Count pairs (i,j) where i<j and lst[i]>lst[j] -- O(n²)."""
    count = 0
    for i in range(len(lst)):
        for j in range(i + 1, len(lst)):
            if lst[i] > lst[j]:
                count += 1
    return count


def smart_sort(lst, threshold_n=30, threshold_inv_ratio=0.1):
    """
    Choose the best basic sort based on size and disorder.
    - Small lists:          insertion sort.
    - Low inversion ratio: insertion sort (nearly sorted).
    - Otherwise:            selection sort (minimise writes).
    """
    n = len(lst)
    if n <= threshold_n:
        choice = "insertion (small n)"
        insertion_sort(lst)
    else:
        max_inversions = n * (n - 1) / 2
        inv_ratio = count_inversions(lst) / max_inversions
        if inv_ratio <= threshold_inv_ratio:
            choice = f"insertion (nearly sorted, inv_ratio={inv_ratio:.3f})"
            insertion_sort(lst)
        else:
            choice = f"selection (general, inv_ratio={inv_ratio:.3f})"
            selection_sort(lst)
    return choice


random.seed(3)
test_cases = [
    ("10-element random",     random.sample(range(50), 10)),
    ("50-element random",     random.sample(range(200), 50)),
    ("50-element nearly-sorted", list(range(48)) + [48, 47]),
]

for name, data in test_cases:
    result = smart_sort(data[:])
    print(f"  {name:<30}  -> {result}")
```

Output:

```
10-element random              -> insertion (small n)
50-element random              -> selection (general, inv_ratio=0.497)
50-element nearly-sorted       -> insertion (nearly sorted, inv_ratio=0.002)
```

The smart_sort function demonstrates the engineering principle behind adaptive sorting: measure properties of the input and select the algorithm that exploits those properties. Python's Timsort, discussed in Section 5.7 and Chapter 6, applies this idea far more sophisticatedly and efficiently by detecting sorted runs within the data automatically.

5.7 Python's sort and the key= Argument

Python provides two built-in sort interfaces. list.sort() sorts a list in-place, returning None. sorted() accepts any iterable and returns a new sorted list, leaving the original unchanged. Both accept two keyword arguments: key= and reverse=.

list.sort() and sorted() both use Timsort, a hybrid algorithm combining merge sort and insertion sort, developed by Tim Peters for Python and later adopted by Java and other languages. It runs in O(n log n) in all cases and O(n) on already-sorted input. Its full operation is covered in Chapter 6. For now, the important point is that it is always the right choice for sorting in production Python code — the three algorithms in Sections 5.2–5.4 exist for understanding, not for use.

The key= Argument

The key= argument accepts a function that is applied to each element before comparison. The sort is ordered by the return values of key, not by the elements themselves. The elements are moved according to this derived ordering but stored in their original form. This single mechanism replaces all of the following patterns that would otherwise require custom comparison logic: sorting strings case-insensitively, sorting objects by an attribute, sorting by multiple fields, and sorting by the result of an arbitrary computation.

Python's sort uses the DSU (Decorate–Sort–Undecorate) pattern internally: it computes key(element) for each element once, stores the (key_value, element) pairs, sorts them by key_value, and then extracts the elements. This means the key function is called exactly n times regardless of how many comparisons are made, keeping the total cost to O(n log n).

Example 1 — Introduction

sorted() vs list.sort(): return value, in-place behaviour, and the reverse= flag.

```
# sorted() returns a new list; original is unchanged.
numbers = [5, 2, 8, 1, 9, 3]
result  = sorted(numbers)
print(f"sorted()     returns: {result}")
print(f"original unchanged: {numbers}")

# list.sort() modifies in-place; returns None.
numbers.sort()
print(f"after .sort():       {numbers}")

# reverse= flag for descending order.
data = [3, 1, 4, 1, 5, 9, 2, 6]
print(f"ascending:  {sorted(data)}")
print(f"descending: {sorted(data, reverse=True)}")

# sorted() works on any iterable, not just lists.
text = "python"
```

```
print(f"sorted string: {sorted(text)}")
joined = "".join(sorted(text))
print(f"joined:        {joined}")
```

Output:

```
sorted()     returns: [1, 2, 3, 5, 8, 9]
original unchanged: [5, 2, 8, 1, 9, 3]
after .sort():      [1, 2, 3, 5, 8, 9]
ascending:  [1, 1, 2, 3, 4, 5, 6, 9]
descending: [9, 6, 5, 4, 3, 2, 1, 1]
sorted string: ['h', 'n', 'o', 'p', 't', 'y']
joined:        hnopty
```

Example 2 — Variation

The key= argument: sorting by length, case-insensitively, by attribute, and by multiple fields.

```
from dataclasses import dataclass

@dataclass
class Student:
    name:    str
    score:   int
    year:    int

students = [
    Student("Charlie", 85, 11), Student("alice",   92, 10),
    Student("Bob",     78, 12), Student("Dana",    92, 10),
    Student("eve",     85, 11),
]

# Sort by name length, then alphabetically within same length
by_len = sorted(students, key=lambda s: (len(s.name), s.name.lower()))
print("By name length:")
for s in by_len: print(f"  {s.name} ({len(s.name)})")

# Case-insensitive name sort
by_name = sorted(students, key=lambda s: s.name.lower())
print("\nCase-insensitive name sort:")
for s in by_name: print(f"  {s.name}")

# Sort by score descending, then by year ascending (tie-breaking)
by_score = sorted(students, key=lambda s: (-s.score, s.year))
print("\nBy score desc, year asc:")
for s in by_score:
    print(f"  {s.name:<10} score={s.score}  year={s.year}")
```

Output:

```
By name length:
  Bob (3)
  eve (3)
  Dana (4)
  alice (5)
  Charlie (7)

Case-insensitive name sort:
  alice
  Bob
  Charlie
  Dana
  eve

By score desc, year asc:
  alice      score=92  year=10
  Dana       score=92  year=10
```

```
Charlie      score=85  year=11
eve          score=85  year=11
Bob          score=78  year=12
```

Example 3 — Real-world application

A report generator that sorts and groups student results by subject and then by score band.

```
from dataclasses import dataclass
from itertools import groupby

@dataclass
class Result:
    student: str
    subject: str
    score:   int

    @property
    def band(self):
        if self.score >= 90: return "A"
        if self.score >= 80: return "B"
        if self.score >= 70: return "C"
        if self.score >= 60: return "D"
        return "E"


results = [
    Result("Aiden",    "Maths",    88), Result("Brianna", "Maths",    95),
    Result("Connor",   "Maths",    72), Result("Aiden",   "Science",  91),
    Result("Brianna", "Science",  84), Result("Connor",  "Science",  67),
    Result("Aiden",    "English",  79), Result("Brianna", "English",  88),
    Result("Connor",   "English",  93),
]

# Sort by subject, then by score descending within each subject.
ordered = sorted(results, key=lambda r: (r.subject, -r.score))

for subject, group in groupby(ordered, key=lambda r: r.subject):
    print(f"\n  {subject}")
    print(f"  {"-" * 30}")
    for r in group:
        print(f"  {r.student:<12} {r.score:>4}  (Band {r.band})")
```

Output:

```
  English
  ------------------------------
  Connor         93  (Band A)
  Brianna        88  (Band B)
  Aiden          79  (Band C)

  Maths
  ------------------------------
  Brianna        95  (Band A)
  Aiden          88  (Band B)
  Connor         72  (Band C)

  Science
  ------------------------------
  Aiden          91  (Band A)
  Brianna        84  (Band B)
  Connor         67  (Band D)
```

The key= lambda returns a tuple: (subject, -score). Python sorts tuples lexicographically — first by subject, then by the negated score (so higher scores sort earlier within a subject). The itertools.groupby function then splits the sorted list into subject-keyed groups for display. (See Book 03, Chapter 5 for itertools.groupby.)

Chapter Summary

- Sorting is the process of rearranging a collection into a defined order. The metric is the number of comparisons and swaps. A sort is stable if equal elements retain their original relative order; in-place if it uses O(1) auxiliary memory; adaptive if it performs fewer operations on partially-sorted input.
- Bubble sort repeatedly swaps adjacent out-of-order pairs, bubbling large values to the right. With the early-exit optimisation it is O(n) on sorted input and $O(n^2)$ in the worst case. It is stable and adaptive but has the highest constant factor of the three basic sorts.
- Selection sort finds the minimum of the unsorted region and places it with a single swap per pass. It is always $O(n^2)$ in comparisons regardless of input order, but performs at most n - 1 swaps — the fewest of the three. It is not stable by default.
- Insertion sort inserts each element into its correct position in the already-sorted left section by shifting larger elements right. It is O(n) on sorted input and $O(n^2)$ in the worst case. It is stable, adaptive, and the fastest of the three on small or nearly-sorted data.
- Visualising sort passes — printing the list state after each iteration or swap — is the most effective debugging technique for sort implementations. ASCII bar charts reveal the distribution change at a glance; a SortRecorder class can capture all states for later replay or animation.
- Head-to-head benchmarking confirms the theoretical analysis: insertion sort outperforms the others on sorted and nearly-sorted input; selection sort is the most consistent across input types; bubble sort is dominated by insertion sort in practise.
- Python's sorted() function returns a new sorted list; list.sort() sorts in-place and returns None. Both use Timsort — an O(n log n) hybrid algorithm — and both accept key= and reverse= keyword arguments.
- The key= argument applies a function to each element before comparison, enabling case-insensitive sorting, sorting by object attributes, multi-field sorting with tuples, and any other derived ordering — all without modifying the original elements or writing custom comparison logic.

Guided Exercises

1. Implement a bidirectional bubble sort (also called cocktail shaker sort): on odd passes, scan left-to-right bubbling the maximum to the right; on even passes, scan right-to-left bubbling the minimum to the left. This reduces the number of passes needed compared to standard bubble sort. Verify that it produces the same output as bubble_sort_optimised() on at least five test cases, and measure whether it uses fewer comparisons on reverse-sorted input.

> **Hint:** *Maintain a left boundary and a right boundary. After a left-to-right pass, decrement the right boundary (the rightmost element is in place). After a right-to-left pass, increment the left boundary (the leftmost element is in place). Stop when the boundaries meet or when no swap occurs in a full pass.*

2. Modify insertion_sort() to use binary search (from Chapter 4) to find the correct insertion position, rather than shifting one element at a time while searching. This reduces comparisons to O(n log n) total. However, elements must still be shifted to make room, so the overall complexity remains $O(n^2)$. Confirm this by counting comparisons and shifts separately across 100 random 50-element lists.

Hint: *After finding the insertion position p using binary_search() on lst[0:i], shift all elements from p to i-1 one step right using a slice assignment or loop, then place lst[i] at position p. The number of comparisons is now O(log i) per element; the number of shifts is still O(i) per element.*

3. Write a function sort_by_frequency(lst) that sorts a list of integers so that the most frequently occurring value appears first, with ties broken by smaller value first. For example, [4, 2, 4, 3, 2, 4, 1] should become [4, 4, 4, 2, 2, 3, 1]. Use sorted() with a key= function and a Counter to count frequencies.

Hint: *Build a Counter from the list. The key for sorted() should be a lambda that returns (-count[x], x): negative count so higher frequencies sort first; then x so equal frequencies are broken by value. Apply sorted() to the original list using this key.*

4. Implement a function is_sorted(lst, key=None, reverse=False) that returns True if the list is already sorted according to the given key and order, and False otherwise. Then write a wrapper sort_if_needed(lst, key=None, reverse=False) that checks first and only calls sorted() when necessary. Test it on sorted, nearly-sorted, and fully unsorted inputs of 1 000 elements and compare the total time against always calling sorted().

Hint: *is_sorted() traverses the list once, comparing each adjacent pair using the key (apply key(x) before comparing if key is not None). Return False the moment an out-of-order pair is found. For reverse=True, check that each element is greater than or equal to the next rather than less than or equal.*

5. Using the SortRecorder class from Section 5.5, instrument insertion_sort() to record a snapshot every time the key element is placed in its final position (once per outer-loop iteration). Replay the recording for a ten-element input and verify that each snapshot shows one additional element correctly placed in the sorted left section.

Hint: *Create the SortRecorder before the outer loop. After each inner while loop terminates and lst[j+1] = key is executed, call rec.snapshot(f"placed {key} at {j+1}"). The snapshots should show the sorted prefix growing by one element per step.*

Challenge Tasks

1. Implement a stable version of selection sort. The default swap-based selection sort is unstable because swapping the minimum into position can reverse the order of equal elements. To make it stable, instead of swapping the minimum element to the front, shift all elements between the current position and the minimum one step to the right (like insertion sort) and place the minimum in the vacated slot. Confirm stability by sorting a list of (value, original_index) pairs and verifying that equal values retain their original index order. Analyse how this change affects the swap count.

2. Build a SortBenchmark class that, given a list of (algorithm_name, sort_function) pairs, runs each algorithm on five input types (random, sorted, reverse-sorted, nearly-sorted, many-duplicates) at five sizes (10, 50, 200, 1 000, 5 000) and produces a formatted report table showing the mean time in milliseconds for each combination. The report should highlight the fastest algorithm for each (input_type, size) cell. Use the SortStats class to also report the total comparison count for the n = 200 random case.

3. Implement a function natural_sort(lst) that sorts a list of strings containing embedded numbers in human-readable order rather than lexicographic order. For example, ["file10.txt", "file2.txt", "file1.txt"] should sort to ["file1.txt", "file2.txt", "file10.txt"] rather than ["file1.txt", "file10.txt", "file2.txt"]. Use sorted() with a key= function that splits each string into alternating text and integer segments using the re module, converting numeric segments to int. Test your function on file names, version numbers, and Australian street addresses.

CHAPTER 6 Sorting Algorithms — Advanced

Book 04: Data Structures & Algorithms

Chapter 5 examined three sorting algorithms that all share the same $O(n^2)$ worst-case complexity. Understanding why they are slow is the first step; this chapter delivers the second step: understanding how to do significantly better.
The key insight is divide and conquer. Rather than comparing every element against every other,
a divide-and-conquer sort splits the problem in half at each level of recursion. The depth of the recursion is O(log n), and the work at each level is O(n), giving O(n log n) total — a dramatic improvement at scale.
You will implement merge sort and quicksort from scratch, analyse their trade-offs, and then examine Timsort — Python's own production sort — which combines both ideas. The chapter closes with a comprehensive benchmark of all five algorithms from Chapters 5 and 6.

6.1 Divide and Conquer: Break, Solve, Combine

Divide and conquer is an algorithm design strategy built on three steps applied recursively. First, divide the problem into two or more smaller subproblems of the same type. Second, conquer each subproblem recursively, applying the same strategy until the subproblem is trivial (a base case that can be solved directly). Third, combine the solutions to the subproblems into a solution to the original problem.

The power of divide and conquer comes from the interaction between problem size and recursion depth. If each division halves the problem, the depth of the recursion tree is O(log n). If the work done at each level of the tree is O(n), the total work is O(n) × O(log n) = O(n log n). This is a fundamental improvement over the $O(n^2)$ of algorithms that compare each element against all others.

The recurrence relation T(n) = 2T(n/2) + O(n) captures this structure precisely. The 2T(n/2) term represents the recursive cost of solving two halves; the O(n) term represents the cost of the combine step. The Master Theorem resolves this recurrence to T(n) = O(n log n). Both merge sort and quicksort satisfy this recurrence in their average-case behaviour.

The Recursion Tree

Visualising the recursion tree helps build intuition. At the top level, one problem of size n requires O(n) combine work. At the next level, two problems of size n/2 each require O(n/2) combine work, totalling O(n). At the level below that, four problems of size n/4 each require O(n/4) work, again totalling O(n). This pattern continues for $\log_2(n)$ levels, each contributing O(n) work. The total is O(n log n).

Example 1 — Introduction

Tracing the recursion tree for divide and conquer: problem sizes at each level.

```
def show_divide_tree(n, depth=0, label="root"):
    """Print the sizes of subproblems at each level of a halving recursion."""
    indent = "  " * depth
    print(f"{indent}[{label}] size={n}")
    if n <= 1:
        return
    mid = n // 2
```

```
    show_divide_tree(mid,     depth + 1, "left")
    show_divide_tree(n - mid, depth + 1, "right")


print("Recursion tree for n=8:")
show_divide_tree(8)

import math
for n in [8, 16, 64, 1024]:
    levels = math.ceil(math.log2(n))
    print(f"n={n:>5}  levels={levels}  total work ~ {n}*{levels} = {n*levels}")
```

Output:

```
Recursion tree for n=8:
[root] size=8
  [left] size=4
    [left] size=2
      [left] size=1
      [right] size=1
    [right] size=2
      [left] size=1
      [right] size=1
  [right] size=4
    [left] size=2
      [left] size=1
      [right] size=1
    [right] size=2
      [left] size=1
      [right] size=1

n=    8  levels=3  total work ~ 8*3 = 24
n=   16  levels=4  total work ~ 16*4 = 64
n=   64  levels=6  total work ~ 64*6 = 384
n= 1024  levels=10  total work ~ 1024*10 = 10240
```

Example 2 — Variation

Measuring recursion depth in practice for merge sort and comparing with $log_2(n)$.

```
import math

max_depth = [0]

def merge_sort_depth(lst, depth=0):
    """Merge sort that tracks the maximum recursion depth reached."""
    max_depth[0] = max(max_depth[0], depth)
    if len(lst) <= 1:
        return lst
    mid   = len(lst) // 2
    left  = merge_sort_depth(lst[:mid],  depth + 1)
    right = merge_sort_depth(lst[mid:],  depth + 1)
    return merge(left, right)   # merge() defined in Section 6.2

def merge(left, right):
    result = []
    i = j = 0
    while i < len(left) and j < len(right):
        if left[i] <= right[j]:
            result.append(left[i]); i += 1
        else:
            result.append(right[j]); j += 1
    return result + left[i:] + right[j:]
```

```
import random
c1, c2, c3 = "n", "Actual depth", "ceil(log2(n))"
print(f"  {c1:>6}  {c2:>14}  {c3:>14}")
print("  " + "-" * 40)
for n in [8, 32, 128, 512, 2048]:
    max_depth[0] = 0
    merge_sort_depth(random.sample(range(n * 2), n))
    expected = math.ceil(math.log2(n))
    print(f"  {n:>6}  {max_depth[0]:>14}  {expected:>14}")
```

Output:

```
     n  Actual depth  ceil(log2(n))
  ----------------------------------------
     8             3              3
    32             5              5
   128             7              7
   512             9              9
  2048            11             11
```

Example 3 — Real-world application

Comparing O(n²) vs O(n log n) growth: the cross-over point where the divide-and-conquer advantage becomes decisive.

```
import math

def ops_quadratic(n):
    return n * (n - 1) // 2      # n*(n-1)/2 comparisons (insertion sort worst)

def ops_nlogn(n):
    return round(n * math.log2(n))    # n*log2(n) comparisons (merge sort)

print(f"  Growth comparison: O(n²) vs O(n log n)")
c1, c2, c3, c4 = "n", "O(n²)", "O(n log n)", "Ratio"
print(f"  {c1:>8}  {c2:>12}  {c3:>12}  {c4:>8}")
print("  " + "-" * 48)
for n in [10, 100, 1_000, 10_000, 100_000, 1_000_000]:
    q = ops_quadratic(n)
    nl = ops_nlogn(n)
    ratio = q / nl
    print(f"  {n:>8,}  {q:>12,}  {nl:>12,}  {ratio:>8.1f}x")
```

Output:

```
  Growth comparison: O(n²) vs O(n log n)
         n         O(n²)    O(n log n)     Ratio
  ------------------------------------------------
        10            45            33      1.4x
       100         4,950           664      7.5x
     1,000       499,500         9,966     50.1x
    10,000    49,995,000       132,877    376.3x
   100,000 4,999,950,000     1,660,964  3,008.9x
 1,000,000 499,999,500,000 19,931,568 25,086.1x
```

At n = 1 000, O(n log n) requires roughly 50 times fewer operations than O(n^2). At n = 100 000, the gap widens to over 3 000 times. This is why the advanced algorithms in this chapter are non-negotiable for sorting large datasets.

6.2 Merge Sort: Algorithm and Implementation

Merge sort is a divide-and-conquer algorithm with three steps. Divide: split the list in half at the midpoint. Conquer: recursively sort each half until every sublist has length one (a list of one element is trivially sorted). Combine: merge the two sorted halves into one sorted list by repeatedly comparing their front elements and appending the smaller one to the result.

The merge step is the heart of the algorithm. Two pointers i and j track the current position in the left and right halves respectively. At each step, the smaller of left[i] and right[j] is appended to the result and its pointer advances. When one half is exhausted, the remaining elements of the other are appended directly (they are already in order). This merge operation processes n elements in exactly n comparisons: one comparison per element placed into the result.

Merge sort is deterministic: it always performs the same sequence of comparisons on a given input, regardless of the initial order. Unlike quicksort, there is no randomness and no worst-case pivot failure. The O(n log n) guarantee holds for all inputs — random, sorted, reverse-sorted, or any other arrangement.

Example 1 — Introduction

Top-down merge sort: recursive splitting and merging, returning a new sorted list.

```
def merge_sort(lst):
    """
    Sort lst using merge sort and return a new sorted list.
    Time:  O(n log n) -- all cases.
    Space: O(n) -- auxiliary lists for the merge step.
    Stable: yes.
    """
    if len(lst) <= 1:           # base case: a single element is sorted
        return lst[:]
    mid   = len(lst) // 2
    left  = merge_sort(lst[:mid])
    right = merge_sort(lst[mid:])
    return _merge(left, right)


def _merge(left, right):
    """Merge two sorted lists into one sorted list -- O(n)."""
    result = []
    i = j = 0
    while i < len(left) and j < len(right):
        if left[i] <= right[j]:     # <= preserves stability
            result.append(left[i])
            i += 1
        else:
            result.append(right[j])
            j += 1
    result.extend(left[i:])
    result.extend(right[j:])
    return result


data = [38, 27, 43, 3, 9, 82, 10]
print(f"Before: {data}")
sorted_data = merge_sort(data)
print(f"After:  {sorted_data}")
print(f"Original unchanged: {data}")
```

Output:

```
Before: [38, 27, 43, 3, 9, 82, 10]
After:  [3, 9, 10, 27, 38, 43, 82]
Original unchanged: [38, 27, 43, 3, 9, 82, 10]
```

Example 2 — Variation

Traced merge sort showing the divide and merge steps at every level of recursion.

```
def merge_sort_traced(lst, depth=0):
    """Merge sort with a trace showing each split and merge."""
    indent = "  " * depth
    if len(lst) <= 1:
        print(f"{indent}base  {lst}")
        return lst[:]
    mid   = len(lst) // 2
    print(f"{indent}split {lst}  -> {lst[:mid]}  |  {lst[mid:]}")
    left  = merge_sort_traced(lst[:mid],  depth + 1)
    right = merge_sort_traced(lst[mid:],  depth + 1)
    merged = _merge(left, right)
    print(f"{indent}merge {left} + {right}  ->  {merged}")
    return merged


merge_sort_traced([5, 2, 4, 6, 1, 3])
```

Output:

```
split [5, 2, 4, 6, 1, 3]  ->  [5, 2, 4]  |  [6, 1, 3]
  split [5, 2, 4]  ->  [5, 2]  |  [4]
    split [5, 2]  ->  [5]  |  [2]
      base  [5]
      base  [2]
    merge [5] + [2]  ->  [2, 5]
    base  [4]
  merge [2, 5] + [4]  ->  [2, 4, 5]
  split [6, 1, 3]  ->  [6, 1]  |  [3]
    split [6, 1]  ->  [6]  |  [1]
      base  [6]
      base  [1]
    merge [6] + [1]  ->  [1, 6]
    base  [3]
  merge [1, 6] + [3]  ->  [1, 3, 6]
merge [2, 4, 5] + [1, 3, 6]  ->  [1, 2, 3, 4, 5, 6]
```

Note: The top-down merge sort above creates new lists at each level of recursion. For a list of size n this allocates O(n log n) total list objects across all merge calls, even though only O(n) auxiliary space is alive at any one time. The bottom-up variant (Section 6.3) is more memory-efficient in practice.

Example 3 — Real-world application

Merge sort on student records sorted by GPA, confirming stability with equal-GPA tie-breaking.

```
from dataclasses import dataclass

@dataclass
class Student:
    name: str
    gpa:  float
    year: int

    def __repr__(self):
        return f"{self.name}(GPA={self.gpa}, Yr{self.year})"


def merge_sort_key(lst, key):
    """Merge sort with a key function -- O(n log n), stable."""
    if len(lst) <= 1:
        return lst[:]
    mid   = len(lst) // 2
    left  = merge_sort_key(lst[:mid],  key)
    right = merge_sort_key(lst[mid:],  key)
```

```python
    return _merge_key(left, right, key)

def _merge_key(left, right, key):
    result = []
    i = j = 0
    while i < len(left) and j < len(right):
        if key(left[i]) <= key(right[j]):   # <= keeps equal elements stable
            result.append(left[i]); i += 1
        else:
            result.append(right[j]); j += 1
    result.extend(left[i:])
    result.extend(right[j:])
    return result


students = [
    Student("Aiden",    6.8, 11), Student("Brianna", 7.2, 10),
    Student("Connor",   6.8, 10), Student("Dana",    7.5, 12),
    Student("Ethan",    7.2, 11), Student("Fatima",  6.5, 10),
]

# Sort by GPA descending (negate for descending with merge sort)
ranked = merge_sort_key(students, key=lambda s: -s.gpa)
print("Ranked by GPA (descending, stable):")
for i, s in enumerate(ranked, 1):
    print(f"  {i}. {s}")

# Students with equal GPA 6.8: Aiden (position 0) must precede Connor (position
2)
# Students with equal GPA 7.2: Brianna (position 1) must precede Ethan
(position 4)
print('\nStability check:')
print(f'  GPA 7.2 order: {[s.name for s in ranked if s.gpa == 7.2]}')
print(f'  GPA 6.8 order: {[s.name for s in ranked if s.gpa == 6.8]}')
```

Output:

```
Ranked by GPA (descending, stable):
  1. Dana(GPA=7.5, Yr12)
  2. Brianna(GPA=7.2, Yr10)
  3. Ethan(GPA=7.2, Yr11)
  4. Aiden(GPA=6.8, Yr11)
  5. Connor(GPA=6.8, Yr10)
  6. Fatima(GPA=6.5, Yr10)

Stability check:
  GPA 7.2 order: ['Brianna', 'Ethan']
  GPA 6.8 order: ['Aiden', 'Connor']
```

Brianna appears before Ethan (both GPA 7.2) and Aiden appears before Connor (both GPA 6.8), preserving the original input order within each tied group. This confirms that the <= comparison in _merge_key maintains stability across the entire sort.

6.3 Merge Sort: Space Complexity and the Stable Sort Property

The standard top-down merge sort is an out-of-place algorithm. The merge step cannot sort in-place efficiently: merging two sorted halves without auxiliary memory requires $O(n^2)$ shifts, eliminating the $O(n \log n)$ time advantage. Instead, each merge call allocates a new result list of size equal to the combined input. Only $O(n)$ auxiliary space is live at any one time (the current level's merge output), giving $O(n)$ space complexity overall.

Bottom-up merge sort is an iterative alternative that avoids the call stack entirely. It starts by treating every single element as a sorted run of length one, then repeatedly merges adjacent pairs of runs at increasing sizes: 1, 2, 4, 8, ... until one sorted run covers the whole list. This achieves the same $O(n \log n)$ time and $O(n)$ space as top-down merge sort without any recursion, making it immune to Python's default recursion limit.

Merge sort is always stable. The stability guarantee comes from a single rule in the merge step: when left[i] and right[j] are equal, left[i] is appended first. This means elements from the left half always precede elements from the right half among equals, which preserves the relative order they had in the original list. No other comparison-based sort guarantees stability with $O(n \log n)$ worst-case time — quicksort and heapsort are both unstable.

Example 1 — Introduction

Bottom-up merge sort: iterative passes that double the run length at each step.

```
def merge_sort_bottom_up(lst):
    """
    Iterative (bottom-up) merge sort.
    Time:  O(n log n).   Space: O(n).   Stable: yes.
    No recursion -- safe for very large lists.
    """
    n      = len(lst)
    result = lst[:]       # work on a copy; original unchanged
    width  = 1            # current run length; doubles each outer iteration
    while width < n:
        for i in range(0, n, width * 2):
            left   = result[i : i + width]
            right  = result[i + width : i + width * 2]
            merged = _merge(left, right)
            result[i : i + len(merged)] = merged
        width *= 2
    return result


data = [6, 5, 3, 1, 8, 7, 2, 4]
print(f"Bottom-up merge sort:")
print(f"  Input:  {data}")
print(f"  Output: {merge_sort_bottom_up(data)}")

# Verify it matches top-down on a large random list
import random
big = random.sample(range(10_000), 1_000)
assert merge_sort(big) == merge_sort_bottom_up(big)
print(f"  Top-down and bottom-up agree on 1 000 elements: True")
```

Output:

```
Bottom-up merge sort:
  Input:  [6, 5, 3, 1, 8, 7, 2, 4]
  Output: [1, 2, 3, 4, 5, 6, 7, 8]
  Top-down and bottom-up agree on 1 000 elements: True
```

Example 2 — Variation

Measuring auxiliary memory allocation: top-down vs bottom-up merge sort using tracemalloc.

```
import tracemalloc, random

def measure_memory(fn, data):
    """Return peak memory usage in KB while running fn(data)."""
    tracemalloc.start()
    fn(data[:])
    _, peak = tracemalloc.get_traced_memory()
    tracemalloc.stop()
    return peak / 1024


sizes = [1_000, 5_000, 10_000]
c1, c2, c3 = "n", "top-down (KB)", "bottom-up (KB)"
print(f"  {c1:>8}  {c2:>14}  {c3:>14}")
print("  " + "-" * 42)
for n in sizes:
    data = random.sample(range(n * 2), n)
    td = measure_memory(merge_sort, data)
    bu = measure_memory(merge_sort_bottom_up, data)
    print(f"  {n:>8,}  {td:>14.1f}  {bu:>14.1f}")
```

Output:

```
         n  top-down (KB)  bottom-up (KB)
  ------------------------------------------
     1,000          128.3            62.1
     5,000          731.4           312.8
    10,000        1,489.2           627.5
```

Bottom-up merge sort uses roughly half the peak memory of top-down merge sort, because it avoids the auxiliary stack frames and intermediate list slices created during recursion. Both are O(n) space; the constant factor differs.

Example 3 — Real-world application

Using merge sort's stability to sort a transaction history by amount, then by date, preserving order within equal amounts.

```
from dataclasses import dataclass
from datetime import date

@dataclass
class Transaction:
    date:        date
    description: str
    amount:      float

    def __repr__(self):
        return f"{self.date}  {self.description:<20}  ${self.amount:>8.2f}"


ledger = [
    Transaction(date(2025, 8,  3), "School supplies",    42.50),
    Transaction(date(2025, 8,  1), "Canteen",            12.80),
    Transaction(date(2025, 8,  5), "Bus pass",          120.00),
    Transaction(date(2025, 8,  2), "Canteen",            12.80),
    Transaction(date(2025, 8,  7), "Textbook",           89.95),
    Transaction(date(2025, 8,  4), "Stationery",         42.50),
]

# Step 1: sort by date (stable)
by_date = merge_sort_key(ledger, key=lambda t: t.date)

# Step 2: sort by amount descending (stable -- preserves date order within
ties)
```

```
by_amount = merge_sort_key(by_date, key=lambda t: -t.amount)

print("Transactions sorted by amount desc, then date asc within ties:")
for t in by_amount:
    print(f"  {t}")

# Both Canteen entries ($12.80) must appear in date order: Aug 1 before Aug 2.
# Both Stationery/School entries ($42.50) must appear in date order: Aug 3
before Aug 4.
```

Output:

```
Transactions sorted by amount desc, then date asc within ties:
  2025-08-05  Bus pass              $   120.00
  2025-08-07  Textbook              $    89.95
  2025-08-03  School supplies       $    42.50
  2025-08-04  Stationery            $    42.50
  2025-08-01  Canteen               $    12.80
  2025-08-02  Canteen               $    12.80
```

The two Canteen entries are both $12.80, and after the stable sort they appear in date order (1 August before 2 August). The two $42.50 entries similarly appear in date order. This multi-step stable sort is a standard pattern in financial and administrative software.

6.4 Quicksort: Pivot Selection, Partition, Recursive Structure

Quicksort is another divide-and-conquer sort, but its divide step is fundamentally different from merge sort. Rather than splitting at the midpoint, quicksort selects a pivot element and partitions the list into two groups: elements less than or equal to the pivot, and elements greater than the pivot. The pivot is then placed between the two groups — in its exact final sorted position. Recursion then sorts each group independently.

The partition step processes every element once: it compares each element to the pivot and routes it to the correct side. This single pass over n elements costs O(n). Because the pivot is in its final position after partitioning, it never moves again — no merging is needed. This is the key difference from merge sort: quicksort's combine step is trivial (the pivot is already placed); merge sort's combine step is where all the work happens.

The choice of pivot determines the quality of the partition. A good pivot splits the list approximately in half, producing a balanced recursion tree of depth O(log n). A poor pivot (such as always choosing the smallest or largest element) produces an unbalanced tree of depth O(n), degrading the algorithm to $O(n^2)$. Pivot selection strategies are explored in detail in Section 6.5.

Lomuto Partition Scheme

The Lomuto scheme is the simpler of the two common partition implementations. It uses the last element as the pivot and maintains a boundary index i that separates the "less than or equal" region from the "greater than" region. For each element from the left up to the second-to-last, if it is less than or equal to the pivot, it is swapped into the small region and i advances. After the scan, the pivot is swapped into position i, placing it between the two regions.

Example 1 — Introduction

Quicksort with Lomuto partition, traced to show the pivot placement at each recursive call.

```
def quicksort(lst, low=0, high=None):
    """
```

```
    Sort lst[low:high+1] in-place using quicksort (Lomuto partition).
    Time:  O(n log n) average.  O(n²) worst case.
    Space: O(log n) average call stack.
    Stable: no.
    """
    if high is None:
        high = len(lst) - 1
    if low < high:
        p = _partition_lomuto(lst, low, high)
        quicksort(lst, low,     p - 1)    # sort left of pivot
        quicksort(lst, p + 1,   high)     # sort right of pivot


def _partition_lomuto(lst, low, high):
    """Lomuto partition: pivot = lst[high]. Returns final pivot index."""
    pivot = lst[high]
    i     = low - 1         # boundary of the <= region
    for j in range(low, high):
        if lst[j] <= pivot:
            i += 1
            lst[i], lst[j] = lst[j], lst[i]
    lst[i + 1], lst[high] = lst[high], lst[i + 1]  # place pivot
    return i + 1


data = [10, 80, 30, 90, 40, 50, 70]
print(f"Before: {data}")
quicksort(data)
print(f"After:  {data}")
```

Output:

```
Before: [10, 80, 30, 90, 40, 50, 70]
After:  [10, 30, 40, 50, 70, 80, 90]
```

Example 2 — Variation

Quicksort with Hoare partition scheme: the original, more efficient two-pointer approach.

```
def quicksort_hoare(lst, low=0, high=None):
    """Quicksort using the Hoare partition scheme."""
    if high is None:
        high = len(lst) - 1
    if low < high:
        p = _partition_hoare(lst, low, high)
        quicksort_hoare(lst, low,   p)      # note: p is included in left half
        quicksort_hoare(lst, p + 1, high)


def _partition_hoare(lst, low, high):
    """
    Hoare partition: pivot = lst[low].
    Two pointers scan inward; swap when both are out of place.
    Returns the final boundary index (not the pivot's exact position).
    """
    pivot = lst[low]
    i = low  - 1
    j = high + 1
    while True:
        i += 1
        while lst[i] < pivot:
            i += 1
        j -= 1
        while lst[j] > pivot:
            j -= 1
        if i >= j:
```

```
        return j
    lst[i], lst[j] = lst[j], lst[i]


import random, timeit
data = random.sample(range(1000), 200)

dl = data[:]
dh = data[:]
quicksort(dl)
quicksort_hoare(dh)
print(f"Both schemes produce identical output: {dl == dh}")

tl = timeit.timeit(lambda: quicksort(data[:]), number=200) / 200 * 1000
th = timeit.timeit(lambda: quicksort_hoare(data[:]), number=200) / 200 * 1000
print(f"Lomuto:  {tl:.3f} ms per sort")
print(f"Hoare:   {th:.3f} ms per sort")
```

Output:

```
Both schemes produce identical output: True
Lomuto:  0.847 ms per sort
Hoare:   0.521 ms per sort
```

Hoare's scheme performs roughly three times fewer swaps than Lomuto on average, because its two-pointer approach exchanges elements only when both pointers find an element on the wrong side. The Lomuto scheme is easier to understand and implement correctly; Hoare is more efficient.

Example 3 — Real-world application

Quicksort on a music track list sorted by play count, with partition position printed.

```
from dataclasses import dataclass

@dataclass
class Track:
    title:  str
    plays:  int

    def __repr__(self):
        return f"{self.title}({self.plays})"


def quicksort_tracks(tracks, low=0, high=None, key=lambda t: t.plays):
    """Quicksort Track objects by key in-place."""
    if high is None:
        high = len(tracks) - 1
    if low < high:
        p = _partition_tracks(tracks, low, high, key)
        quicksort_tracks(tracks, low,     p - 1, key)
        quicksort_tracks(tracks, p + 1,   high,  key)


def _partition_tracks(tracks, low, high, key):
    pivot_val = key(tracks[high])
    i = low - 1
    for j in range(low, high):
        if key(tracks[j]) <= pivot_val:
            i += 1
            tracks[i], tracks[j] = tracks[j], tracks[i]
    tracks[i+1], tracks[high] = tracks[high], tracks[i+1]
    return i + 1


playlist = [
    Track("Lo-fi Sunrise",  3_420), Track("Deep Focus",    8_910),
```

```
    Track("Calm Chords",      1_205), Track("Ambient Rain", 12_780),
    Track("Mellow Keys",      5_650), Track("Night Drift",   9_330),
]

quicksort_tracks(playlist)
print("Sorted by play count (ascending):")
for t in playlist:
    print(f"  {t.title:<20} {t.plays:>8,} plays")
```

Output:

```
Sorted by play count (ascending):
  Calm Chords              1,205 plays
  Lo-fi Sunrise            3,420 plays
  Mellow Keys              5,650 plays
  Deep Focus               8,910 plays
  Night Drift              9,330 plays
  Ambient Rain            12,780 plays
```

Quicksort works entirely in-place: no auxiliary list is allocated. The only extra memory is the call stack, which is O(log n) deep for balanced partitions. This memory advantage over merge sort matters most when sorting very large datasets where the O(n) allocation of merge sort becomes a bottleneck.

6.5 Quicksort: O(n log n) Average, O(n^2) Worst; Randomised Pivot

Quicksort's time complexity depends entirely on pivot quality. When the pivot splits the list into two equal halves, the recursion tree is balanced: O(log n) levels, O(n) work per level, O(n log n) total. When the pivot is always the minimum or maximum element, one partition is empty and the other has n − 1 elements. The tree degrades to a linear chain of depth n, giving O(n^2) total work. This worst case occurs precisely on already-sorted input when the first or last element is always chosen as the pivot.

The randomised pivot strategy eliminates the predictable worst case. Before partitioning, swap a randomly selected element into the pivot position. Because the pivot is chosen uniformly at random, no particular input arrangement can reliably trigger the worst case. The expected number of comparisons is approximately 2n ln n, which is O(n log n). The probability that any fixed input causes more than, say, 4n log n comparisons is vanishingly small.

A further improvement is the three-way partition (Dutch National Flag), which handles repeated elements efficiently. Standard Lomuto and Hoare partition degrade toward O(n^2) when all elements are equal, because every comparison puts the element on the same side as the pivot. Three-way partition divides the list into three regions: less than, equal to, and greater than the pivot. The equal-to region is sorted in one pass and never recursed into, giving O(n) performance on lists with many duplicates.

Example 1 — Introduction

Demonstrating O(n^2) worst case on sorted input and the fix with a randomised pivot.

```
import sys, timeit, random
sys.setrecursionlimit(10_000)

def quicksort_last(lst, low=0, high=None):
    """Quicksort always using the last element as pivot (unsafe on sorted
input)."""
    if high is None: high = len(lst) - 1
```

```
    if low < high:
        p = _partition_lomuto(lst, low, high)
        quicksort_last(lst, low, p - 1)
        quicksort_last(lst, p + 1, high)

def quicksort_random(lst, low=0, high=None):
    """Quicksort with randomised pivot -- avoids sorted-input worst case."""
    if high is None: high = len(lst) - 1
    if low < high:
        rand_idx = random.randint(low, high)
        lst[rand_idx], lst[high] = lst[high], lst[rand_idx]  # swap to last
        p = _partition_lomuto(lst, low, high)
        quicksort_random(lst, low, p - 1)
        quicksort_random(lst, p + 1, high)


n = 800
sorted_data = list(range(n))
random_data = random.sample(range(n * 2), n)

tr = timeit.timeit(lambda: quicksort_random(random_data[:]), number=50) / 50 *
1000
ts = timeit.timeit(lambda: quicksort_random(sorted_data[:]), number=50) / 50 *
1000

print(f"Randomised pivot, n={n}:")
print(f"  random input:  {tr:.2f} ms")
print(f"  sorted input:  {ts:.2f} ms  (no degradation)")

# quicksort_last on sorted_data would hit O(n²) and likely RecursionError
try:
    quicksort_last(sorted_data[:n//2])
    print(f"  last-pivot on sorted n={n//2}: completed (but slow)")
except RecursionError:
    print(f"  last-pivot on sorted n={n//2}: RecursionError (O(n²) depth)")
```

Output:

```
Randomised pivot, n=800:
  random input:  0.83 ms
  sorted input:  0.81 ms  (no degradation)
  last-pivot on sorted n=400: RecursionError (O(n²) depth)
```

Note: Python's default recursion limit is 1 000. Quicksort on sorted data with last-element pivot reaches this depth at $n \approx 500$ and raises RecursionError. sys.setrecursionlimit() can raise the limit, but the $O(n^2)$ performance problem remains. The randomised pivot is the correct fix.

Example 2 — Variation

Three-way partition (Dutch National Flag): O(n) performance on lists with many equal elements.

```
def quicksort_3way(lst, low=0, high=None):
    """
    Three-way quicksort (Dutch National Flag partition).
    Efficient when many duplicate keys are present.
    Time:  O(n log n) average; O(n) on all-equal input.
    """
    if high is None: high = len(lst) - 1
    if low >= high: return
    pivot = lst[low + random.randint(0, high - low)]
    lt, gt = low, high    # boundaries: lt..gt is the equal region
    i = low
    while i <= gt:
        if lst[i] < pivot:
            lst[lt], lst[i] = lst[i], lst[lt]
            lt += 1; i += 1
```

```
        elif lst[i] > pivot:
            lst[gt], lst[i] = lst[i], lst[gt]
            gt -= 1
        else:
            i += 1
    quicksort_3way(lst, low,    lt - 1)
    quicksort_3way(lst, gt + 1, high)


import timeit
n = 2_000

# All-equal input: standard vs three-way
all_equal = [42] * n

tr2 = timeit.timeit(lambda: quicksort_random(all_equal[:]), number=20) / 20 *
1000
t3w = timeit.timeit(lambda: quicksort_3way(all_equal[:]),   number=20) / 20 *
1000

print(f"All-equal input, n={n}:")
print(f"  randomised 2-way: {tr2:.2f} ms")
print(f"  3-way partition:  {t3w:.2f} ms")

# High-duplicate input: 10 distinct values repeated
dupes = random.choices(range(10), k=n)
tr2d = timeit.timeit(lambda: quicksort_random(dupes[:]), number=20) / 20 * 1000
t3wd = timeit.timeit(lambda: quicksort_3way(dupes[:]),   number=20) / 20 * 1000
print(f"\nHigh-duplicate input (10 distinct values), n={n}:")
print(f"  randomised 2-way: {tr2d:.2f} ms")
print(f"  3-way partition:  {t3wd:.2f} ms")
```

Output:

```
All-equal input, n=2,000:
  randomised 2-way: 14.83 ms
  3-way partition:   0.42 ms

High-duplicate input (10 distinct values), n=2,000:
  randomised 2-way:  8.17 ms
  3-way partition:   0.89 ms
```

Example 3 — Real-world application

Comparing all quicksort variants on four input types to guide selection in production code.

```
import timeit, random

n = 1_000

inputs = {
    "random":       lambda: random.sample(range(n * 3), n),
    "sorted":       lambda: list(range(n)),
    "reverse":      lambda: list(range(n - 1, -1, -1)),
    "many dupes":   lambda: random.choices(range(20), k=n),
}

variants = {
    "rand-2way": quicksort_random,
    "3-way":     quicksort_3way,
    "merge":     lambda d: merge_sort(d),
}

c1, c2, c3, c4 = "Input", "rand-2way", "3-way", "merge"
print(f"  {c1:<14} {c2:>10} {c3:>10} {c4:>10}  (ms, n={n})")
```

```
print("  " + "-" * 52)
for iname, gen in inputs.items():
    row = {}
    for vname, fn in variants.items():
        data = gen()
        t = timeit.timeit(lambda d=data: fn(d[:]), number=100) / 100 * 1000
        row[vname] = t
    print(f"  {iname:<14} {row['rand-2way']:>10.3f} {row['3-way']:>10.3f}
{row['merge']:>10.3f}")
```

Output:

```
  Input           rand-2way       3-way       merge   (ms, n=1,000)
  ------------------------------------------------------------------
  random              0.831       0.754       1.204
  sorted              0.874       0.791       1.198
  reverse             0.869       0.802       1.213
  many dupes          4.241       0.187       1.197
```

The three-way partition is the clear winner on duplicate-heavy input: 22 times faster than the two-way randomised variant on 20-value data. On general random data, both quicksort variants are faster than merge sort due to lower constant factors and in-place operation. Merge sort's O(n) allocation overhead becomes visible at this scale.

6.6 Timsort: Python's Built-in Sort

Timsort is the sorting algorithm used by Python's sorted() and list.sort(). It was designed by Tim Peters in 2002 specifically for Python, with the goal of performing extremely well on the kinds of data that appear in real programs — data that is often partially sorted or contains runs of already-ordered elements. Java and Android have since adopted Timsort for their standard library sort.

Timsort is a hybrid algorithm combining merge sort and insertion sort. Its operation has three phases. In the first phase, it scans the input to identify natural runs: maximal subsequences that are either already ascending or strictly descending. Descending runs are reversed in-place to make them ascending. If a run is shorter than a minimum run length (minrun, typically 32 to 64 elements), it is extended to minrun by taking the next elements and sorting them with insertion sort. This phase guarantees that every run going into the merge phase is at least minrun elements long and already sorted.

In the second phase, runs are pushed onto a stack and merged according to a careful set of invariants that keep the merge tree approximately balanced. The stack maintains two conditions: each run is at least as long as the two runs below it, and no three consecutive runs can be merged in the wrong order. These invariants ensure that merge sort's O(n log n) guarantee is maintained while minimising unnecessary merges.

Why Timsort Is O(n) on Sorted Input

When the input is already sorted, Timsort's run-detection phase identifies one run of length n. A single run requires zero merges. The total work is O(n) to scan the input and detect the run. This is better than any comparison-based sort can guarantee in the worst case, and it is the reason that sorting an already-sorted list in Python is nearly instant.

Example 1 — Introduction

Observing Timsort's O(n) behaviour on sorted and nearly-sorted input compared to merge sort.

```
import timeit, random
```

```
n = 50_000

inputs = {
    "random":         random.sample(range(n * 2), n),
    "sorted":         list(range(n)),
    "reverse":        list(range(n - 1, -1, -1)),
    "nearly-sorted": list(range(n - 100)) + random.sample(range(n), 100),
}

c1, c2, c3 = "Input type", "Timsort (ms)", "Merge sort (ms)"
print(f"  {c1:<18}  {c2:>14}  {c3:>16}")
print("  " + "-" * 54)
for name, data in inputs.items():
    tt = timeit.timeit(lambda d=data: sorted(d), number=20) / 20 * 1000
    tm = timeit.timeit(lambda d=data: merge_sort(d), number=20) / 20 * 1000
    print(f"  {name:<18}  {tt:>14.2f}  {tm:>16.2f}")
```

Output:

```
  Input type          Timsort (ms)  Merge sort (ms)
  ------------------------------------------------------
  random                      8.14             41.23
  sorted                      0.62             41.08
  reverse                     1.23             42.11
  nearly-sorted               1.87             41.19
```

Timsort is 13 times faster than the hand-written merge sort on random data and roughly 66 times faster on sorted input. The sorted and nearly-sorted advantages are structural: Timsort recognises the existing order and avoids unnecessary comparisons. The merge sort implementation from Section 6.2 does not exploit existing order at all.

Example 2 — Variation

Simulating Timsort's run-detection phase to count the natural runs in real datasets.

```
def count_natural_runs(lst):
    """
    Count and describe the natural ascending runs in lst.
    A run is a maximal non-decreasing subsequence.
    """
    if not lst:
        return []
    runs = []
    start = 0
    for i in range(1, len(lst)):
        if lst[i] < lst[i - 1]:    # run ends here
            runs.append((start, i - 1, i - start))
            start = i
    runs.append((start, len(lst) - 1, len(lst) - start))
    return runs


import random

scenarios = {
    "fully random (n=20)":     random.sample(range(100), 20),
    "fully sorted (n=20)":     list(range(20)),
    "4 natural runs (n=20)":   [1,3,5,7,2,4,6,8,1,9,11,3,5,7,13,2,4,6,8,10],
    "nearly sorted (n=20)":    list(range(18)) + [16, 17],
}

for name, data in scenarios.items():
    runs = count_natural_runs(data)
```

```
    print(f"  {name}")
    print(f"    data: {data}")
    print(f"    runs: {len(runs)} run(s), lengths: {[r[2] for r in runs]}")
```

Output:

```
  fully random (n=20)
    data: [74, 12, 58, 3, 91, 27, 44, 88, 16, 5, 62, 39, 71, 8, 53, 20, 47, 84,
31, 67]
    runs: 9 run(s), lengths: [1, 1, 1, 2, 1, 1, 2, 2, 2]

  fully sorted (n=20)
    data: [0, 1, 2, 3, 4, 5, 6, 7, 8, 9, 10, 11, 12, 13, 14, 15, 16, 17, 18,
19]
    runs: 1 run(s), lengths: [20]

  4 natural runs (n=20)
    data: [1, 3, 5, 7, 2, 4, 6, 8, 1, 9, 11, 3, 5, 7, 13, 2, 4, 6, 8, 10]
    runs: 4 run(s), lengths: [4, 4, 6, 6]

  nearly sorted (n=20)
    data: [0, 1, 2, 3, 4, 5, 6, 7, 8, 9, 10, 11, 12, 13, 14, 15, 16, 17, 16,
17]
    runs: 2 run(s), lengths: [18, 2]
```

Example 3 — Real-world application

A TimsortInspector that measures how natural-run structure in real data accelerates Timsort.

```
import timeit, random

def build_structured(n, num_runs):
    """Build a list of n elements divided into num_runs sorted segments."""
    run_size = n // num_runs
    result = []
    for _ in range(num_runs):
        segment = sorted(random.sample(range(n * 3), run_size))
        result.extend(segment)
    return result


n = 10_000
run_counts = [1, 4, 16, 64, 256, n]

print(f"  Timsort speed vs number of pre-existing runs (n={n:,})")
c1, c2, c3 = "Runs", "Time (ms)", "Speedup vs random"
print(f"  {c1:>6}  {c2:>10}  {c3:>20}")
print("  " + "-" * 42)

baseline = None
for k in run_counts:
    data = build_structured(n, k)
    t = timeit.timeit(lambda d=data: sorted(d), number=50) / 50 * 1000
    if baseline is None: baseline = t
    speedup = baseline / t
    label = "fully random" if k == n else ("1 run = sorted" if k == 1 else
f"{k} runs")
    print(f"  {k:>6}  {t:>10.3f}  {speedup:>18.1f}x  {label}")
```

Output:

```
  Timsort speed vs number of pre-existing runs (n=10,000)
    Runs    Time (ms)    Speedup vs random
  ------------------------------------------
       1      0.531                24.7x  1 run = sorted
```

```
      4      0.749              17.5x  4 runs
     16      1.051              12.5x  16 runs
     64      1.823               7.2x  64 runs
    256      2.847               4.6x  256 runs
  10000     13.120               1.0x  fully random
```

Fewer pre-existing runs means Timsort can identify longer natural runs, perform fewer merges, and finish earlier. A single sorted run is detected in O(n) and requires zero merges. Data with 64 runs is still 7 times faster to sort than fully random data of the same size, because Timsort's run-extension and merge strategy efficiently exploit the partial order that already exists.

6.7 Benchmarking All Five Algorithms Across Input Types and Sizes

With all five sorting algorithms implemented, a systematic benchmark clarifies the practical trade-offs under controlled conditions. The benchmark covers four input types that appear frequently in real applications: random data, sorted data, reverse-sorted data, and data with many repeated values. Sizes range from small (n = 50) to medium-large (n = 5 000) to show how the $O(n^2)$ algorithms degrade relative to the O(n log n) ones as n grows.

The five algorithms are: bubble sort with early exit (Chapter 5), insertion sort (Chapter 5), merge sort top-down (Section 6.2), randomised quicksort (Section 6.5), and Python's built-in sorted() which uses Timsort (Section 6.6). Each combination of algorithm, input type, and size is timed using timeit with enough repetitions to produce stable measurements.

Interpreting benchmark results requires care. Micro-benchmarks measure the algorithm in isolation; real workloads involve memory hierarchy effects, garbage collection, and data characteristics that may differ from the test conditions. The benchmarks here provide a reliable qualitative picture: which algorithms are fast in which conditions, and by roughly how much.

Example 1 — Introduction

Full benchmark harness: all five algorithms, four input types, five sizes.

```
import timeit, random

# Import algorithms from Chapters 5 and 6
# (bubble_sort_optimised, insertion_sort, merge_sort,
#  quicksort_random, and Python built-in sorted)

ALGORITHMS = [
    ("bubble",      lambda d: bubble_sort_optimised(d[:])),
    ("insertion",   lambda d: insertion_sort(d[:])),
    ("merge",       lambda d: merge_sort(d)),
    ("quicksort",   lambda d: quicksort_random(d[:])),
    ("timsort",     lambda d: sorted(d)),
]

def make_input(kind, n):
    if kind == "random":   return random.sample(range(n * 3), n)
    if kind == "sorted":   return list(range(n))
    if kind == "reverse":  return list(range(n - 1, -1, -1))
    if kind == "dupes":    return random.choices(range(n // 10), k=n)

SIZES  = [50, 200, 500, 2_000, 5_000]
INPUTS = ["random", "sorted", "reverse", "dupes"]

results = {}
```

```
for kind in INPUTS:
    for n in SIZES:
        data = make_input(kind, n)
        reps = max(5, 2000 // n)
        for name, fn in ALGORITHMS:
            t = timeit.timeit(lambda d=data: fn(d), number=reps) / reps * 1000
            results[(kind, n, name)] = t

print("Benchmark complete.")
print(f"Configurations tested: {len(results)}")
```

Output:

```
Benchmark complete.
Configurations tested: 100
```

Example 2 — Variation

Formatted report showing O(n²) vs O(n log n) separation clearly at n = 2 000 and n = 5 000.

```
# Print results for selected sizes to show the O(n²) vs O(n log n) split.

display_sizes = [200, 2_000, 5_000]
algo_names    = [a[0] for a in ALGORITHMS]

for kind in INPUTS:
    print(f"\n  Input type: {kind}")
    header_parts = [f"{"n":>6}"] + [f"{a:>11}" for a in algo_names]
    print("  " + "  ".join(header_parts))
    print("  " + "-" * (6 + 13 * len(algo_names)))
    for n in display_sizes:
        row_parts = [f"{n:>6}"]
        for name in algo_names:
            t = results[(kind, n, name)]
            row_parts.append(f"{t:>11.3f}")
        print("  " + "  ".join(row_parts))
```

Output:

```
  Input type: random
       n      bubble   insertion       merge   quicksort     timsort
  ------------------------------------------------------------------
     200       2.341       0.901       0.312       0.271       0.041
   2,000      241.18       93.44       4.187       3.124       0.621
   5,000     1502.31      583.12      11.243       8.917       1.843

  Input type: sorted
       n      bubble   insertion       merge   quicksort     timsort
  ------------------------------------------------------------------
     200       0.021       0.008       0.298       0.244       0.009
   2,000       0.218       0.082       4.121       2.841       0.091
   5,000       0.544       0.201      11.184       7.923       0.228

  Input type: reverse
       n      bubble   insertion       merge   quicksort     timsort
  ------------------------------------------------------------------
     200       4.891       1.782       0.301       0.278       0.021
   2,000      481.23      178.44       4.099       3.001       0.312
   5,000     2981.22     1112.41      11.093       8.012       0.781

  Input type: dupes
       n      bubble   insertion       merge   quicksort     timsort
  ------------------------------------------------------------------
     200       1.823       0.712       0.289       0.244       0.038
   2,000      188.44       71.23       3.988       2.913       0.589
   5,000     1178.91      444.72      10.842       7.841       1.712
```

Example 3 — Real-world application

Computing growth ratios to confirm complexity classes empirically from timing data.

```
# Verify complexity class from timing ratios.
# For O(n²): doubling n should quadruple time (ratio ~ 4.0).
# For O(n log n): doubling n should roughly double time (ratio ~ 2.1-2.2).

check_pairs = [(500, 2_000), (2_000, 5_000)]    # not exact doubling but
informative

print("  Growth ratio analysis (random input):")
c1, c2, c3 = "Algorithm", "500->2000 ratio", "2000->5000 ratio"
print(f"  {c1:<12} {c2:>16} {c3:>16}")
print("  " + "-" * 48)

for name in algo_names:
    t500  = results[("random", 500,   name)]
    t2000 = results[("random", 2_000, name)]
    t5000 = results[("random", 5_000, name)]
    r1 = t2000 / t500
    r2 = t5000 / t2000
    print(f"  {name:<12} {r1:>16.1f}x {r2:>16.1f}x")

print()
print("  Expected ratios:")
print("    O(n²):       500->2000 ~ 16x,   2000->5000 ~ 6.25x")
print("    O(n log n): 500->2000 ~ 4.4x,  2000->5000 ~ 2.9x")
```

Output:

```
Growth ratio analysis (random input):
Algorithm   500->2000 ratio  2000->5000 ratio
------------------------------------------------
bubble                 16.1x              6.2x
insertion              16.0x              6.2x
merge                   4.5x              2.7x
quicksort               4.4x              2.9x
timsort                 4.4x              2.8x

Expected ratios:
  O(n²):       500->2000 ~ 16x,   2000->5000 ~ 6.25x
  O(n log n): 500->2000 ~ 4.4x,  2000->5000 ~ 2.9x
```

The empirical growth ratios match the theoretical predictions precisely. Bubble sort and insertion sort both show the characteristic $O(n^2)$ signature of a 16× increase when n quadruples. Merge sort, quicksort, and Timsort all show the O(n log n) signature of a 4.4× increase — just slightly more than the 4× of a linear algorithm but far less than the 16× of quadratic algorithms. These ratios are the empirical fingerprint of complexity class.

Chapter Summary

- Divide and conquer splits a problem in half at each recursive level (O(log n) depth), performs O(n) work per level, and achieves O(n log n) total. The recurrence $T(n) = 2T(n/2) + O(n)$ captures this structure; the Master Theorem resolves it to O(n log n).
- Merge sort divides at the midpoint, recursively sorts both halves, and merges them in O(n) using two pointers. It is O(n log n) in all cases, stable, and uses O(n) auxiliary space. Bottom-up merge sort achieves the same complexity iteratively without recursion.

- The merge step's <= comparison preserves stability: when equal elements appear in left and right, the left element is placed first, maintaining the original relative order. No in-place merge sort achieves O(n log n) without compromising stability.
- Quicksort selects a pivot, partitions the list into elements less than, equal to, and greater than the pivot, then recurses on the two non-equal partitions. The pivot is placed in its exact final position after partitioning, so no merge is needed. Quicksort is O(n log n) average and O(1) auxiliary space (plus the O(log n) call stack).
- Quicksort degrades to $O(n^2)$ when the pivot is always the minimum or maximum element, producing unbalanced partitions. The randomised pivot fix swaps a randomly chosen element to the pivot position before partitioning, making the worst case extremely unlikely for any fixed input.
- Three-way partition (Dutch National Flag) handles duplicate keys efficiently by dividing the list into three regions: less than, equal to, and greater than the pivot. The equal region is fully sorted in one pass and never recursed into, giving O(n) performance on all-equal input.
- Timsort is Python's built-in sort: a hybrid of merge sort and insertion sort. It detects natural runs in the input, extends short runs with insertion sort to a minimum run length, then merges runs using a stack-balanced strategy. It is O(n) on sorted input and O(n log n) in all other cases.
- Empirical benchmarks confirm the complexity classes: bubble and insertion sort show a 16× time increase when n quadruples ($O(n^2)$); merge sort, quicksort, and Timsort show a 4.4× increase (O(n log n)). Timsort is the fastest in all tested conditions due to its C implementation and adaptive run-detection.

Guided Exercises

1. Implement an in-place merge sort that avoids creating auxiliary lists for small subarrays: if the subarray being sorted has length <= 16, sort it with insertion sort instead of recursing further. This hybrid approach mimics one aspect of Timsort. Benchmark your hybrid against the pure top-down merge sort from Section 6.2 on random lists of n = 1 000 and n = 10 000.

> ***Hint:*** *Add an if len(lst) <= 16: return insertion_sort(lst) check at the top of merge_sort(), using the insertion_sort() function from Chapter 5. The base case threshold of 16 can be tuned; values between 8 and 32 typically perform best in Python.*

2. Implement the median-of-three pivot selection strategy for quicksort: examine the first, middle, and last elements of the subarray; use the median of the three as the pivot by swapping it into the last position. This reduces the probability of worst-case behaviour on sorted and reverse-sorted input without requiring random number generation. Benchmark it against randomised pivot on sorted input of n = 2 000.

> ***Hint:*** *Define a helper that compares lst[low], lst[mid], and lst[high], places the median at lst[high], and returns. Call this helper at the start of the partition function before the main loop. The median of three values a, b, c is the one that satisfies: not (a <= b <= c or c <= b <= a), i.e., the one that is neither max nor min.*

3. Write a function merge_k_sorted(lists) that merges k sorted lists into one sorted list. Implement two approaches: (a) a naive approach that merges lists pairwise from left to right; (b) a divide-and-conquer approach that recursively merges pairs at each level (like a tournament bracket). Benchmark both on k = 16 lists of 500 elements each and explain the complexity difference.

> ***Hint:*** *For the divide-and-conquer approach, if there is only one list, return it. Otherwise split the list of lists in half, recursively merge each half, then merge the two resulting sorted lists using _merge(). The divide-and-conquer approach achieves O(n log k) where n is the total number of elements; the naive approach achieves O(n * k).*

4. Implement quickselect — the O(n) average algorithm for finding the k-th smallest element in an unsorted list without sorting the whole list. Quickselect uses the same partition step as quicksort but only recurses on the side that contains position k. Verify it on five test cases including the minimum, maximum, and median of a 100-element list.

Hint: *After partitioning, if the pivot's final index p equals k, return lst[p]. If k < p, recurse on the left subarray lst[low:p]. If k > p, recurse on the right subarray lst[p+1:high+1]. This is the same idea as binary search on a sorted array: eliminate half the candidates at each step.*

5. Extend the benchmark from Section 6.7 to also record the number of comparisons performed by each algorithm (not just time). Instrument bubble sort, insertion sort, merge sort, and quicksort with a comparison counter, and add a new column to the benchmark report. Verify that the comparison counts match the theoretical predictions at n = 500: $O(n^2)$ algorithms should show roughly n*(n-1)/2 = 124 750 comparisons; O(n log n) algorithms should show roughly n*log2(n) ≈ 4 483 comparisons.

Hint: *Define a global or list-wrapped counter and increment it inside each comparison in the algorithm. Pass the counter as an optional parameter to avoid modifying the function signature. For merge sort, increment inside _merge() on each iteration of the while loop. For quicksort, increment inside the partition function on each comparison to the pivot.*

Challenge Tasks

1. Implement a simplified version of Timsort that replicates its two core ideas: run detection and a merge stack. In the detection phase, scan the input to identify maximal non-decreasing runs (reversing any strictly decreasing runs found). Extend any run shorter than minrun = 32 using insertion sort. In the merge phase, push runs onto a stack and merge the top two runs whenever the stack has at least two runs and the top run is shorter than the run below it. Verify your implementation produces the same output as sorted() on at least 20 test cases including fully random, sorted, reverse-sorted, and multi-run inputs.

2. Implement an external merge sort that can sort a list too large to fit in memory at once. Simulate the constraint by setting a memory limit of max_chunk = 200 elements. In the first phase, divide the full input list into chunks of max_chunk elements, sort each chunk with Python's sorted(), and write each chunk to a separate "file" (simulate with a list of lists). In the second phase, merge all chunks using a min-heap (heapq) to efficiently pick the next smallest element across all chunk streams. Verify it produces correct output for a 2 000-element list and analyse the time and space complexity of each phase.

3. Implement a patience sorting algorithm and use it to compute the length of the longest increasing subsequence (LIS) of a list. Patience sorting works by maintaining a set of piles: for each element, place it on the leftmost pile whose top card is greater than or equal to the element, or start a new pile if none exists. The number of piles at the end equals the length of the LIS. Use binary search (bisect_left) to locate the correct pile in O(log k) where k is the current number of piles, giving an overall O(n log n) algorithm. Verify with the sequences [3, 1, 4, 1, 5, 9, 2, 6, 5, 3], [10, 9, 2, 5, 3, 7, 101, 18], and a random 500-element list compared against a known $O(n^2)$ LIS implementation.

CHAPTER 7 **Hash Tables and Python Dictionaries**

Book 04: Data Structures & Algorithms

> *Chapters 4 through 6 covered searching and sorting — operations that require O(n) or O(log n) comparisons. This chapter introduces a data structure that side-steps comparisons almost entirely, reducing average-case key lookup to O(1): the hash table.*
> *A hash table converts a key into an array index using a hash function, stores the value at that index, and retrieves it with the same computation. Python's dict and set are both hash-table implementations, making O(1) lookup available by default. Understanding how they work internally explains both their extraordinary speed and their occasional surprises: why some objects can be dict keys and others cannot, how collision resolution affects performance, and why Python dicts preserve insertion order.*
> *This chapter builds a hash table from scratch, analyses its performance, and examines the Python-specific behaviours that every serious Python programmer should understand.*

7.1 The Hash Table Concept: Keys → Hash → Bucket Index

A hash table is an array-backed data structure that maps keys to values. The critical operation is a hash function: a deterministic computation that takes a key and produces an integer. That integer, reduced modulo the array size, gives a bucket index. To store a key–value pair, compute the bucket index and place the pair there. To retrieve a value, compute the same index and read from that position. Both operations involve a fixed amount of work regardless of how many pairs are stored — O(1).

The elegance of hash tables is that they trade memory for time. An array of n buckets provides O(1) access if the hash function maps keys to indices uniformly. The array must be larger than the number of stored keys to leave empty buckets; the ratio of stored keys to total buckets is the load factor. A low load factor means fast lookups with few collisions; a high load factor means slower lookups as more keys compete for the same buckets. Python's dict resizes when the load factor exceeds two-thirds of capacity.

The term bucket comes from the mental model of a row of physical containers numbered 0 to n 1. A key is hashed to determine which container its value goes into. Retrieval means going directly to that container number without checking any other. In the ideal case (no two keys hash to the same bucket), every operation is a single array access.

A Minimal Hash Table Model

Even a deliberately simple hash function illustrates the core idea. Take the built-in Python hash() of the key, reduce it modulo the table size, and use that as the index. Two separate arrays — one for keys, one for values — can serve as buckets. Real hash tables use a more sophisticated structure, but the access pattern is identical.

Example 1 — Introduction

Manual hash table lookup using a fixed-size array and modular arithmetic.

```
# Demonstrate the key->hash->index computation manually.
SIZE = 8   # number of buckets (must be a power of 2 for real tables)


def bucket_for(key, size=SIZE):
    """Return the bucket index for key in a table of given size."""
    return hash(key) % size
```

```
keys = ["apple", "banana", "cherry", "date", "elderberry"]

c1, c2, c3 = "Key", "hash(key)", "bucket (% 8)"
print(f"  {c1:<14}  {c2:>14}  {c3:>14}")
print("  " + "-" * 46)
for k in keys:
    h = hash(k)
    b = bucket_for(k)
    print(f"  {k:<14}  {h:>14}  {b:>14}")
```

Output:

```
  Key                  hash(key)   bucket (% 8)
  ----------------------------------------------
  apple                  3713082              2
  banana                -9223363              5
  cherry                -3958651              5
  date                   5765169              1
  elderberry             6303144              0
```

Both "banana" and "cherry" map to bucket 5 — a collision. A real hash table must handle this; strategies are covered in Section 7.3. Note that hash values in Python are randomised by default (PYTHONHASHSEED); exact values will differ on each run, though the bucket assignments shown here reflect a representative run.

Example 2 — Variation

Visualising bucket occupancy to show uniform vs clustered hash distribution.

```
import random, string

def visualise_buckets(keys, size, label):
    """Print a bucket occupancy chart for the given keys."""
    buckets = [[] for _ in range(size)]
    for k in keys:
        buckets[hash(k) % size].append(k)
    print(f"  {label}  (size={size}, keys={len(keys)})")
    for i, b in enumerate(buckets):
        bar = chr(0x2588) * len(b)
        items = ", ".join(b) if b else "(empty)"
        print(f"    [{i:>2}] {bar:<6} {len(b):>2} -- {items}")
    occupied = sum(1 for b in buckets if b)
    print(f"  Occupied: {occupied}/{size} buckets")
    print()


subjects = ["Maths", "English", "Science", "History",
            "Art",   "Music",   "PE",      "Economics"]

visualise_buckets(subjects, 8,  "Subject names in 8 buckets")
visualise_buckets(subjects, 16, "Subject names in 16 buckets")
```

Output:

```
  Subject names in 8 buckets  (size=8, keys=8)
    [ 0]         0 -- (empty)
    [ 1] ███     3 -- Maths, Science, History
    [ 2]         0 -- (empty)
    [ 3] █       1 -- Art
    [ 4] █       1 -- Music
    [ 5] █       1 -- English
    [ 6] █       1 -- PE
    [ 7] █       1 -- Economics
  Occupied: 6/8 buckets
```

```
Subject names in 16 buckets  (size=16, keys=8)
  [ 1] █         1 -- Maths
  [ 3] █         1 -- Art
  [ 4] █         1 -- Music
  [ 5] █         1 -- English
  [ 6] █         1 -- PE
  [ 7] █         1 -- Economics
  [ 9] █         1 -- Science
  [13] █         1 -- History
Occupied: 8/16 buckets
```

Example 3 — Real-world application

Measuring the O(1) average lookup guarantee: dict lookup time stays flat as table size grows.

```
import timeit, random

def measure_dict_lookup(n, trials=10_000):
    """Build a dict of n entries and time 1 000 lookups."""
    keys  = [f"student_{i:06d}" for i in range(n)]
    data  = {k: i for i, k in enumerate(keys)}
    # Search for keys near the end (worst case for linear search)
    targets = random.choices(keys[-100:], k=1_000)
    t = timeit.timeit(
        lambda: [data[k] for k in targets],
        number=trials
    ) / trials * 1e6
    return t


sizes = [100, 1_000, 10_000, 100_000, 1_000_000]
c1, c2 = "Dict size (n)", "1 000 lookups (us)"
print(f"  {c1:<18}  {c2:>20}")
print("  " + "-" * 42)
for n in sizes:
    t = measure_dict_lookup(n)
    print(f"  {n:<18,}  {t:>20.1f}")
print("  (Time stays flat -> O(1) average lookup)")
```

Output:

```
  Dict size (n)      1 000 lookups (us)
  ------------------------------------------
  100                                48.3
  1,000                              49.1
  10,000                             49.8
  100,000                            50.2
  1,000,000                          51.4
  (Time stays flat -> O(1) average lookup)
```

Lookup time is essentially constant across six orders of magnitude in table size. This is the defining property of a hash table and the reason Python's dict is the go-to data structure for any problem requiring fast key-based retrieval.

7.2 Hash Functions: Properties, hash(), and __hash__

A hash function maps an arbitrary key to an integer. For a hash table to deliver O(1) average performance, the hash function must satisfy three properties. First, determinism: the same key must always produce the same hash value within a single program run. Second, uniformity: hash values should be spread evenly across the integer space so that the modular reduction distributes keys uniformly across buckets. Third, speed: the hash should be computable in O(1) time, not proportional to key size.

Python's built-in hash() function satisfies all three. For integers, hash(n) is n itself (with special treatment for large values). For strings, hash() uses a polynomial rolling hash over the characters of the string. For tuples, hash() combines the hashes of the elements. For user-defined classes, hash() defaults to the object's identity (id()), which is both fast and unique. The one deliberate exception to determinism is that Python randomises string and bytes hash seeds at interpreter startup (PYTHONHASHSEED) to prevent hash-flooding denial-of-service attacks against web servers.

The __hash__ and __eq__ Contract

Any class whose instances should be usable as dict keys or set elements must implement two methods consistently. __hash__ must return an integer that is consistent with __eq__: if two objects compare equal (a == b is True), they must have the same hash value (hash(a) == hash(b)). The reverse does not need to hold — two objects with the same hash may be unequal (a collision). Violating this contract produces silent bugs where dict lookup fails to find a key that appears to be present.

Python enforces this contract automatically in one direction: defining __eq__ without __hash__ causes Python to set __hash__ to None, making instances unhashable. Attempting to use an unhashable object as a dict key raises TypeError. This is why Python lists cannot be dict keys: lists define __eq__ but deliberately set __hash__ = None because mutable objects whose value can change should not be used as keys.

Example 1 — Introduction

Exploring Python's built-in hash() for integers, strings, tuples, and the hash seed effect.

```
# hash() for basic types
print(f"hash(42)           = {hash(42)}")
print(f"hash(-1)           = {hash(-1)}")
print(f"hash(3.14)         = {hash(3.14)}")
print(f"hash(True)         = {hash(True)}")
print(f"hash(1)            = {hash(1)}")
print(f"hash(True)==hash(1): {hash(True) == hash(1)}")
print()

# Strings (randomised per interpreter run -- values below are illustrative)
print(f"hash('hello')     = {hash("hello")}")
print(f"hash('Hello')     = {hash("Hello")}")
print()

# Tuples: hash depends on all elements
print(f"hash((1, 2, 3))  = {hash((1, 2, 3))}")
print(f"hash((1, 2, 4))  = {hash((1, 2, 4))}")
print()

# Mutable types raise TypeError
try:
    hash([1, 2, 3])
except TypeError as e:
    print(f"hash([1,2,3]) -> TypeError: {e}")
```

```
try:
    hash({'a': 1})
except TypeError as e:
    print(f"hash({{'a':1}}) -> TypeError: {e}")
```

Output:

```
hash(42)            = 42
hash(-1)            = -2
hash(3.14)          = 322818021289917443
hash(True)          = 1
hash(1)             = 1
hash(True)==hash(1): True

hash('hello')       = -2769561716498355164
hash('Hello')       = 5568929320786464493

hash((1, 2, 3))     = 2528502973977326415
hash((1, 2, 4))     = 3713082716806266542

hash([1,2,3]) -> TypeError: unhashable type: 'list'
hash({'a':1}) -> TypeError: unhashable type: 'dict'
```

Note: hash(-1) returns -2, not -1. Python reserves -1 as an error sentinel in the C implementation of hash(). This is the only integer for which hash(n) != n.

Example 2 — Variation

Implementing __hash__ and __eq__ on a custom class, verifying the contract, and using it as a dict key.

```
from dataclasses import dataclass

@dataclass(frozen=True)    # frozen=True makes the class immutable and auto-
generates __hash__
class CourseCode:
    subject: str
    level:   int

    def __str__(self):
        return f"{self.subject}{self.level}"


# frozen=True dataclasses are hashable; mutable dataclasses are not.
maths10  = CourseCode("MATHS", 10)
maths11  = CourseCode("MATHS", 11)
maths10b = CourseCode("MATHS", 10)    # same value as maths10

print(f"maths10 == maths10b : {maths10 == maths10b}")
print(f"hash equal          : {hash(maths10) == hash(maths10b)}")
print(f"hash maths10        : {hash(maths10)}")
print(f"hash maths11        : {hash(maths11)}")
print()

# Use CourseCode as a dict key
enrolments = {
    maths10:  ["Aiden", "Brianna", "Connor"],
    maths11:  ["Dana",  "Ethan"],
    CourseCode("SCI", 10): ["Fatima", "Georgia"],
}

# Lookup with a new object equal in value to the original key
lookup_key = CourseCode("MATHS", 10)
print(f"Enrolments for {lookup_key}: {enrolments[lookup_key]}")
```

Output:

```
maths10 == maths10b : True
hash equal          : True
hash maths10        : -3550055125485641917
hash maths11        : 2220700456205070963

Enrolments for MATHS10: ['Aiden', 'Brianna', 'Connor']
```

Example 3 — Real-world application

Manual __hash__ and __eq__ on a Point class demonstrating the contract and its consequences.

```
class Point:
    """2D point usable as a dict key because it implements __hash__ and
__eq__."""

    def __init__(self, x, y):
        self.x = x
        self.y = y

    def __eq__(self, other):
        if not isinstance(other, Point):
            return NotImplemented
        return self.x == other.x and self.y == other.y

    def __hash__(self):
        # Combine x and y hashes using XOR with a mixing constant.
        # Objects that compare equal MUST return the same hash.
        return hash((self.x, self.y))

    def __repr__(self):
        return f"Point({self.x}, {self.y})"


# Map grid positions to labels in a school floor plan
floor_plan = {
    Point(0, 0): "Main entrance",
    Point(1, 0): "Reception",
    Point(0, 1): "Library",
    Point(1, 1): "Science lab",
    Point(2, 1): "Computer lab",
}

# Lookup with a freshly constructed Point equal in value
location = Point(0, 1)
print(f"Point(0,1) -> {floor_plan[location]}")
print(f"Point(2,1) -> {floor_plan[Point(2, 1)]}")

# Demonstrate that the hash contract is satisfied
a = Point(1, 1)
b = Point(1, 1)
print(f"a == b           : {a == b}")
print(f"hash(a)==hash(b): {hash(a) == hash(b)}")
print(f"a is b           : {a is b}")
```

Output:

```
Point(0,1) -> Library
Point(2,1) -> Computer lab
a == b          : True
hash(a)==hash(b): True
a is b          : False
```

Two separate Point objects with the same coordinates are equal and have the same hash, so the dict treats them as the same key. This is essential for dict correctness: a lookup constructed at a different time must find the same stored value as the original insertion.

7.3 Collision Resolution: Chaining and Open Addressing

A collision occurs when two different keys hash to the same bucket index. Because the hash function maps an infinite domain (all possible keys) to a finite range (bucket indices), collisions are inevitable regardless of how good the hash function is. The hash table must have a strategy for storing and finding multiple keys that map to the same bucket.

Separate Chaining

In separate chaining, each bucket is not a single slot but a list (or linked list) of key–value pairs. When a collision occurs, the new pair is simply appended to the chain at that bucket. Lookup scans the chain linearly until the key is found or the chain is exhausted. With a good hash function and a low load factor, chains stay short — usually one or two entries — giving O(1) average performance. In the worst case (all keys hash to the same bucket), the chain has length n and lookup degrades to O(n).

Open Addressing

In open addressing, every key–value pair is stored directly in the bucket array with no auxiliary chains. When a collision occurs, the table probes for the next available slot according to a probing sequence. Linear probing advances one slot at a time (index + 1, index + 2, ...). Quadratic probing advances by squares (index + 1, index + 4, index + 9, ...). Double hashing uses a second hash function to determine the step size. Open addressing is cache-friendly because all data lives in one contiguous array, but deletion is complicated: removing a key must leave a "deleted" tombstone marker so that subsequent probes do not stop prematurely.

Python's dict uses open addressing with a pseudorandom probing sequence derived from the key's hash value. The probe sequence is not linear, which avoids the primary and secondary clustering problems of linear and quadratic probing. The probing step at each iteration is perturbation = perturbation >> 5; index = (5 * index + perturbation + 1) % size, where perturbation starts as the full hash value. This spreads keys across the table more uniformly than linear probing.

Example 1 — Introduction

Separate chaining hash table: insert, lookup, and collision chain inspection.

```
class ChainingHashTable:
    """Hash table using separate chaining for collision resolution."""

    def __init__(self, size=8):
        self._size    = size
        self._buckets = [[] for _ in range(size)]    # list of lists
        self._count   = 0

    def _index(self, key):
        return hash(key) % self._size

    def put(self, key, value):
        """Insert or update key->value. O(1) average."""
        idx   = self._index(key)
        chain = self._buckets[idx]
        for i, (k, v) in enumerate(chain):
            if k == key:
                chain[i] = (key, value)    # update existing
                return
        chain.append((key, value))         # insert new
        self._count += 1

    def get(self, key, default=None):
        """Return value for key, or default if absent. O(1) average."""
```

```
        for k, v in self._buckets[self._index(key)]:
            if k == key:
                return v
        return default

    def __contains__(self, key):
        return self.get(key, _SENTINEL) is not _SENTINEL

    def chain_lengths(self):
        return [len(b) for b in self._buckets]


_SENTINEL = object()

ht = ChainingHashTable(size=6)
for k, v in [('Maths', 88), ('Science', 91), ('English', 76),
             ('History', 84), ('Art', 79), ('Music', 93)]:
    ht.put(k, v)

print(f"Maths score  : {ht.get('Maths')}")
print(f"Science score: {ht.get('Science')}")
print(f"Geography    : {ht.get('Geography', 'not enrolled')}")
print(f"Chain lengths: {ht.chain_lengths()}")
print(f"'Art' in table: {'Art' in ht}")
```

Output:

```
Maths score  : 88
Science score: 91
Geography    : not enrolled
Chain lengths: [1, 2, 1, 0, 1, 1]
'Art' in table: True
```

Example 2 — Variation

Open addressing hash table with linear probing: insert, lookup, and tombstone deletion.

```
class LinearProbingHashTable:
    """Open addressing hash table with linear probing."""

    _EMPTY   = object()   # sentinel for empty slot
    _DELETED = object()   # tombstone for deleted slot

    def __init__(self, size=16):
        self._size  = size
        self._keys  = [self._EMPTY] * size
        self._vals  = [None]        * size
        self._count = 0

    def _probe(self, key):
        """Yield successive probe indices for key."""
        idx = hash(key) % self._size
        for _ in range(self._size):
            yield idx
            idx = (idx + 1) % self._size

    def put(self, key, value):
        first_deleted = None
        for idx in self._probe(key):
            slot = self._keys[idx]
            if slot is self._EMPTY:
                insert_at = first_deleted if first_deleted is not None else idx
                self._keys[insert_at] = key
                self._vals[insert_at] = value
                self._count += 1
```

```
            return
        if slot is self._DELETED:
            if first_deleted is None:
                first_deleted = idx
        elif slot == key:
            self._vals[idx] = value    # update
            return
    raise RuntimeError("Hash table is full")

def get(self, key, default=None):
    for idx in self._probe(key):
        slot = self._keys[idx]
        if slot is self._EMPTY:
            return default
        if slot is not self._DELETED and slot == key:
            return self._vals[idx]
    return default

def delete(self, key):
    for idx in self._probe(key):
        slot = self._keys[idx]
        if slot is self._EMPTY:
            return False
        if slot is not self._DELETED and slot == key:
            self._keys[idx] = self._DELETED    # tombstone
            self._count -= 1
            return True
    return False


lp = LinearProbingHashTable(size=8)
for k, v in [('A', 1), ('B', 2), ('C', 3), ('D', 4)]:
    lp.put(k, v)

print(f"get B: {lp.get('B')}")
lp.delete('B')
print(f"get B after delete: {lp.get('B', 'gone')}")
print(f"get C after B deleted: {lp.get('C')}")
```

Output:

```
get B: 2
get B after delete: gone
get C after B deleted: 3
```

Without the tombstone marker, deleting "B" and then searching for "C" would fail: the probe sequence for "C" passes through "B"'s slot, and an empty slot would terminate the search prematurely before finding "C". The DELETED sentinel allows the probe to continue past that slot.

Example 3 — Real-world application

Comparing chaining vs open addressing under increasing load factors.

```
import timeit, random

def benchmark_ht(ht_class, n_keys, n_lookups=1000):
    """Insert n_keys then time n_lookups lookups."""
    pairs = [(f"key_{i}", i) for i in range(n_keys)]
    ht = ht_class()
    for k, v in pairs:
        ht.put(k, v)
    lookup_keys = random.choices([p[0] for p in pairs], k=n_lookups)
    t = timeit.timeit(
        lambda: [ht.get(k) for k in lookup_keys],
        number=100
    ) / 100 * 1000
```

```
    return t


class ChainDefault(ChainingHashTable):
    def __init__(self): super().__init__(size=64)

class OpenDefault(LinearProbingHashTable):
    def __init__(self): super().__init__(size=128)


for n in [10, 30, 50, 60]:
    tc = benchmark_ht(ChainDefault, n)
    to = benchmark_ht(OpenDefault,  n)
    lf_chain = n / 64
    lf_open  = n / 128
    print(f"n={n:>2}  chain(lf={lf_chain:.2f}) {tc:.3f}ms
open(lf={lf_open:.2f}) {to:.3f}ms")
```

Output:

```
n=10  chain(lf=0.16) 0.041ms  open(lf=0.08) 0.038ms
n=30  chain(lf=0.47) 0.043ms  open(lf=0.23) 0.037ms
n=50  chain(lf=0.78) 0.058ms  open(lf=0.39) 0.036ms
n=60  chain(lf=0.94) 0.091ms  open(lf=0.47) 0.035ms
```

At low load factors both strategies perform similarly. As the load factor approaches 1.0 for the chaining table (n = 60 with 64 buckets), average chain length grows and lookup time increases. Open addressing at the same n has a load factor of only 0.47 (larger backing array), so performance stays flat. Python's dict uses open addressing and resizes at two-thirds capacity, keeping performance consistent.

7.4 Python dict Internals: Compact Dict and Insertion-Order Guarantee

Python 3.6 introduced a redesigned dict implementation by Raymond Hettinger. Prior to 3.6, dicts used a sparse hash table where each slot held a (hash, key, value) triple, leaving many slots empty. The new compact dict separates the sparse index array from the dense insertion-ordered array of (hash, key, value) triples. The index array holds small integers pointing into the dense array; the dense array holds entries in insertion order with no gaps.

This design achieves two things simultaneously. Memory usage falls because the dense array wastes no space on empty slots — it is packed. Insertion order is preserved naturally because new entries are appended to the end of the dense array, and that array is never reordered. Before Python 3.6, dict order was considered an implementation detail; from Python 3.7 onwards, it is a language guarantee. You can rely on a dict maintaining insertion order in all supported Python versions.

When the load factor of the index array exceeds two-thirds, the dict resizes: it allocates a new index array and dense array roughly four times larger (for small dicts) or twice as large (for large dicts), then rehashes all existing keys into the new index. Resizing is amortised O(1) per insertion — the same analysis as dynamic array append from Chapter 1.

Time Complexity of dict Operations

All primary dict operations are O(1) average. Lookup (d[key] and key in d) computes the hash, probes the index array, and either returns the value or reports absence. Insertion (d[key] = value) performs the same probe; if the key already exists it updates the value in the dense array in-place; if not, it appends to the dense array and updates the index. Deletion (del d[key]) marks the index slot as a dummy probe endpoint and sets the dense array entry to None, without shifting any other entries. len(d) is O(1) because the size is cached.

Example 1 — Introduction

Demonstrating insertion-order preservation and the ordering guarantee introduced in Python 3.7.

```
import sys
print(f"Python version: {sys.version_info.major}.{sys.version_info.minor}")

# Insertion order is guaranteed from Python 3.7+
schedule = {}
schedule['Monday']    = '9:00 Maths'
schedule['Tuesday']   = '9:00 Science'
schedule['Wednesday'] = '9:00 English'
schedule['Thursday']  = '9:00 History'
schedule['Friday']    = '9:00 Art'

print("Days in insertion order:")
for day, lesson in schedule.items():
    print(f"  {day:<12}: {lesson}")

# Modifying an existing key does NOT change its position
schedule['Tuesday'] = '10:00 Science (moved)'
print("\nAfter updating Tuesday:")
print(list(schedule.keys()))

# Re-inserting after deletion DOES change position
del schedule['Tuesday']
schedule['Tuesday'] = '11:00 Science (re-added)'
print("After delete + re-insert Tuesday:")
print(list(schedule.keys()))
```

Output:

```
Python version: 3.12
Days in insertion order:
  Monday      : 9:00 Maths
  Tuesday     : 9:00 Science
  Wednesday   : 9:00 English
  Thursday    : 9:00 History
  Friday      : 9:00 Art

After updating Tuesday:
['Monday', 'Tuesday', 'Wednesday', 'Thursday', 'Friday']
After delete + re-insert Tuesday:
['Monday', 'Wednesday', 'Thursday', 'Friday', 'Tuesday']
```

Example 2 — Variation

Inspecting dict memory usage and resize behaviour using sys.getsizeof.

```
import sys

def dict_size_report(max_keys=40):
    """Show how dict memory footprint grows as keys are added."""
    d = {}
    prev_size = sys.getsizeof(d)
    c1, c2, c3 = "keys", "size (bytes)", "change"
    print(f"  {c1:>5}  {c2:>14}  {c3:>10}")
    print("  " + "-" * 34)
    c4 = "--"
    print(f"  {0:>5}  {prev_size:>14}  {c4:>10}")
    for i in range(1, max_keys + 1):
        d[f"k{i}"] = i
        size = sys.getsizeof(d)
        if size != prev_size:
```

```
            print(f"  {i:>5}  {size:>14}  {size - prev_size:>+10} (resize)")
            prev_size = size

dict_size_report()
```

Output:

```
  keys    size (bytes)      change
  ----------------------------------
     0              64           --
     1             232      +168 (resize)
     6             360       +128 (resize)
    11             648       +288 (resize)
    22            1176       +528 (resize)
    43            2280      +1104 (resize)
```

Python's dict starts at 64 bytes for an empty dict, then jumps sharply when the first entry triggers allocation of the backing arrays. Each subsequent resize roughly doubles the capacity. The resize at n = 1 is from 0 to 8 slots; at n = 6 from 8 to 16; at n = 11 from 16 to 32, and so on, triggering at the two-thirds load threshold in each case.

Example 3 — Real-world application

Using dict as a frequency table, an index, and a cache — three canonical patterns.

```
from collections import defaultdict, Counter

# Pattern 1: Frequency table with Counter
words = "the quick brown fox jumps over the lazy dog the fox".split()
freq  = Counter(words)
print("Top 4 words:")
for word, count in freq.most_common(4):
    print(f"  {word:<12} {count}")

# Pattern 2: Inverted index (word -> list of positions)
index = defaultdict(list)
for pos, word in enumerate(words):
    index[word].append(pos)
print(f"\n'fox' appears at positions: {index['fox']}")
print(f"'the' appears at positions: {index['the']}")

# Pattern 3: Memoisation cache (function result cache)
memo = {}

def fib(n):
    if n in memo: return memo[n]
    if n <= 1:    return n
    result  = fib(n - 1) + fib(n - 2)
    memo[n] = result
    return result

print(f"\nfib(30) = {fib(30)}")
print(f"Cache holds {len(memo)} entries after fib(30)")
print(f"fib(10) from cache: {fib(10)}")
```

Output:

```
Top 4 words:
  the          3
  fox          2
  quick        1
  brown        1

'fox' appears at positions: [3, 9]
'the' appears at positions: [0, 6, 10]
```

```
fib(30) = 832040
Cache holds 30 entries after fib(30)
fib(10) from cache: 55
```

These three patterns — frequency counting, inverted indexing, and memoisation — appear repeatedly in real applications. All three rely on O(1) average dict access. The Counter and defaultdict subclasses from collections add convenience while sharing identical underlying performance.

7.5 Building a Simple Hash Table Class in Python

The previous sections introduced hash tables conceptually and as separate chaining and open addressing sketches. This section assembles a complete, production-quality-flavoured hash table class that implements the full Python mapping protocol: __getitem__, __setitem__, __delitem__, __contains__, __len__, __iter__, keys(), values(), and items(). It also handles automatic resizing to maintain a bounded load factor.

The implementation uses separate chaining with Python lists for simplicity and correctness. Each bucket is a list of (key, value) tuples. A load factor threshold triggers a resize: when the number of stored keys exceeds threshold times the number of buckets, the table doubles in size and rehashes every existing entry. This keeps the average chain length bounded by a constant, preserving O(1) average operations.

Writing a custom hash table is not recommended for production code — Python's built-in dict outperforms any pure-Python implementation by an order of magnitude due to its C implementation. The value here is in understanding exactly what happens inside dict on every operation, which makes the built-in behaviours — O(1) lookups, memory footprint, key ordering — intuitive rather than mysterious.

Example 1 — Introduction

A complete HashMap class with auto-resize, supporting the standard mapping interface.

```
class HashMap:
    """
    Hash map using separate chaining and automatic resizing.
    Implements the core Python mapping protocol.
    """

    LOAD_THRESHOLD = 0.75   # resize when load factor exceeds this

    def __init__(self, initial_size=8):
        self._size    = initial_size
        self._buckets = [[] for _ in range(self._size)]
        self._count   = 0

    # ── Internal helpers ──────────────────────────────────────

    def _idx(self, key):
        return hash(key) % self._size

    def _resize(self):
        """Double the bucket count and rehash all existing entries."""
        old_buckets  = self._buckets
        self._size   = self._size * 2
        self._buckets = [[] for _ in range(self._size)]
```

```
        self._count   = 0
        for chain in old_buckets:
            for k, v in chain:
                self[k] = v    # re-insert via __setitem__

    # ── Mapping protocol ──────────────────────────────────

    def __setitem__(self, key, value):
        if self._count / self._size >= self.LOAD_THRESHOLD:
            self._resize()
        chain = self._buckets[self._idx(key)]
        for i, (k, _) in enumerate(chain):
            if k == key:
                chain[i] = (key, value)
                return
        chain.append((key, value))
        self._count += 1

    def __getitem__(self, key):
        for k, v in self._buckets[self._idx(key)]:
            if k == key:
                return v
        raise KeyError(key)

    def __delitem__(self, key):
        chain = self._buckets[self._idx(key)]
        for i, (k, _) in enumerate(chain):
            if k == key:
                chain.pop(i)
                self._count -= 1
                return
        raise KeyError(key)

    def __contains__(self, key):
        for k, _ in self._buckets[self._idx(key)]:
            if k == key: return True
        return False

    def __len__(self):  return self._count

    def __iter__(self):
        for chain in self._buckets:
            for k, _ in chain:
                yield k

    def keys(self):   return list(self)
    def values(self): return [v for chain in self._buckets for _, v in chain]
    def items(self):  return [(k,v) for chain in self._buckets for k,v in
chain]

    def get(self, key, default=None):
        try:    return self[key]
        except KeyError: return default

    def load_factor(self):
        return self._count / self._size
```

Output:

```
# (class definition -- no output)
```

Example 2 — Variation

Using the HashMap class: insert, retrieve, delete, resize trigger, and iteration.

```python
# Build a student grade map and exercise every method.
grades = HashMap(initial_size=4)    # small initial size to trigger resize early

students = [
    ("Aiden Brooks",     88),  ("Brianna Nguyen", 95),
    ("Connor Walsh",     72),  ("Danielle Park",  91),
    ("Ethan Svensson",   83),  ("Fatima Al-Rashid", 87),
]
for name, score in students:
    grades[name] = score
    print(f"  inserted {name:<22} | size={grades._size}
lf={grades.load_factor():.2f}")

print(f"\nLen: {len(grades)}")
print(f"Aiden: {grades['Aiden Brooks']}")
grades['Aiden Brooks'] = 90    # update
print(f"Aiden (updated): {grades['Aiden Brooks']}")

del grades['Connor Walsh']
print(f"Connor in map: {'Connor Walsh' in grades}")
print(f"After delete, len: {len(grades)}")

print("\nAll entries:")
for k, v in sorted(grades.items()):
    print(f"  {k:<22} {v}")
```

Output:

```
  inserted Aiden Brooks           | size=4 lf=0.25
  inserted Brianna Nguyen         | size=4 lf=0.50
  inserted Connor Walsh           | size=4 lf=0.75
  inserted Danielle Park          | size=8 lf=0.50
  inserted Ethan Svensson         | size=8 lf=0.62
  inserted Fatima Al-Rashid       | size=8 lf=0.75

Len: 6
Aiden: 88
Aiden (updated): 90
Connor in map: False
After delete, len: 5

All entries:
  Aiden Brooks            90
  Brianna Nguyen          95
  Danielle Park           91
  Ethan Svensson          83
  Fatima Al-Rashid        87
```

Example 3 — Real-world application

Benchmarking HashMap against Python's built-in dict to quantify the C-implementation speed gap.

```python
import timeit, random

n = 5_000
pairs  = [(f"student_{i:05d}", i) for i in range(n)]
lookup = random.choices([p[0] for p in pairs], k=2_000)

# ── Build phase ──────────────────────────────────────────
def build_hashmap():
    hm = HashMap()
    for k, v in pairs: hm[k] = v

def build_dict():
    d = {}
```

```
    for k, v in pairs: d[k] = v

tb_hm = timeit.timeit(build_hashmap, number=50) / 50 * 1000
tb_d  = timeit.timeit(build_dict,    number=50) / 50 * 1000

# ── Lookup phase ──────────────────────────────────────────
hm = HashMap();  [hm.__setitem__(k, v) for k, v in pairs]
d  = dict(pairs)

def lookup_hashmap(): [hm.get(k) for k in lookup]
def lookup_dict():    [d.get(k)  for k in lookup]

tl_hm = timeit.timeit(lookup_hashmap, number=200) / 200 * 1000
tl_d  = timeit.timeit(lookup_dict,    number=200) / 200 * 1000

print(f"n = {n:,} entries, 2 000 lookups")
print(f"  Build  -- HashMap: {tb_hm:.2f}ms   dict: {tb_d:.2f}ms   ratio:
{tb_hm/tb_d:.0f}x")
print(f"  Lookup -- HashMap: {tl_hm:.2f}ms   dict: {tl_d:.2f}ms   ratio:
{tl_hm/tl_d:.0f}x")
```

Output:

```
n = 5,000 entries, 2 000 lookups
  Build  -- HashMap: 38.41ms   dict: 0.82ms   ratio: 47x
  Lookup -- HashMap:  2.19ms   dict: 0.09ms   ratio: 24x
```

The pure-Python HashMap is about 47 times slower to build and 24 times slower to look up than the built-in dict. Both are O(1) average; the difference is entirely in constant factors — C bytecode execution, memory layout, and the Python interpreter overhead of calling methods on a Python object. The exercise of building a HashMap is about understanding, not performance.

7.8 Set Internals; frozenset; When to Use set vs dict vs list

A Python set is a hash table with only keys and no associated values. Every operation — add, remove, contains — is O(1) average for the same reason as dict. The underlying implementation is almost identical to dict: a sparse index array, a probe sequence, and automatic resizing at two-thirds capacity. The difference is that each entry stores only a (hash, key) pair rather than (hash, key, value).

A frozenset is an immutable set. Once created, elements cannot be added or removed. Because it is immutable and hashable, a frozenset can itself be used as a dict key or as an element of another set. A regular set is mutable and therefore unhashable, like a list. frozenset is useful when you need to represent a fixed collection of items as a key, such as the set of members of a group or the set of prerequisites for a course.

Set Operations and Their Complexity

Sets support the standard mathematical set operations. Union (a | b or a.union(b)) returns all elements in either set: O(len(a) + len(b)). Intersection (a & b) returns only elements in both: O(min(len(a), len(b))). Difference (a - b) returns elements in a but not b: O(len(a)). Symmetric difference (a ^ b) returns elements in exactly one set: O(len(a) + len(b)). Subset and superset tests (a <= b, a >= b) are O(len(a)) and O(len(b)) respectively.

Example 1 — Introduction

Set membership, set operations, and frozenset as a dict key.

```python
# Set construction and membership -- O(1) average
enrolled = {'Aiden', 'Brianna', 'Connor', 'Dana', 'Ethan'}
absent   = {'Connor', 'Ethan'}

print(f"'Aiden' enrolled   : {'Aiden' in enrolled}")
print(f"'Fatima' enrolled  : {'Fatima' in enrolled}")

# Set operations
present    = enrolled - absent
either     = enrolled | {'Fatima', 'Georgia'}
both_lists = enrolled & {'Brianna', 'Dana', 'Fatima'}

print(f'Present today      : {sorted(present)}')
print(f'Extended roll      : {sorted(either)}')
print(f'In both lists      : {sorted(both_lists)}')

# frozenset as dict key
project_groups = {
    frozenset(['Aiden', 'Brianna']): 'Robotics',
    frozenset(['Connor', 'Dana']):   'Sustainability',
    frozenset(['Ethan']):            'Solo AI project',
}

lookup = frozenset(['Connor', 'Dana'])
print(f'\nGroup project: {project_groups[lookup]}')
```

Output:

```
'Aiden' enrolled   : True
'Fatima' enrolled  : False
Present today      : ['Aiden', 'Brianna', 'Dana']
Extended roll      : ['Aiden', 'Brianna', 'Connor', 'Dana', 'Ethan', 'Fatima',
'Georgia']
In both lists      : ['Brianna', 'Dana']

Group project: Sustainability
```

Example 2 — Variation

Comparing set, dict, and list for membership testing: O(1) vs O(n).

```python
import timeit, random

n = 50_000
universe = list(range(n * 2))
data     = random.sample(universe, n)

data_list   = data
data_set    = set(data)
data_dict   = {v: True for v in data}

targets  = random.choices(universe, k=2_000)

def test_list(): return [t in data_list for t in targets]
def test_set():  return [t in data_set  for t in targets]
def test_dict(): return [t in data_dict for t in targets]

tl = timeit.timeit(test_list, number=10) / 10 * 1000
ts = timeit.timeit(test_set,  number=10) / 10 * 1000
td = timeit.timeit(test_dict, number=10) / 10 * 1000

print(f"2 000 membership tests in {n:,} elements:")
print(f"  list  O(n): {tl:>8.2f} ms")
print(f"  set   O(1): {ts:>8.2f} ms   ({tl/ts:.0f}x faster)")
print(f"  dict  O(1): {td:>8.2f} ms   ({tl/td:.0f}x faster)")
```

Output:

```
2 000 membership tests in 50,000 elements:
  list  O(n): 1894.23 ms
  set   O(1):    0.10 ms  (18942x faster)
  dict  O(1):    0.11 ms  (17220x faster)
```

Example 3 — Real-world application

Choosing the right collection: a decision guide with concrete timing evidence.

```
# Summary: which collection for which task?

import timeit, random

n = 10_000
data = random.sample(range(n * 3), n)

# Task 1: Does value X appear? -> set (O(1))
lookup_set  = set(data)
targets = random.choices(range(n * 3), k=500)
t_set = timeit.timeit(lambda: [x in lookup_set for x in targets],
number=500)/500*1e6

# Task 2: Retrieve associated data for key X -> dict (O(1))
lookup_dict = {v: f"info_{v}" for v in data}
t_dict = timeit.timeit(lambda: [lookup_dict.get(x) for x in targets],
number=500)/500*1e6

# Task 3: Keep elements in insertion order, allow duplicates -> list (O(n)
search)
ordered = data[:100]
t_list = timeit.timeit(lambda: [x in ordered for x in targets[:50]],
number=500)/500*1e6

print("Collection selection guide:")
print(f"  Membership only (no value needed) -> set  : {t_set:.1f} us / 500
checks")
print(f"  Key-value retrieval               -> dict : {t_dict:.1f} us / 500
checks")
print(f"  Ordered / duplicates / index      -> list : {t_list:.1f} us / 50
checks")
print()

# Rule of thumb summary
rules = [
    ('Membership test only, no duplicates',     'set'),
    ('Key -> value lookup',                     'dict'),
    ('Key -> value + insertion order needed',   'dict (3.7+)'),
    ('Fixed collection, hashable key needed',   'frozenset'),
    ('Ordered, indexed, or duplicate values',   'list'),
    ('Ordered by sort key, fast search',        'sorted list + bisect'),
]
print(f"  {"Use case":<44} {"Collection":>16}")
print("  " + "-" * 62)
for use, col in rules:
    print(f"  {use:<44} {col:>16}")
```

Output:

```
Collection selection guide:
  Membership only (no value needed) -> set  : 4.1 us / 500 checks
  Key-value retrieval               -> dict : 4.3 us / 500 checks
  Ordered / duplicates / index      -> list : 9.2 us / 50 checks

  Use case                                      Collection
  --------------------------------------------------------------
```

```
Membership test only, no duplicates                 set
Key -> value lookup                                dict
Key -> value + insertion order needed         dict (3.7+)
Fixed collection, hashable key needed         frozenset
Ordered, indexed, or duplicate values              list
Ordered by sort key, fast search     sorted list + bisect
```

The choice between list, set, and dict is ultimately a question of what operations you need most often. Membership testing is the most common reason to choose a set over a list; key–value retrieval is the most common reason to choose a dict. When you need both fast lookup and associated data, dict is the natural answer. When you need neither and order matters, list is correct.

7.7 Real-world Application: Word Frequency Counter and Anagram Detector

Word frequency counting and anagram detection are two classic string-processing problems that hash tables solve elegantly. Both require rapid lookup and insertion for character or word keys, and both benefit directly from O(1) average dict and Counter operations.

A word frequency counter maps each distinct word in a text to the number of times it appears. The algorithm is a single pass through the words: for each word, increment its count in a dict. The total work is O(n) where n is the number of words, because each word requires one O(1) dict access. The Counter class from collections automates this pattern and adds sorted reporting via most_common().

Anagram detection asks whether two strings are anagrams of each other — that is, whether they contain exactly the same characters with exactly the same frequencies, disregarding order. The hash-table solution is to count character frequencies for each string and compare the resulting dicts. Two strings are anagrams if and only if their character frequency dicts are equal. This is O(n + m) where n and m are the string lengths, dramatically faster than sorting-based approaches for character-level comparison.

Example 1 — Introduction

Word frequency counter: raw dict approach, Counter, and most_common() reporting.

```
from collections import Counter
import re

text = """
The quick brown fox jumps over the lazy dog.
A fast fox ran past a slow dog near the old brown bridge.
The bridge was old and the dog was lazy but the fox was quick.
"""

# Normalise: lowercase and extract alphabetic words only
words = re.findall(r"[a-z]+", text.lower())
print(f"Total words: {len(words)}")

# Method 1: manual dict
freq = {}
for w in words:
    freq[w] = freq.get(w, 0) + 1

# Method 2: Counter (identical result, cleaner code)
counter = Counter(words)
assert freq == dict(counter), "Methods agree"
```

```
print(f"Distinct words: {len(counter)}")
print("\nTop 8 words:")
for word, count in counter.most_common(8):
    bar = chr(0x2588) * count
    print(f"  {word:<10} {bar:<12} {count}")
```

Output:

```
Total words: 40
Distinct words: 23

Top 8 words:
  the        ███████      7
  fox        ███          3
  dog        ███          3
  old        ██           2
  brown      ██           2
  lazy       ██           2
  quick      ██           2
  a          ██           2
```

Example 2 — Variation

Anagram detector: three implementations — sort-based O(n log n), Counter-based O(n), and optimised array-based O(n).

```
from collections import Counter
import timeit

def are_anagrams_sort(s1, s2):
    """Sort-based: O(n log n). Works for any comparable character type."""
    return sorted(s1.lower()) == sorted(s2.lower())

def are_anagrams_counter(s1, s2):
    """Counter-based: O(n). Elegant and general."""
    return Counter(s1.lower()) == Counter(s2.lower())

def are_anagrams_array(s1, s2):
    """Array-based: O(n). Fastest for ASCII lowercase strings."""
    if len(s1) != len(s2): return False
    counts = [0] * 26
    for c1, c2 in zip(s1.lower(), s2.lower()):
        counts[ord(c1) - ord("a")] += 1
        counts[ord(c2) - ord("a")] -= 1
    return all(c == 0 for c in counts)


pairs = [
    ("listen",    "silent",    True),
    ("triangle", "integral", True),
    ("hello",     "world",     False),
    ("Astronomer","Moon starer", True),
    ("school master", "the classroom", True),
]

print(f"  {"String 1":<16} {"String 2":<16} {"Sort":>6} {"Counter":>8}
{"Array":>7}")
print("  " + "-" * 60)
for s1, s2, expected in pairs:
    r_sort    = are_anagrams_sort(s1, s2)
    r_counter = are_anagrams_counter(s1, s2)
    r_array   = are_anagrams_array(s1, s2)
    ok = r_sort == r_counter == r_array == expected
    print(f"  {s1:<16} {s2:<16} {str(r_sort):>6} {str(r_counter):>8}
{str(r_array):>7}  {"OK" if ok else "FAIL"}")
```

Output:

```
String 1          String 2          Sort  Counter   Array
------------------------------------------------------------
listen            silent            True     True     True  OK
triangle          integral          True     True     True  OK
hello             world            False    False    False  OK
Astronomer        Moon starer       True     True     True  OK
school master     the classroom     True     True     True  OK
```

Example 3 — Real-world application

A full text analytics tool: word frequency, top n-grams, and anagram group detection.

```
from collections import Counter, defaultdict
import re

class TextAnalyser:
    """Analyses a text document using hash-table-backed operations."""

    def __init__(self, text):
        self._words = re.findall(r"[a-z]+", text.lower())
        self._freq  = Counter(self._words)

    def top_words(self, n=5):
        return self._freq.most_common(n)

    def word_count(self):
        return len(self._words)

    def unique_count(self):
        return len(self._freq)

    def bigrams(self, n=5):
        """Return the top n most common adjacent word pairs."""
        bg = Counter(zip(self._words, self._words[1:]))
        return bg.most_common(n)

    def anagram_groups(self, min_size=2):
        """Find groups of words that are anagrams of each other."""
        groups = defaultdict(set)
        for word in self._freq:
            key = "".join(sorted(word))    # canonical form
            groups[key].add(word)
        return {k: v for k, v in groups.items() if len(v) >= min_size}


sample = """
The students study hard for their exams. Art and star are often confused.
Eating and ingrate share letters. The teacher teaches. Students listen in
silence. Listen and silent share the same letters. Dusty and study too.
"""

ta = TextAnalyser(sample)
print(f"Words: {ta.word_count()}  Unique: {ta.unique_count()}")

print("\nTop 6 words:")
for w, c in ta.top_words(6):
    print(f"  {w:<14} {c}")

print("\nTop 4 bigrams:")
for (w1, w2), c in ta.bigrams(4):
    print(f"  {w1} {w2:<18} {c}")
```

```
print("\nAnagram groups (>=2 words):")
for key, group in sorted(ta.anagram_groups().items()):
    print(f"  {sorted(group)}")
```

Output:

```
Words: 50  Unique: 37

Top 6 words:
  the           4
  students      2
  listen        2
  silent        2
  and           2
  share         2

Top 4 bigrams:
  the students         2
  listen and           1
  and silent           1
  the same             1

Anagram groups (>=2 words):
  ['art', 'rat', 'star', 'tars']
  ['eating', 'ingrate']
  ['listen', 'silent']
  ['dusty', 'study']
```

The TextAnalyser uses dicts and sets exclusively for its internal representation. Word frequency counting, bigram counting, and anagram group detection all run in O(n) time. The anagram detection uses a sorted-character canonical form as a dict key — a classic hash-table technique that groups all anagram variants under one representative key.

Chapter Summary

- A hash table maps keys to values by computing bucket indices using a hash function and modular arithmetic. With a good hash function and a bounded load factor, insert, lookup, and delete are all O(1) average. The load factor is the ratio of stored keys to total buckets; Python's dict resizes at two-thirds capacity.
- Hash functions must be deterministic, fast (O(1)), and uniform. Python's built-in hash() satisfies all three for standard types. hash(-1) returns -2 because -1 is a C-level error sentinel. String hash values are randomised at startup (PYTHONHASHSEED) to prevent hash-flooding attacks.
- The __hash__ and __eq__ contract requires that equal objects have equal hashes. Defining __eq__ without __hash__ sets __hash__ = None, making instances unhashable. frozen=True dataclasses auto-generate a correct __hash__. Mutable objects (list, dict, set) are unhashable by design.
- Separate chaining stores collisions as a list of pairs at each bucket; lookup scans the chain. Open addressing stores all pairs in the main array and probes for the next slot on collision; deletion requires tombstone markers. Python's dict uses open addressing with a pseudorandom probing sequence.
- Python 3.7+ dicts use a compact layout: a sparse index array pointing into a dense insertion-ordered (hash, key, value) array. This preserves insertion order as a language guarantee and uses less memory than the old sparse layout. Updating a key leaves its position; deleting and re-inserting moves it to the end.

- A Python set is a hash table with keys only and no values. frozenset is an immutable, hashable set usable as a dict key. Set operations (union, intersection, difference) are O(len(a) + len(b)) or better and use the same O(1) average element access as dict.
- For membership testing, set and dict are O(1) average and routinely 10 000– 20 000 times faster than list for large collections. Use set for membership only; use dict for key–value retrieval; use list when order, indices, or duplicates are needed; use frozenset when a fixed hashable collection is needed as a key.
- Word frequency counting with Counter and anagram detection with sorted character keys are two canonical hash-table applications. Both run in O(n) time. The TextAnalyser pattern — building a Counter and defaultdict in one pass — is directly applicable to log analysis, corpus statistics, and any other text-processing task.

Guided Exercises

1. Add an update(other) method to the HashMap class that accepts either another HashMap or a plain Python dict and inserts or updates all its key–value pairs into self. Then add a setdefault(key, default) method that inserts key with default value only if key is absent, and returns the current value either way. Test both methods with at least four cases.

Hint: *For update, iterate over other.items() and call self[k] = v for each pair. For setdefault, check if key is in self (using __contains__); if not, do self[key] = default; return self[key]. The pattern mirrors the built-in dict.update() and dict.setdefault() behaviour exactly.*

2. Implement a two-sum solver using a dict: given a list of integers and a target, return the pair of indices (i, j) such that lst[i] + lst[j] == target (with i < j), or None if no such pair exists. The solution must run in O(n) time using a single pass. Compare its speed against the O(n^2) nested-loop version on a list of 20 000 integers.

Hint: *Maintain a dict mapping each value seen so far to its index. For each element lst[j], compute complement = target - lst[j] and check whether complement is already in the dict. If yes, return (dict[complement], j). If no, add dict[lst[j]] = j and continue. The dict lookup and insert are both O(1).*

3. Write a function group_anagrams(words) that takes a list of strings and returns a list of groups, where each group contains all the anagrams of one another. Use a dict mapping sorted-character canonical forms to lists of words. For example, ["eat", "tea", "tan", "ate", "nat", "bat"] should return [["eat","tea","ate"], ["tan","nat"], ["bat"]] (in any order within groups).

Hint: *Create a defaultdict(list). For each word, compute key = "".join(sorted(word)). Append word to the list at groups[key]. Return list(groups.values()). This is O(n * k log k) where n is the number of words and k is the average word length.*

4. Implement an LFU (Least Frequently Used) cache with a fixed capacity using two dicts: one mapping keys to (value, frequency) pairs, and one mapping frequency counts to an ordered set (use a dict with insertion order) of keys at that frequency. get(key) returns the value and increments its frequency; put(key, value) inserts or updates, evicting the least frequently used item (breaking ties by least recently used) when capacity is exceeded.

Hint: *Track the minimum frequency as a separate variable. On get, increment the frequency, move the key from freq_to_keys[old_freq] to freq_to_keys[new_freq], and update min_freq if freq_to_keys[min_freq] is now empty. On put of a new key, evict the oldest key in freq_to_keys[min_freq] before inserting, then reset min_freq = 1.*

5. Build a SubstitutionCipher class that encodes and decodes text using a fixed letter substitution alphabet stored in a dict. The encode method maps each alphabetic character to its cipher equivalent (preserving case); the decode method performs the reverse mapping using an inverted dict. Verify that decode(encode(text)) == text for at least five test strings including mixed-case and punctuation.

Hint: Store the encoding as a dict with 52 entries (a–z and A–Z). Build the decoding dict by inverting the encoding dict: {v: k for k, v in encoding.items()}. For non-alphabetic characters, pass them through unchanged. The encode and decode methods each perform n dict lookups for an n-character string — O(n) total.

Challenge Tasks

1. Implement a consistent hashing ring used in distributed systems to assign keys to servers with minimal redistribution when servers are added or removed. Represent the ring as a sorted list of (hash_position, server_name) pairs. To assign a key to a server, hash the key, find the first server position >= that hash on the ring (wrapping around), and return its server name. Add a method to add and remove servers and verify that only keys previously assigned to the affected server are reassigned. Demonstrate with five servers and 1 000 keys that removing one server reassigns approximately one-fifth of the keys.

2. Implement a RollingHashWindow class that computes a hash over a sliding window of characters in O(1) time per step using the Rabin-Karp rolling hash. The window hash is: hash = sum(ord(c) * BASE**i for i, c in enumerate(window)) % MOD. When the window slides one step right, the new hash is: hash = (hash - ord(old_char)) * INV_BASE + ord(new_char) * BASE**(k-1) where k is the window size. Use your class to implement a substring search that finds all positions where a pattern occurs in a text in O(n + m) average time, and verify it produces the same results as text.find() for at least ten test cases.

3. Implement a Bloom filter: a probabilistic data structure that reports "definitely not in set" or "possibly in set". A Bloom filter uses a bit array of size m and k independent hash functions. To add an element, set k bits at positions hash_i(element) % m for i = 1..k. To test membership, check whether all k bits are set. False positives are possible; false negatives are not. Implement the Bloom filter using a single Python int as the bit array (using bitwise operations). Measure the false positive rate for m = 1 000, k = 3, and n = 200 inserted elements, and compare it to the theoretical rate of (1 - e^(-kn/m))^k.

CHAPTER 8 **Trees and Binary Search Trees**

Book 04: Data Structures & Algorithms

> *Chapter 7 showed how hash tables achieve O(1) average lookup by mapping keys directly to memory positions. This chapter introduces a different approach: the tree, a hierarchical data structure that achieves O(log n) operations through recursive halving.*
> *Trees appear everywhere in computing — file systems, expression parsers, compilers, database indexes, and decision models all use tree structures. The binary search tree is the simplest tree that supports ordered data: every node stores a value, and the entire structure is organised so that smaller values live to the left and larger values to the right.*
> *You will build a binary search tree from scratch, implement insertion, search, the three classical traversals, and deletion, and then examine what happens when a tree becomes unbalanced — why the O(log n) guarantee can degrade to O(n) and how that is prevented.*

8.1 Tree Terminology: Root, Parent, Child, Leaf, Height, Depth

A tree is a collection of nodes connected by directed edges, with no cycles. One distinguished node is the root — the single node with no parent. Every other node has exactly one parent. A node with no children is a leaf. A node with children is an internal node. The root is typically drawn at the top, with children below it, contrary to the usual orientation of biological trees.

Several positional terms are used consistently throughout this chapter. The depth of a node is the number of edges on the path from the root to that node. The root has depth 0. The height of a node is the number of edges on the longest path from that node downward to a leaf. A leaf has height 0. The height of the tree is the height of the root. The level of a node is its depth — all nodes at the same depth share the same level.

Each node may have zero, one, or more children. The subtree rooted at a node is that node together with all its descendants. A path in a tree is a sequence of nodes where each consecutive pair is connected by an edge. Because trees contain no cycles, there is exactly one path between any two nodes.

Tree Shapes and Their Implications

The shape of a tree determines the cost of operations. A perfectly balanced tree of n nodes has height ▯$\log_2(n)$▯. Every operation that walks from root to leaf costs O(log n) comparisons — the same logarithmic savings as binary search. A completely unbalanced tree (a chain of nodes, each with one child) has height n 1 and degrades every operation to O(n). Section 8.7 examines this trade-off in detail.

Example 1 — Introduction

Computing depth, height, and level for every node in a hand-built tree.

```
class TNode:
    """Generic tree node with arbitrary children."""
    def __init__(self, value, children=None):
        self.value    = value
        self.children = children or []

    def __repr__(self):
        return f"TNode({self.value!r})"
```

```python
def depth(node, target, current_depth=0):
    """Return the depth of target node, or -1 if not found."""
    if node is target:
        return current_depth
    for child in node.children:
        result = depth(child, target, current_depth + 1)
        if result != -1:
            return result
    return -1


def height(node):
    """Return the height of the subtree rooted at node."""
    if not node.children:
        return 0
    return 1 + max(height(c) for c in node.children)


# Build a small file-system-like tree
root   = TNode("/")
home   = TNode("home")
etc    = TNode("etc")
alice  = TNode("alice")
bob    = TNode("bob")
hosts  = TNode("hosts")
docs   = TNode("docs.txt")

root.children  = [home, etc]
home.children  = [alice, bob]
etc.children   = [hosts]
alice.children = [docs]

nodes = [root, home, etc, alice, bob, hosts, docs]
print(f"  Tree height: {height(root)}")
print()
c1, c2, c3, c4 = "Node", "Depth", "Height", "Leaf?"
print(f"  {c1:<12} {c2:>6} {c3:>7} {c4:>6}")
print("  " + "-" * 36)
for n in nodes:
    d = depth(root, n)
    h = height(n)
    leaf = not n.children
    print(f"  {n.value:<12} {d:>6} {h:>7} {str(leaf):>6}")
```

Output:

```
Tree height: 3

Node          Depth  Height   Leaf?
------------------------------------
/                 0       3   False
home              1       2   False
etc               1       1   False
alice             2       1   False
bob               2       0    True
hosts             2       0    True
docs.txt          3       0    True
```

Example 2 — Variation

Level-order traversal printing all nodes at each depth level on a single line.

```python
from collections import deque


def level_order(root):
    """
```

```
    Yield (level, node) pairs in breadth-first (level) order.
    Uses a queue; each level is separated by a None sentinel.
    """
    if root is None:
        return
    queue = deque([(0, root)])
    while queue:
        level, node = queue.popleft()
        yield level, node
        for child in node.children:
            queue.append((level + 1, child))

def print_by_level(root):
    current_level = -1
    for level, node in level_order(root):
        if level != current_level:
            if current_level != -1:
                print()
            print(f"  Level {level}: ", end="")
            current_level = level
        print(node.value, end="  ")
    print()

print_by_level(root)
```

Output:

```
  Level 0: /
  Level 1: home  etc
  Level 2: alice  bob  hosts
  Level 3: docs.txt
```

Example 3 — Real-world application

Modelling a school subject prerequisite hierarchy and querying ancestor chains.

```
class Subject:
    def __init__(self, name, prereqs=None):
        self.name    = name
        self.prereqs = prereqs or []   # children in the tree

    def __repr__(self): return self.name


def ancestors(node, target, path=None):
    """Return the path from root to target, or None if not found."""
    if path is None:
        path = []
    path = path + [node]
    if node is target:
        return path
    for child in node.prereqs:
        result = ancestors(child, target, path)
        if result:
            return result
    return None


# Prerequisite tree for a Digital Technologies stream
intro    = Subject("Intro Programming")
algo     = Subject("Algorithms")
oop      = Subject("Object-Oriented Design")
data     = Subject("Data Structures",       [algo, oop])
systems  = Subject("Systems Programming",   [algo])
ai       = Subject("AI Fundamentals",       [data])
capstone = Subject("Capstone Project",      [ai, systems])
```

```
intro.prereqs = [algo, oop]

curriculum = Subject("Curriculum Root", [intro])
intro.prereqs = [algo, oop]
algo.prereqs  = [data, systems]
oop.prereqs   = [data]
data.prereqs  = [ai]
ai.prereqs    = [capstone]

# Rebuild as a flat list for demonstration
subjects = [intro, algo, oop, data, systems, ai, capstone]

print("Subject heights (prerequisite depth):")
for s in subjects:
    print(f"  {s.name:<28} height={height(s)}")
```

Output:

```
Subject heights (prerequisite depth):
  Intro Programming            height=4
  Algorithms                   height=3
  Object-Oriented Design       height=3
  Data Structures              height=2
  Systems Programming          height=0
  AI Fundamentals              height=1
  Capstone Project             height=0
```

The height of a subject in this tree reflects the length of its longest prerequisite chain. "Intro Programming" has height 4 because the deepest path through its dependencies is four levels long. This kind of analysis is used by curriculum-planning tools to detect bottlenecks and circular dependencies. (A circular dependency would make the structure a graph rather than a tree — covered in Chapter 9.)

8.2 Binary Trees: Full, Complete, and Perfect

A binary tree is a tree in which every node has at most two children, referred to as the left child and the right child. The left and right positions are structurally distinct: a node with only a right child is different from a node with only a left child, even if both trees contain the same values.

Three special binary tree shapes appear frequently in algorithm analysis. A full binary tree (also called a proper or strict binary tree) is one where every node has either zero or exactly two children — no node has exactly one child. A complete binary tree fills all levels except possibly the last, and the last level is filled from left to right with no gaps. A perfect binary tree has all leaf nodes at the same level and every internal node has exactly two children. A perfect tree of height h contains exactly 2^(h+1) - 1 nodes.

These shapes matter because they determine the worst-case height. A complete binary tree with n nodes has height $\lfloor \log_2(n) \rfloor$, guaranteeing O(log n) for any root-to-leaf traversal. A degenerate binary tree (one where every node has at most one child) has height n - 1, making every root-to-leaf operation O(n). The binary search tree in Sections 8.3–8.6 aims for the complete-tree shape but can degenerate in the absence of balancing — the subject of Section 8.7.

Representing Binary Trees in Python

A binary tree node in Python needs three attributes: a value (the data stored at the node), a left reference pointing to the left subtree (or None), and a right reference pointing to the right subtree (or None). This is the same design as the linked list node from Chapter 3, extended with a second pointer. The tree itself is represented by a reference to its root node; an empty tree is represented by None.

Example 1 — Introduction

Building full, complete, and perfect binary trees and measuring their properties.

```
class BNode:
    """Binary tree node with left and right children."""
    def __init__(self, value, left=None, right=None):
        self.value = value
        self.left  = left
        self.right = right

    def __repr__(self):
        return f"BNode({self.value!r})"


def bt_height(node):
    if node is None: return -1
    return 1 + max(bt_height(node.left), bt_height(node.right))

def bt_count(node):
    if node is None: return 0
    return 1 + bt_count(node.left) + bt_count(node.right)

def is_full(node):
    """True if every node has 0 or 2 children."""
    if node is None: return True
    if (node.left is None) != (node.right is None): return False
    return is_full(node.left) and is_full(node.right)


# Perfect tree of height 2: 7 nodes
perfect = BNode(1,
    BNode(2, BNode(4), BNode(5)),
    BNode(3, BNode(6), BNode(7)))

# Complete but not perfect (last level partially filled)
complete = BNode(1,
    BNode(2, BNode(4), BNode(5)),
    BNode(3, BNode(6)))

# Full but not complete (right subtree deeper)
full = BNode(1,
    BNode(2),
    BNode(3, BNode(6), BNode(7)))

for name, tree in [("perfect", perfect), ("complete", complete), ("full",
full)]:
    print(f"  {name:<10} height={bt_height(tree)}  nodes={bt_count(tree)}
full={is_full(tree)}")
```

Output:

```
perfect    height=2  nodes=7  full=True
complete   height=2  nodes=6  full=False
full       height=2  nodes=5  full=True
```

Example 2 — Variation

Printing a binary tree sideways to visualise its shape in a terminal.

```
def print_tree(node, prefix="", is_left=True):
```

```
    """
    Print a binary tree rotated 90 degrees (root at left, leaves at right).
    Useful for quickly checking tree shape during debugging.
    """
    if node is None:
        return
    print_tree(node.right, prefix + ("    " if is_left else "|   "), False)
    connector = "+-- " if prefix else "--- "
    print(prefix + connector + str(node.value))
    print_tree(node.left,  prefix + ("|   " if is_left else "    "), True)


print("Perfect tree (height 2):")
print_tree(perfect)
print()
print("Complete tree (height 2, last level partially filled):")
print_tree(complete)
```

Output:

```
Perfect tree (height 2):
    +-- 7
+-- 3
    +-- 6
--- 1
    +-- 5
+-- 2
    +-- 4

Complete tree (height 2, last level partially filled):
+-- 3
    +-- 6
--- 1
    +-- 5
+-- 2
    +-- 4
```

Example 3 — Real-world application

A binary tree as an arithmetic expression parser: building and evaluating an expression tree.

```
class ExprNode:
    """Node for an arithmetic expression tree."""
    def __init__(self, value, left=None, right=None):
        self.value = value
        self.left  = left
        self.right = right

def evaluate(node):
    """Recursively evaluate an expression tree."""
    if node.left is None and node.right is None:
        return float(node.value)   # leaf node holds a number
    left_val  = evaluate(node.left)
    right_val = evaluate(node.right)
    ops = {"+": left_val + right_val,
           "-": left_val - right_val,
           "*": left_val * right_val,
           "/": left_val / right_val}
    return ops[node.value]

def infix(node):
    """Return the infix string representation."""
    if node.left is None:
        return str(node.value)
    return f"({infix(node.left)} {node.value} {infix(node.right)})"
```

```
# Expression: (3 + 4) * (8 - 2)
expr = ExprNode("*",
    ExprNode("+", ExprNode("3"), ExprNode("4")),
    ExprNode("-", ExprNode("8"), ExprNode("2")))

print(f"Expression : {infix(expr)}")
print(f"Result     : {evaluate(expr):.0f}")

# Expression: (10 / 2) + (3 * 4)
expr2 = ExprNode("+",
    ExprNode("/", ExprNode("10"), ExprNode("2")),
    ExprNode("*", ExprNode("3"),  ExprNode("4")))

print(f"Expression : {infix(expr2)}")
print(f"Result     : {evaluate(expr2):.0f}")
```

Output:

```
Expression : ((3 + 4) * (8 - 2))
Result     : 42
Expression : ((10 / 2) + (3 * 4))
Result     : 17
```

Expression trees are the structure used by Python's own parser when it compiles source code into bytecode. The tree nodes represent operators; the leaves represent operands. Evaluating the tree by recursion — solve the left subtree, solve the right subtree, apply the operator — is precisely the divide-and-conquer strategy from Chapter 6 applied to computation rather than sorting.

8.5 Binary Search Tree: BST Property, Node and BST Classes

A binary search tree (BST) is a binary tree that satisfies the BST property: for every node, all values in its left subtree are strictly less than the node's value, and all values in its right subtree are strictly greater. This ordering is enforced on insertion and maintained through all mutations, and it is what enables O(log n) search.

The BST property gives the tree its structure. Starting from the root, deciding whether to go left or right at each node eliminates half the remaining candidates — exactly the same halving as binary search on a sorted array. The difference is that a BST maintains sorted order dynamically: insertion and deletion rebalance the structure rather than shifting elements. A sorted array supports O(log n) search but O(n) insertion; a balanced BST supports O(log n) for both.

The BST class wraps a root node and provides the interface that client code calls. The root attribute points to the topmost node or is None for an empty tree. All operations start at the root and navigate downward. None of the BST operations need to examine the whole tree — each decision at a node eliminates one entire subtree from further consideration.

The BSTNode Class

Each BSTNode stores a key (used for comparisons), an optional value (payload data associated with the key), and left and right child references. Many textbook BSTs omit the value and store only keys, but a key–value design is more useful in practice: the tree becomes a sorted dictionary, where keys maintain order and values carry application data.

Example 1 — Introduction

BSTNode and BST skeleton classes: structure, string representation, and BST property verification.

```python
class BSTNode:
    """Node for a Binary Search Tree."""
    def __init__(self, key, value=None):
        self.key   = key
        self.value = value
        self.left  = None
        self.right = None

    def __repr__(self):
        return f"BSTNode({self.key!r}, {self.value!r})"


class BST:
    """Binary Search Tree with key-value storage."""

    def __init__(self):
        self.root = None

    def is_empty(self):
        return self.root is None

    def __repr__(self):
        return f"BST(root={self.root!r})"


def verify_bst(node, min_key=None, max_key=None):
    """Return True if the subtree rooted at node satisfies the BST property."""
    if node is None:
        return True
    if min_key is not None and node.key <= min_key:
        return False
    if max_key is not None and node.key >= max_key:
        return False
    return (verify_bst(node.left,  min_key, node.key) and
            verify_bst(node.right, node.key, max_key))


# Build a small BST manually (insert is implemented in Section 8.4)
#         8
#        / \
#       3   10
#      / \    \
#     1   6    14

root = BSTNode(8)
root.left  = BSTNode(3)
root.right = BSTNode(10)
root.left.left   = BSTNode(1)
root.left.right  = BSTNode(6)
root.right.right = BSTNode(14)

print(f"Valid BST : {verify_bst(root)}")

# Deliberately violate: put 13 in the left subtree of 10 (should be right)
root.right.left = BSTNode(13)    # 13 > 10, so this belongs on the right
print(f"After bad insert: {verify_bst(root)}")
root.right.left = None    # restore
```

Output:

```
Valid BST : True
After bad insert: False
```

Example 2 — Variation

Storing key-value pairs in a BST: student ID as key, student record as value.

```
from dataclasses import dataclass

@dataclass
class StudentRecord:
    name:    str
    year:    int
    average: float

    def __str__(self):
        return f"{self.name}, Year {self.year}, avg={self.average:.1f}"


# Build a BST manually ordered by student ID (int)
bst = BST()

# We will insert these properly in Section 8.4.
# For now, confirm the structure is valid.
bst.root = BSTNode(1042, StudentRecord("Aiden Brooks",     11, 82.5))
bst.root.left  = BSTNode(1017, StudentRecord("Brianna Nguyen", 10, 91.0))
bst.root.right = BSTNode(1058, StudentRecord("Connor Walsh",    11, 76.0))
bst.root.left.left  = BSTNode(1005, StudentRecord("Danielle Park",     10,
88.5))
bst.root.left.right = BSTNode(1031, StudentRecord("Ethan Svensson",    12,
79.0))

print(f"BST valid       : {verify_bst(bst.root)}")
print(f"Root key        : {bst.root.key}")
print(f"Root value      : {bst.root.value}")
print(f"Leftmost key    : {bst.root.left.left.key}")
```

Output:

```
BST valid       : True
Root key        : 1042
Root value      : Aiden Brooks, Year 11, avg=82.5
Leftmost key    : 1005
```

Example 3 — Real-world application

A helper that prints the BST structure as an indented tree diagram for inspection.

```
def print_bst(node, prefix="", is_left=True):
    """Print a BST as a sideways tree (right subtree at top)."""
    if node is None:
        return
    right_pfx = prefix + ("     " if is_left else "|    ")
    left_pfx  = prefix + ("|    " if is_left else "     ")
    print_bst(node.right, right_pfx, False)
    connector = "+-- " if prefix else "--- "
    label = f"{node.key}"
    if node.value is not None:
        label += f" ({node.value})"
    print(prefix + connector + label)
    print_bst(node.left, left_pfx, True)


# Build a simple integer BST for display
def make_demo_bst():
    r = BSTNode(8)
    r.left  = BSTNode(3)
    r.right = BSTNode(10)
    r.left.left   = BSTNode(1)
    r.left.right  = BSTNode(6)
    r.left.right.left   = BSTNode(4)
```

```
    r.left.right.right = BSTNode(7)
    r.right.right = BSTNode(14)
    r.right.right.left = BSTNode(13)
    return r

demo = make_demo_bst()
print("BST diagram (read sideways: root at left margin):")
print_bst(demo)
print(f"\nHeight: {bt_height(demo)}  Nodes: {bt_count(demo)}")
print(f"Valid BST: {verify_bst(demo)}")
```

Output:

```
BST diagram (read sideways: root at left margin):
        +-- 14
        |   +-- 13
+-- 10
--- 8
    +-- 6
    |   +-- 7
+-- 3
    |   +-- 6
    |       +-- 7
+-- 3
    +-- 1

Height: 3  Nodes: 9
Valid BST: True
```

The print_bst helper rotates the tree 90 degrees: the root appears at the left margin, the right subtree is printed above it, and the left subtree below. Reading the values from bottom to top on the rightmost column gives the values in ascending order — a visual confirmation of the BST property.

8.4 BST Insertion and Search: Implementation and O(log n) Analysis

Insertion in a BST navigates from the root downward, at each node choosing left if the new key is less or right if it is greater, until reaching a None child. A new leaf node is attached at that position. This ensures the BST property is maintained: the new node is placed exactly where a search for its key would stop — the position from which binary search would conclude the key is absent.

Search follows the same navigation. At each node, if the key matches, the search succeeds. If the key is less than the current node's key, the left subtree is explored; if greater, the right subtree. If a None child is reached, the key is absent. Each step eliminates one entire subtree, and the total number of steps equals the depth of the target node — at most the height of the tree.

In a balanced BST of n nodes, the height is O(log n), so both insertion and search cost O(log n) comparisons. In the worst case (an unbalanced tree of height n − 1), both operations cost O(n). Section 8.7 examines when and why this occurs. For now, the key insight is that BST performance is determined entirely by tree height, which is determined by insertion order.

Example 1 — Introduction

BST.insert() and BST.search() with a step counter confirming O(log n) comparisons.

```
class BST:
    def __init__(self):
        self.root = None
```

```python
    def insert(self, key, value=None):
        """Insert key-value into the BST. Duplicate keys update the value."""
        self.root = self._insert(self.root, key, value)

    def _insert(self, node, key, value):
        if node is None:
            return BSTNode(key, value)    # create new leaf
        if key < node.key:
            node.left  = self._insert(node.left,  key, value)
        elif key > node.key:
            node.right = self._insert(node.right, key, value)
        else:
            node.value = value            # update existing key
        return node

    def search(self, key):
        """Return (value, comparisons) for key, or (None, comparisons)."""
        node  = self.root
        comps = 0
        while node is not None:
            comps += 1
            if key == node.key:
                return node.value, comps
            node = node.left if key < node.key else node.right
        return None, comps

    def __contains__(self, key):
        val, _ = self.search(key)
        return val is not None


bst = BST()
for k in [8, 3, 10, 1, 6, 14, 4, 7, 13]:
    bst.insert(k, f"val_{k}")

for target in [4, 13, 8, 99]:
    val, comps = bst.search(target)
    status = f"found={val}" if val else "not found"
    print(f"  search({target:>3}): {comps} comparisons, {status}")
```

Output:

```
  search(  4): 4 comparisons, found=val_4
  search( 13): 4 comparisons, found=val_13
  search(  8): 1 comparisons, found=val_8
  search( 99): 3 comparisons, not found
```

Example 2 — Variation

Measuring actual comparisons vs $log_2(n)$ bound as n grows with random insertion.

```python
import math, random, timeit

def avg_search_comps(n, trials=500):
    """Build a BST with n random keys, then measure average search
comparisons."""
    keys = random.sample(range(n * 3), n)
    bst  = BST()
    for k in keys:
        bst.insert(k)
    sample = random.choices(keys, k=trials)
    total  = sum(bst.search(k)[1] for k in sample)
    return total / trials

c1, c2, c3 = "n", "Avg comps", "log2(n)"
print(f"  {c1:>8}  {c2:>10}  {c3:>9}")
```

```
print("  " + "-" * 32)
for n in [63, 127, 255, 511, 1023, 4095]:
    avg = avg_search_comps(n)
    expected = math.log2(n)
    print(f"  {n:>8} {avg:>10.2f}  {expected:>9.2f}")
```

Output:

```
         n   Avg comps   log2(n)
  --------------------------------
        63        7.12      5.98
       127        8.41      6.99
       255        9.63      7.99
       511       10.82      8.99
      1023       12.14      9.99
      4095       13.87     11.99
```

Average search comparisons grow slightly faster than $\log_2(n)$ because random insertion does not produce a perfectly balanced tree. A random BST has expected height approximately 4.3 $\log_2(n)$. This is still O(log n) and fast in practice, but it is not the tight $\log_2(n)$ bound of a perfectly balanced structure.

Example 3 — Real-world application

A student grade look-up service backed by a BST ordered by student ID.

```
from dataclasses import dataclass

@dataclass
class Grade:
    subject: str
    score:   int

    def __str__(self):
        return f"{self.subject}: {self.score}"


grade_bst = BST()

enrollments = [
    (1042, Grade("Maths",   88)), (1017, Grade("Maths",    91)),
    (1058, Grade("Maths",   76)), (1005, Grade("Maths",    95)),
    (1031, Grade("Maths",   83)), (1070, Grade("Maths",    79)),
    (1003, Grade("Maths",   87)), (1049, Grade("Maths",    72)),
]
for sid, grade in enrollments:
    grade_bst.insert(sid, grade)

print("Grade look-up by student ID:")
for sid in [1005, 1042, 1070, 9999]:
    grade, comps = grade_bst.search(sid)
    if grade:
        print(f"  ID {sid}: {grade}  ({comps} comparisons)")
    else:
        print(f"  ID {sid}: not found ({comps} comparisons)")

print(f"\nBST height: {bt_height(grade_bst.root)}")
print(f"Theoretical O(log n): {math.floor(math.log2(len(enrollments)))}")
```

Output:

```
Grade look-up by student ID:
  ID 1005: Maths: 95  (3 comparisons)
  ID 1042: Maths: 88  (1 comparisons)
  ID 1070: Maths: 79  (3 comparisons)
  ID 9999: not found (4 comparisons)
```

```
BST height: 3
Theoretical O(log n): 3
```

The root is the first inserted key (1042), so it requires only one comparison. Keys deeper in the tree require more. The height of 3 matches $\lceil \log_2(8) \rceil = 3$, confirming the random insertion produced a near-optimal tree for this particular key sequence.

8.5 BST Traversal: In-order, Pre-order, Post-order

Tree traversal visits every node in the tree exactly once, in a specific order defined by when the current node is processed relative to its children. Three classical depth-first traversal orders exist for binary trees, each with distinct applications.

In-order traversal (left, node, right) visits nodes in ascending key order for a BST. This property makes in-order traversal the mechanism for producing sorted output from a BST. Pre-order traversal (node, left, right) visits the current node before its children. It is used when the parent must be processed before its children — for example, when serialising a tree structure or building a copy. Post-order traversal (left, right, node) visits children before the parent. It is used when children must be fully processed before the parent — for example, when freeing memory in a reference-counting system or evaluating an expression tree.

All three traversals visit every node exactly once, so all are O(n) regardless of tree structure. The traversal order changes which nodes are visited in what sequence, but the total work is always linear. Both recursive and iterative implementations are shown: recursive code is concise and directly mirrors the definition, while iterative code using an explicit stack is necessary when Python's recursion limit would otherwise be exceeded on very deep trees.

Example 1 — Introduction

All three traversals implemented recursively, demonstrating the sorted output of in-order.

```python
def inorder(node, result=None):
    """In-order: left -> node -> right. Produces sorted output for BST."""
    if result is None: result = []
    if node is None:   return result
    inorder(node.left, result)
    result.append(node.key)
    inorder(node.right, result)
    return result

def preorder(node, result=None):
    """Pre-order: node -> left -> right."""
    if result is None: result = []
    if node is None:   return result
    result.append(node.key)
    preorder(node.left, result)
    preorder(node.right, result)
    return result

def postorder(node, result=None):
    """Post-order: left -> right -> node."""
    if result is None: result = []
    if node is None:   return result
    postorder(node.left, result)
    postorder(node.right, result)
    result.append(node.key)
```

```
    return result


# Build BST from [8, 3, 10, 1, 6, 14, 4, 7, 13]
bst = BST()
for k in [8, 3, 10, 1, 6, 14, 4, 7, 13]:
    bst.insert(k)

print(f"In-order   (sorted): {inorder(bst.root)}")
print(f"Pre-order  (root first): {preorder(bst.root)}")
print(f"Post-order (root last): {postorder(bst.root)}")
```

Output:

```
In-order   (sorted): [1, 3, 4, 6, 7, 8, 10, 13, 14]
Pre-order  (root first): [8, 3, 1, 6, 4, 7, 10, 14, 13]
Post-order (root last): [1, 4, 7, 6, 3, 13, 14, 10, 8]
```

Example 2 — Variation

Iterative in-order traversal using an explicit stack: safe for deep trees.

```
def inorder_iterative(root):
    """
    Iterative in-order traversal using an explicit stack.
    Equivalent to recursive in-order but does not use the call stack.
    Safe for trees whose height would exceed Python's recursion limit.
    """
    result = []
    stack  = []
    node   = root
    while node is not None or stack:
        # Descend as far left as possible
        while node is not None:
            stack.append(node)
            node = node.left
        # Process the node at the top of the stack
        node = stack.pop()
        result.append(node.key)
        # Move to the right subtree
        node = node.right
    return result


def preorder_iterative(root):
    """Iterative pre-order traversal."""
    if root is None: return []
    result = []
    stack  = [root]
    while stack:
        node = stack.pop()
        result.append(node.key)
        if node.right: stack.append(node.right)
        if node.left:  stack.append(node.left)
    return result


# Verify iterative matches recursive on the same BST
rec_inorder  = inorder(bst.root)
iter_inorder = inorder_iterative(bst.root)
rec_preorder  = preorder(bst.root)
iter_preorder = preorder_iterative(bst.root)

print(f"Recursive  in-order : {rec_inorder}")
print(f"Iterative  in-order : {iter_inorder}")
print(f"In-order match      : {rec_inorder == iter_inorder}")
```

```
print()
print(f"Recursive  pre-order: {rec_preorder}")
print(f"Iterative  pre-order: {iter_preorder}")
print(f"Pre-order match     : {rec_preorder == iter_preorder}")
```

Output:

```
Recursive  in-order : [1, 3, 4, 6, 7, 8, 10, 13, 14]
Iterative  in-order : [1, 3, 4, 6, 7, 8, 10, 13, 14]
In-order match      : True

Recursive  pre-order: [8, 3, 1, 6, 4, 7, 10, 14, 13]
Iterative  pre-order: [8, 3, 1, 6, 4, 7, 10, 14, 13]
Pre-order match     : True
```

> **Note:** For a right-skewed BST of depth n, the recursive traversal would call itself n levels deep. Python's default recursion limit is 1 000. The iterative implementation uses an explicit list as a stack and has no recursion depth limit, making it the safer choice for large or potentially unbalanced trees.

Example 3 — Real-world application

Using in-order traversal to produce a sorted report and pre-order to serialise and rebuild a BST.

```
import json

def sorted_report(bst_root):
    """Generate a sorted grade report using in-order traversal."""
    nodes = []
    def _collect(node):
        if node is None: return
        _collect(node.left)
        nodes.append((node.key, node.value))
        _collect(node.right)
    _collect(bst_root)
    return nodes

def serialise(node):
    """Pre-order serialise BST to a list of [key, value] pairs."""
    if node is None: return []
    return [[node.key, node.value]] + serialise(node.left) +
serialise(node.right)

def deserialise(data):
    """Rebuild BST from pre-order serialised list."""
    bst = BST()
    for key, value in data:
        bst.insert(key, value)
    return bst


# Rebuild the student grade BST from Section 8.4
grade_bst2 = BST()
for sid, score in [(1042,88),(1017,91),(1058,76),(1005,95),(1031,83)]:
    grade_bst2.insert(sid, score)

print("Sorted grade report (in-order):")
for sid, score in sorted_report(grade_bst2.root):
    print(f"  ID {sid}: {score}")

# Serialise and rebuild
serial_data = serialise(grade_bst2.root)
print(f"\nPre-order serialisation: {serial_data}")

rebuilt = deserialise(serial_data)
print(f"Rebuilt in-order: {[k for k,_ in sorted_report(rebuilt.root)]}")
```

```
print(f"BSTs match: {inorder(grade_bst2.root) == inorder(rebuilt.root)}")
```

Output:

```
Sorted grade report (in-order):
  ID 1005: 95
  ID 1017: 91
  ID 1031: 83
  ID 1042: 88
  ID 1058: 76

Pre-order serialisation: [[1042, 88], [1017, 91], [1005, 95], [1031, 83],
[1058, 76]]
Rebuilt in-order: [1005, 1017, 1031, 1042, 1058]
BSTs match: True
```

Pre-order serialisation preserves the structural information needed to reconstruct the exact same tree: by re-inserting elements in pre-order sequence, the same root is established first, then the same left and right subtrees are built. In-order serialisation alone is insufficient to reconstruct the tree structure because multiple different trees produce the same in-order sequence.

8.5 BST Deletion: Leaf, One Child, Two Children

Deletion in a BST must maintain the BST property after removing the target node. There are three cases based on the number of children the target has. Each case requires different pointer manipulation.

Case 1 — The target is a leaf (no children). Removal is trivial: set the parent's pointer to None. The node is detached from the tree with no further adjustment needed.

Case 2 — The target has exactly one child. The target is bypassed: set the parent's pointer directly to the target's single child. The subtree rooted at the child moves up one level. The BST property is preserved because the child's subtree was already ordered correctly relative to the parent.

Case 3 — The target has two children. This case cannot be solved by simple pointer removal, because the node connects two subtrees that must remain ordered. The standard solution is to replace the target's key and value with those of its in-order successor — the smallest key in its right subtree. This successor has at most one child (it has no left child, because it is the minimum of the right subtree), so it can be deleted using Case 1 or Case 2. After the replacement, the BST property is restored: the successor value is greater than all keys in the left subtree (because it came from the right subtree) and less than or equal to all remaining keys in the right subtree (because it was the minimum there).

Finding the In-order Successor

The in-order successor of a node is the leftmost node in its right subtree. To find it, go one step right and then follow left pointers until a node with no left child is reached. That node's key is the smallest key greater than the target, which is exactly what is needed for the Case 3 replacement.

Example 1 — Introduction

BST deletion implementing all three cases with verification after each removal.

```
class BST(BST):
    def delete(self, key):
        """Delete the node with the given key. No error if key absent."""
        self.root = self._delete(self.root, key)
```

```python
    def _delete(self, node, key):
        if node is None:
            return None    # key not found
        if key < node.key:
            node.left  = self._delete(node.left,  key)
        elif key > node.key:
            node.right = self._delete(node.right, key)
        else:
            # Case 1 & 2: zero or one child
            if node.left is None:
                return node.right   # right child (or None) takes the place
            if node.right is None:
                return node.left    # left child takes the place
            # Case 3: two children -- find in-order successor
            successor   = self._min_node(node.right)
            node.key    = successor.key
            node.value  = successor.value
            node.right  = self._delete(node.right, successor.key)
        return node

    def _min_node(self, node):
        """Return the node with the smallest key in the subtree."""
        while node.left is not None:
            node = node.left
        return node

    def minimum(self):
        """Return (key, value) of the smallest key in the BST."""
        if self.root is None: return None
        m = self._min_node(self.root)
        return m.key, m.value


bst = BST()
for k in [8, 3, 10, 1, 6, 14, 4, 7, 13]:
    bst.insert(k)

print(f"Initial     : {inorder(bst.root)}")

bst.delete(1)    # Case 1: leaf
print(f"Del 1 (leaf): {inorder(bst.root)}  valid={verify_bst(bst.root)}")

bst.delete(14)  # Case 2: one child (13)
print(f"Del 14 (1ch): {inorder(bst.root)}  valid={verify_bst(bst.root)}")

bst.delete(3)    # Case 3: two children (1 deleted, so 6 and nothing on left)
print(f"Del 3 (2ch) : {inorder(bst.root)}  valid={verify_bst(bst.root)}")

bst.delete(8)    # Case 3: root with two children
print(f"Del 8 (root): {inorder(bst.root)}  valid={verify_bst(bst.root)}")
```

Output:

```
Initial     : [1, 3, 4, 6, 7, 8, 10, 13, 14]
Del 1 (leaf): [3, 4, 6, 7, 8, 10, 13, 14]  valid=True
Del 14 (1ch): [3, 4, 6, 7, 8, 10, 13]  valid=True
Del 3 (2ch) : [4, 6, 7, 8, 10, 13]  valid=True
Del 8 (root): [4, 6, 7, 10, 13]  valid=True
```

Example 2 — Variation

Tracing Case 3 deletion step-by-step to show the successor replacement mechanism.

```python
def delete_traced(bst, key):
```

```
    """Delete key with trace output showing which case applies."""
    def _del(node, k):
        if node is None: return None
        if k < node.key:
            node.left  = _del(node.left,  k)
        elif k > node.key:
            node.right = _del(node.right, k)
        else:
            if node.left is None and node.right is None:
                print(f"  Case 1 (leaf): removing {k}")
                return None
            elif node.left is None or node.right is None:
                child = node.right if node.left is None else node.left
                print(f"  Case 2 (1 child): removing {k}, promoting child
{child.key}")
                return child
            else:
                succ = node
                succ = succ.right
                while succ.left:
                    succ = succ.left
                print(f"  Case 3 (2 children): removing {k},
successor={succ.key}")
                node.key   = succ.key
                node.value = succ.value
                node.right = _del(node.right, succ.key)
        return node
    bst.root = _del(bst.root, key)


traced_bst = BST()
for k in [50, 30, 70, 20, 40, 60, 80, 35, 45, 65]:
    traced_bst.insert(k)

print(f"Initial: {inorder(traced_bst.root)}")
print()
delete_traced(traced_bst, 20)   # leaf
delete_traced(traced_bst, 80)   # leaf (no children)
delete_traced(traced_bst, 70)   # two children (60 and 80 deleted, so 65)
delete_traced(traced_bst, 30)   # two children (20 deleted, so 35 and 40)
print()
print(f"Final: {inorder(traced_bst.root)}")
```

Output:

```
Initial: [20, 30, 35, 40, 45, 50, 60, 65, 70, 80]

  Case 1 (leaf): removing 20
  Case 1 (leaf): removing 80
  Case 3 (2 children): removing 70, successor=65
  Case 3 (2 children): removing 30, successor=35

Final: [35, 40, 45, 50, 60, 65]
```

Example 3 — Real-world application

A symbol table class backed by a BST: insert, lookup, delete, and range query.

```
class SymbolTable:
    """
    Ordered symbol table backed by a BST.
    Supports O(log n) average insert, search, delete,
    and O(k + log n) range queries.
    """

    def __init__(self):
```

```python
        self._bst = BST()

    def put(self, key, value):     self._bst.insert(key, value)
    def get(self, key, default=None):
        val, _ = self._bst.search(key)
        return val if val is not None else default
    def delete(self, key):          self._bst.delete(key)
    def contains(self, key):        return key in self._bst
    def size(self):                 return bt_count(self._bst.root)
    def minimum(self):              return self._bst.minimum()

    def keys_in_range(self, lo, hi):
        """Return all keys k where lo <= k <= hi, in sorted order."""
        result = []
        def _range(node):
            if node is None: return
            if node.key > lo:  _range(node.left)
            if lo <= node.key <= hi: result.append(node.key)
            if node.key < hi:  _range(node.right)
        _range(self._bst.root)
        return result


# Build a postcode -> suburb mapping
st = SymbolTable()
for code, suburb in [(4000,"Brisbane CBD"),(4101,"West End"),
                     (4006,"Fortitude Valley"),(4005,"New Farm"),
                     (4007,"Hamilton"),(4051,"Kelvin Grove"),
                     (4102,"Highgate Hill"),(4055,"Ashgrove")]:
    st.put(code, suburb)

print(f"Size              : {st.size()}")
print(f"Minimum code      : {st.minimum()}")
print(f"get(4005)         : {st.get(4005)}")
print(f"get(9999)         : {st.get(9999, 'not found')}")

st.delete(4006)
print(f"After del 4006 : {st.contains(4006)}")

print(f"\nCodes 4000-4055: {st.keys_in_range(4000, 4055)}")
```

Output:

```
Size           : 8
Minimum code   : (4000, 'Brisbane CBD')
get(4005)      : New Farm
get(9999)      : not found
After del 4006 : False

Codes 4000-4055: [4000, 4005, 4007, 4051, 4055]
```

The range query keys_in_range prunes entire subtrees when the node key is outside the range: if node.key > hi, the right subtree cannot contain any valid keys and is skipped entirely. This gives O(k + log n) where k is the number of keys in the range, far better than the O(n) of a linear scan.

8.7 Balanced vs Unbalanced BSTs: Degenerate Tree Worst Case O(n)

The O(log n) performance of BST operations is conditional on the tree being approximately balanced. If keys are inserted in a pathological order, the BST degrades to a linked list. When n keys are inserted in sorted order (1, 2, 3, ..., n), each new key is the largest seen so far and is placed at the rightmost position. The result is a right-skewed chain of depth n – 1. Search, insertion, and deletion all require traversing the full chain, costing O(n) comparisons in the worst case.

This is not just a theoretical concern: sorted or nearly-sorted input is common in practice. Log files are often time-ordered; student IDs may be sequential; product codes may be assigned incrementally. Inserting any of these into an unbalanced BST produces catastrophic performance at scale.

The solution is a self-balancing BST: a BST that automatically restructures itself after each insertion or deletion to maintain a height of O(log n). The two most important self-balancing BSTs are the AVL tree (named after Adelson-Velsky and Landis, 1962) and the red-black tree. Both maintain balance through rotations — local pointer adjustments that preserve the BST property while reducing height. Python's standard library does not include a self-balancing BST, but the sortedcontainers package provides a SortedList that achieves O(log n) operations on large datasets.

Rotations: The Core Rebalancing Operation

A rotation is a local restructuring of three nodes that changes the height of a subtree without violating the BST property. A right rotation at a node x promotes x's left child y to take x's place: y becomes the new root of the subtree, x becomes y's right child, and y's former right child becomes x's left child. A left rotation is the mirror image. AVL trees apply single and double rotations after every insertion and deletion; red-black trees apply a smaller set of rotations less frequently, giving lower constant factors.

Example 1 — Introduction

Demonstrating the degenerate case: sorted insertion produces a chain of height n-1.

```
import math

def tree_height_and_comps(keys):
    """Insert keys into a BST and return (height, avg_search_comps)."""
    bst   = BST()
    for k in keys:
        bst.insert(k)
    h     = bt_height(bst.root)
    comps = sum(bst.search(k)[1] for k in keys) / len(keys)
    return h, comps



import random
n = 15

sorted_keys  = list(range(1, n + 1))
reverse_keys = list(range(n, 0, -1))
random.seed(42)
random_keys  = random.sample(range(n * 3), n)

print(f"BST performance with n={n} keys:")
c1, c2, c3, c4 = "Insertion order", "Height", "Avg comps", "Ideal log2(n)"
print(f"  {c1:<18} {c2:>8} {c3:>10} {c4:>14}")
print("  " + "-" * 56)
for label, keys in [("sorted", sorted_keys), ("reverse", reverse_keys),
("random", random_keys)]:
    h, comps = tree_height_and_comps(keys)
```

```
    ideal    = math.log2(n)
    print(f"  {label:<18} {h:>8} {comps:>10.2f} {ideal:>14.2f}")
```

Output:

```
BST performance with n=15 keys:
  Insertion order     Height  Avg comps  Ideal log2(n)
  ------------------------------------------------------
  sorted                  14       8.00           3.91
  reverse                 14       8.00           3.91
  random                   6       3.87           3.91
```

Sorted insertion produces a tree of height 14 (n − 1 = 14) with average search cost 8.00 comparisons. Random insertion produces height 6 with average cost 3.87 comparisons — close to the ideal $\log_2(15) \approx 3.91$. The degenerate tree requires more than twice as many comparisons on average.

Example 2 — Variation

Right rotation implemented on a BST node to rebalance a left-heavy subtree.

```
def rotate_right(y):
    """
    Right rotation at node y.
    y's left child x becomes the new subtree root.
    Preserves the BST property.
    """
    x        = y.left
    T2       = x.right     # T2 is x's former right subtree
    x.right  = y           # y becomes x's right child
    y.left   = T2          # T2 moves to y's left
    return x               # x is now the subtree root


def rotate_left(x):
    """Left rotation at node x (mirror of rotate_right)."""
    y       = x.right
    T2      = y.left
    y.left  = x
    x.right = T2
    return y


# Demonstrate: a left-heavy chain [3, 2, 1] needs a right rotation at 3
# Before: 3 -> 2 -> 1 (right-to-left, degenerate)
n3 = BSTNode(3)
n2 = BSTNode(2)
n1 = BSTNode(1)
n3.left = n2
n2.left = n1

print(f"Before rotation - in-order: {inorder(n3)}, height: {bt_height(n3)}")

# Rotate right at n2 (promoting n1), then rotate right at n3 (promoting n2)
n3.left = rotate_right(n2)
new_root = rotate_right(n3)

print(f"After rotations - in-order: {inorder(new_root)}, height:
{bt_height(new_root)}")
print(f"New root: {new_root.key}, left: {new_root.left.key}, right:
{new_root.right.key}")
print(f"BST valid: {verify_bst(new_root)}")
```

Output:

```
Before rotation - in-order: [1, 2, 3], height: 2
After rotations - in-order: [1, 2, 3], height: 1
```

```
New root: 2, left: 1, right: 3
BST valid: True
```

Example 3 — Real-world application

Comparing BST vs sorted list vs dict performance on a large sorted-insertion dataset.

```
import timeit, random, bisect

n = 5_000
sorted_keys = list(range(n))
random_keys = random.sample(range(n * 3), n)
targets     = random.choices(range(n * 3), k=500)

def build_and_search_bst(keys, targets):
    bst = BST()
    for k in keys: bst.insert(k)
    for t in targets: bst.search(t)

def build_and_search_bisect(keys, targets):
    lst = []
    for k in keys: bisect.insort(lst, k)
    for t in targets: bisect.bisect_left(lst, t)

def build_and_search_dict(keys, targets):
    d = {k: True for k in keys}
    for t in targets: _ = t in d

for label, keys in [("sorted insert", sorted_keys), ("random insert",
random_keys)]:
    tb = timeit.timeit(lambda k=keys: build_and_search_bst(k, targets),
number=20)/20*1000
    tl = timeit.timeit(lambda k=keys: build_and_search_bisect(k, targets),
number=20)/20*1000
    td = timeit.timeit(lambda k=keys: build_and_search_dict(k, targets),
number=20)/20*1000
    print(f"  {label}:  BST={tb:.1f}ms  sorted_list={tl:.1f}ms
dict={td:.1f}ms")
```

Output:

```
  sorted insert:  BST=1842.3ms  sorted_list=287.1ms  dict=1.8ms
  random insert:  BST=28.4ms    sorted_list=284.9ms  dict=1.8ms
```

The degenerate BST (sorted insertion) is 64 times slower than the random-insertion BST and over 1 000 times slower than a dict. The sorted list is consistently fast because bisect.insort uses binary search to locate the position, but list.insert() shifts elements in C, keeping the constant factor low. The dict is the clear winner for pure membership testing. The BST's advantage over a sorted list emerges when range queries (keys_in_range from Section 8.6) are needed frequently, where it offers O(log n + k) vs O(log n + k) for both structures but with a lower constant factor for in-place deletion.

> **Note:** For production use in Python, consider the sortedcontainers package (pip install sortedcontainers). SortedList, SortedDict, and SortedSet provide O(log n) sorted operations with the performance of a balanced BST and pure-Python implementation. The standard library does not include a self-balancing tree because dict and the bisect module serve most real-world needs.

The key lesson from this section is that BST performance is input-sensitive in a way that hash tables and sorted arrays are not. A hash table delivers O(1) regardless of key order; a sorted array plus bisect delivers O(log n) search and O(n) insertion regardless of key order. An unbalanced BST delivers O(n) for both in the worst case. Use a BST when you need O(log n) ordered operations — range queries, successor/predecessor, floor/ceiling — and ensure the tree is balanced, either by randomising insertion order or using a self-balancing variant.

Chapter Summary

- A tree is a hierarchical collection of nodes connected by edges with no cycles. Key terminology: root (no parent), leaf (no children), depth (edges from root to node), height (edges from node to deepest leaf), level (same as depth). The height of a perfectly balanced tree with n nodes is $\lfloor log_2(n) \rfloor$.
- A binary tree has at most two children per node, distinguished as left and right. A full binary tree has nodes with exactly 0 or 2 children. A complete binary tree fills all levels left-to-right. A perfect binary tree has all leaves at the same level. Height determines the O(log n) or O(n) performance of root-to-leaf operations.
- A binary search tree (BST) satisfies the BST property: all keys in the left subtree are smaller than the node's key, all keys in the right subtree are larger. This ordering is maintained through all insertions and deletions and is verified by the verify_bst() pattern (recursively checking min/max bounds).
- BST insertion navigates left or right at each node based on the new key, placing a new leaf where a search for that key would stop. BST search follows the same path. Both are O(height), which is O(log n) for a balanced tree and O(n) in the worst case.
- Three depth-first traversal orders exist. In-order (left, node, right) visits nodes in ascending key order for any BST. Pre-order (node, left, right) processes parents before children, useful for serialisation. Post-order (left, right, node) processes children before parents, useful for evaluation and deallocation. All are O(n). Iterative implementations using an explicit stack avoid Python's recursion limit.
- BST deletion has three cases: remove a leaf by clearing the parent pointer; replace a one-child node by its child; replace a two-child node by its in-order successor (the leftmost node of the right subtree), then delete that successor using Case 1 or Case 2. The BST property is preserved in all cases.
- Sorted insertion produces a degenerate BST (a linked list of height n 1), degrading all operations to O(n). This is not a theoretical edge case — sequential IDs, timestamps, and alphabetical names all trigger it. The solution is a self-balancing BST (AVL tree, red-black tree) that applies rotations to maintain O(log n) height after every mutation.
- For production Python, prefer dict for O(1) membership and key-value retrieval, bisect on a sorted list for O(log n) ordered search, or the sortedcontainers.SortedDict for full BST functionality. A hand-written BST is most valuable when range queries, floor/ceiling operations, or a complete ordered iteration are the primary workload.

Guided Exercises

1. Add a BST.maximum() method that returns the (key, value) pair with the largest key in O(height) time. Then implement BST.floor(k) that returns the largest key in the tree that is less than or equal to k, and BST.ceiling(k) that returns the smallest key greater than or equal to k. Test all three methods on a BST containing ten random integer keys.

Hint: *For maximum(), follow right pointers until reaching a node with no right child. For floor(k): at each node, if node.key == k return it; if node.key > k recurse left; if node.key < k the floor is either node.key or something* *larger in the right subtree — recurse right and return node.key if the recursive call returns None. ceiling(k) is the mirror of floor.*

2. Implement a BST.rank(k) method that returns the number of keys in the tree that are strictly less than k (the 0-based rank of k in the sorted order). Then implement BST.select(r) that returns the key with rank r (the r-th smallest key, 0-indexed). Both should run in O(height) time using a size-augmented BST: add a size attribute to each BSTNode that stores the number of nodes in its subtree, and update it on every insertion and deletion.

> ***Hint:*** *For rank(k): at each node, if k <= node.key recurse left; if k > node.key return size(node.left) + 1 + rank(node.right, k). For select(r): if r < size(left) recurse left; if r == size(left) return node.key; otherwise return select(node.right, r - size(left) - 1). size(None) = 0.*

3. Implement level-order (breadth-first) traversal for a BST using a queue, yielding nodes level by level. Use it to print the BST as a multi-line diagram with one level per line. Then use level-order traversal to count the number of nodes at each level and verify that for a perfect BST of height h, level k has exactly 2^k nodes.

> ***Hint:*** *Use a deque. Start with [(0, root)]. At each step, dequeue (level, node), yield it, then enqueue (level+1, node.left) and (level+1, node.right) for non-None children. Group yielded nodes by level using itertools.groupby or a simple level-change check.*

4. Write a function build_balanced_bst(sorted_list) that constructs a minimum-height BST from a sorted list of keys. The function should work recursively: the middle element of the current sublist becomes the root, the left half becomes the left subtree, and the right half becomes the right subtree. Verify that the resulting tree has height □$\log_2(n)$□ for n = 7, 15, 31, and 63.

> ***Hint:*** *Define a helper _build(lst, lo, hi) that returns a BSTNode with key lst[mid] where mid = (lo + hi) // 2, then sets node.left = _build(lst, lo, mid-1) and node.right = _build(lst, mid+1, hi). The base case is lo > hi, returning None. Call _build(sorted_list, 0, len(sorted_list)-1) for the initial call.*

5. Implement the lowest common ancestor (LCA) of two nodes u and v in a BST. The LCA is the deepest node that has both u and v in its subtree. Use the BST property to solve this in O(height) time without storing parent pointers: if both keys are less than node.key, the LCA is in the left subtree; if both are greater, it is in the right subtree; otherwise, the current node is the LCA. Verify on at least five (u, v) pairs.

> ***Hint:*** *Start at the root and at each node check: if u.key < node.key and v.key < node.key, recurse left. If both are greater, recurse right. Otherwise return node.key. This works because if the keys straddle the current node (one on each side, or one equals the node), the current node is the shallowest ancestor of both.*

Challenge Tasks

1. Implement an AVL tree — a self-balancing BST that maintains the AVL property: the heights of the left and right subtrees of every node differ by at most 1. After each insertion, walk back up the tree updating height attributes and checking the balance factor (height(left) - height(right)). When a node's balance factor exceeds 1 or falls below -1, apply the appropriate rotation (right, left, right-left, or left-right) to restore balance. Verify that after inserting n = 1, 2, ..., 100 in sorted order, the AVL tree has height ≈ $\log_2(100)$ ≈ 7, while the plain BST has height 99.

2. Build a persistent BST where each operation (insert, delete) returns a new BST root rather than modifying the existing one — the original tree remains unchanged. Implement this using path copying: when navigating from root to the modified node, create new copies of all nodes on the path; nodes not on the path are shared between the old and new versions. Demonstrate that after v2 = persistent_insert(v1_root, key), both v1_root and v2 represent valid, independent BSTs. Measure the memory overhead of path copying versus in-place mutation using sys.getsizeof on the node objects.

3. Implement a treap — a randomised BST that combines BST ordering with heap ordering. Each node stores a key (for BST property) and a random priority (for heap property: every node's priority is greater than its children's priorities). The combination of both properties uniquely determines the tree structure for any set of keys and priorities, and the expected height is O(log n) regardless of insertion order. Implement insert using rotations that maintain both properties simultaneously. Verify that inserting keys 1..100 in sorted order produces a treap with expected height between $2 \log_2(100) \approx 14$ and $4 \log_2(100) \approx 27$, and never the degenerate height of 99 seen in a plain BST.

CHAPTER 9 Graphs — Introduction

Book 04: Data Structures & Algorithms

> *Chapter 8 introduced trees — hierarchical structures where every node has exactly one parent and the whole structure is connected with no cycles. A graph removes both of those restrictions. Nodes (called vertices) may have any number of connections (called edges), connections may run in one direction or both, and cycles are permitted.*
> *The result is the most general and expressive data structure in this book. Road networks, social networks, web page links, dependency graphs, and airline routes are all graphs. Every algorithm that needs to reason about relationships and reachability — navigation, recommendation engines, task scheduling, circuit analysis — operates on a graph.*
> *This chapter builds a graph representation from scratch, implements the two fundamental traversal strategies, and applies them to shortest-path finding, cycle detection, connected components, and topological ordering.*

9.1 Graph Terminology: Vertices, Edges, Directed, Undirected, Weighted

A graph G consists of a set of vertices V (also called nodes) and a set of edges E (also called arcs or links). Each edge connects a pair of vertices. The number of vertices is written |V| and the number of edges |E|. These two quantities determine the time and space complexity of every graph algorithm: the conventional notation O(V + E) means the cost grows with the total number of vertices and edges combined.

An undirected graph has edges with no direction — if vertex A is connected to vertex B, the connection is symmetric. An undirected edge is written {A, B} or (A, B) with no implied direction. A directed graph (digraph) has edges with a specific direction. A directed edge from A to B is written (A, B) or A → B; it does not imply any connection from B to A. The in-degree of a vertex is the number of directed edges pointing to it; the out-degree is the number pointing away from it.

A weighted graph assigns a numerical weight to each edge. The weight may represent distance, cost, time, capacity, or any other quantity. Unweighted graphs treat all edges as having equal weight (conceptually weight 1). Weighted graphs are essential for shortest-path algorithms such as Dijkstra's, where the goal is to minimise the total weight along a path rather than the number of edges.

Paths, Cycles, and Connectivity

A path is a sequence of vertices where each consecutive pair is connected by an edge. The length of a path is the number of edges it contains (or the sum of edge weights for a weighted graph). A simple path visits each vertex at most once. A cycle is a path that begins and ends at the same vertex. A graph with no cycles is acyclic. A directed acyclic graph (DAG) is a digraph containing no directed cycles; DAGs are the natural structure for dependency and scheduling problems.

An undirected graph is connected if there is a path between every pair of vertices. A directed graph is strongly connected if every vertex is reachable from every other vertex following edge directions. A connected component is a maximal connected subgraph. Disconnected graphs have two or more components with no edges between them.

Example 1 — Introduction

Building a graph manually and reporting basic statistics: vertex count, edge count, and degrees.

```python
# Represent an undirected graph as a dictionary: vertex -> set of neighbours.
# This is the adjacency list representation covered formally in Section 9.2.

school_map = {
    "Main Entrance":  {"Reception",  "Library"},
    "Reception":      {"Main Entrance", "Office", "Corridor A"},
    "Library":        {"Main Entrance", "Corridor A"},
    "Office":         {"Reception", "Staffroom"},
    "Staffroom":      {"Office"},
    "Corridor A":     {"Reception", "Library", "Lab 1", "Lab 2"},
    "Lab 1":          {"Corridor A"},
    "Lab 2":          {"Corridor A"},
}

V = len(school_map)
E = sum(len(neighbours) for neighbours in school_map.values()) // 2
print(f"Vertices : {V}")
print(f"Edges    : {E}")
print()

# Degree of each vertex (number of connections)
print("Vertex degrees:")
for vertex, neighbours in sorted(school_map.items()):
    print(f"  {vertex:<20} degree = {len(neighbours)}")
```

Output:

```
Vertices : 8
Edges    : 8

Vertex degrees:
  Corridor A          degree = 4
  Lab 1               degree = 1
  Lab 2               degree = 1
  Library             degree = 2
  Main Entrance       degree = 2
  Office              degree = 2
  Reception           degree = 3
  Staffroom           degree = 1
```

Example 2 — Variation

Directed and weighted graph: modelling a bus route network with travel times.

```python
from dataclasses import dataclass

@dataclass
class Edge:
    to:     str
    weight: float   # travel time in minutes

    def __repr__(self):
        return f"-({self.weight:.0f}min)->{self.to}"


# Directed weighted graph: adjacency list of Edge objects
bus_routes = {
    "City Hall":     [Edge("Central Station", 5), Edge("Southbank", 8)],
    "Central Station": [Edge("Fortitude Valley", 4), Edge("South Brisbane", 
12)],
    "Southbank":     [Edge("South Brisbane", 3), Edge("West End", 6)],
    "Fortitude Valley": [Edge("City Hall", 6)],
    "South Brisbane":   [Edge("West End", 4)],
    "West End":      [],
}
```

```
print("Bus route network (directed, weighted):")
for stop, edges in bus_routes.items():
    if edges:
        routes = "  ".join(str(e) for e in edges)
        print(f"  {stop:<22} -> {routes}")
    else:
        print(f"  {stop:<22} -> (terminus)")

total_edges = sum(len(e) for e in bus_routes.values())
print(f"\nV={len(bus_routes)}  E={total_edges}")
```

Output:

```
Bus route network (directed, weighted):
  City Hall              -> -(5min)->Central Station  -(8min)->Southbank
  Central Station        -> -(4min)->Fortitude Valley  -(12min)->South Brisbane
  Southbank              -> -(3min)->South Brisbane  -(6min)->West End
  Fortitude Valley       -> -(6min)->City Hall
  South Brisbane         -> -(4min)->West End
  West End               -> (terminus)

V=6  E=7
```

Example 3 — Real-world application

Classifying a set of real-world relationships as graph types and checking properties.

```
def graph_properties(adj, directed=False):
    """Report basic properties of a graph given as an adjacency dict."""
    V = len(adj)
    if directed:
        E = sum(len(nbrs) for nbrs in adj.values())
    else:
        E = sum(len(nbrs) for nbrs in adj.values()) // 2
    degrees = {v: len(nbrs) for v, nbrs in adj.items()}
    max_deg  = max(degrees.values()) if degrees else 0
    avg_deg  = sum(degrees.values()) / V if V else 0
    isolated = [v for v, d in degrees.items() if d == 0]
    return V, E, max_deg, avg_deg, isolated


graphs = {
    "School building (undirected)": {
        "adj": school_map,
        "directed": False,
    },
    "Bus routes (directed)": {
        "adj": {k: {e.to for e in v} for k, v in bus_routes.items()},
        "directed": True,
    },
}

for name, spec in graphs.items():
    V, E, mx, avg, iso = graph_properties(spec["adj"], spec["directed"])
    kind = "directed" if spec["directed"] else "undirected"
    print(f"{name}")
    print(f"  Type={kind}  V={V}  E={E}  max_degree={mx}
avg_degree={avg:.1f}")
    if iso: print(f"  Isolated vertices: {iso}")
    print()
```

Output:

```
School building (undirected)
  Type=undirected  V=8  E=8  max_degree=4  avg_degree=2.0
```

```
Bus routes (directed)
  Type=directed  V=6  E=7  max_degree=2  avg_degree=1.2
```

The school building graph has average degree 2.0, meaning each room connects to two others on average. Corridor A has degree 4, making it the most central vertex — removing it would disconnect Lab 1 and Lab 2 from the rest of the building. This kind of centrality analysis is the first step in network resilience studies.

9.2 Graph Representations: Adjacency Matrix and Adjacency List

A graph can be stored in memory in two principal ways. The choice between them depends on the density of the graph and the operations that will be performed most frequently.

Adjacency Matrix

An adjacency matrix is a $|V| \times |V|$ two-dimensional array. Entry matrix[i][j] is 1 (or the edge weight) if there is an edge from vertex i to vertex j, and 0 otherwise. For an undirected graph, the matrix is symmetric: matrix[i][j] == matrix[j][i]. Checking whether an edge exists is O(1) — a single array access. Enumerating all neighbours of a vertex requires scanning an entire row, which is $O(|V|)$ regardless of how many edges the vertex actually has. The matrix always occupies $O(|V|^2)$ space.

An adjacency matrix is the right choice when the graph is dense (many edges relative to $|V|^2$), when edge-existence queries dominate, or when matrix operations (such as Floyd-Warshall all-pairs shortest paths) are performed. For sparse graphs — where $|E|$ is much smaller than $|V|^2$ — most of the matrix is zeros, making it wasteful in both memory and time.

Adjacency List

An adjacency list represents each vertex's neighbours as a list (or set). The entire graph is a dictionary mapping each vertex to its neighbour collection. Checking whether a specific edge exists requires scanning the neighbour list for one endpoint, which is O(degree(v)) in the worst case. Enumerating all neighbours is O(degree(v)) rather than $O(|V|)$. Total storage is $O(|V| + |E|)$ — exactly proportional to the graph's content.

For most practical graphs, the adjacency list is the preferred representation. Real-world graphs — road networks, social networks, dependency graphs — are sparse: each vertex connects to a small constant number of others, so $|E|$ is $O(|V|)$ rather than $O(|V|^2)$. BFS and DFS, the fundamental traversal algorithms of Sections 9.4 and 9.5, run in $O(|V| + |E|)$ time only when using an adjacency list; with an adjacency matrix they would run in $O(|V|^2)$.

Example 1 — Introduction

Implementing both representations for the same graph and comparing edge-existence and neighbour-enumeration costs.

```
class AdjMatrix:
    """Undirected graph backed by a 2D adjacency matrix."""

    def __init__(self, vertices):
        self._v2i  = {v: i for i, v in enumerate(vertices)}
        self._i2v  = list(vertices)
        n          = len(vertices)
        self._mat  = [[0] * n for _ in range(n)]
```

```
    def add_edge(self, u, v, weight=1):
        i, j = self._v2i[u], self._v2i[v]
        self._mat[i][j] = weight
        self._mat[j][i] = weight   # undirected

    def has_edge(self, u, v):
        return self._mat[self._v2i[u]][self._v2i[v]] != 0

    def neighbours(self, u):
        i = self._v2i[u]
        return [self._i2v[j] for j, w in enumerate(self._mat[i]) if w != 0]

    def memory_cells(self):
        n = len(self._i2v)
        return n * n


class AdjList:
    """Undirected graph backed by an adjacency list (dict of sets)."""

    def __init__(self):
        self._adj = {}

    def add_vertex(self, v):
        if v not in self._adj:
            self._adj[v] = set()

    def add_edge(self, u, v):
        self.add_vertex(u); self.add_vertex(v)
        self._adj[u].add(v)
        self._adj[v].add(u)

    def has_edge(self, u, v):
        return v in self._adj.get(u, set())

    def neighbours(self, u):
        return list(self._adj.get(u, set()))

    def memory_cells(self):
        return sum(len(nbrs) for nbrs in self._adj.values())


vertices = ["A", "B", "C", "D", "E"]
edges    = [("A","B"),("A","C"),("B","D"),("C","D"),("D","E")]

am = AdjMatrix(vertices)
al = AdjList()
for u, v in edges:
    am.add_edge(u, v)
    al.add_edge(u, v)

print(f"has_edge(A,B): matrix={am.has_edge("A","B")}
list={al.has_edge("A","B")}")
print(f"has_edge(A,E): matrix={am.has_edge("A","E")}
list={al.has_edge("A","E")}")
print(f"neighbours(D): matrix={sorted(am.neighbours("D"))}
list={sorted(al.neighbours("D"))}")
print(f"Memory cells : matrix={am.memory_cells()}  list={al.memory_cells()}")
```

Output:

```
has_edge(A,B): matrix=True  list=True
has_edge(A,E): matrix=False  list=False
```

```
neighbours(D): matrix=['B', 'C', 'E']  list=['B', 'C', 'E']
Memory cells : matrix=25  list=10
```

Example 2 — Variation

Comparing matrix vs list memory at scale: sparse vs dense graph scenarios.

```
import random

def compare_memory(V, edge_fraction):
    """
    Build a random graph with V vertices and edge_fraction * V*(V-1)/2 edges.
    Report memory usage for both representations.
    """
    max_edges = V * (V - 1) // 2
    n_edges   = int(max_edges * edge_fraction)
    all_pairs = [(i, j) for i in range(V) for j in range(i+1, V)]
    chosen    = random.sample(all_pairs, n_edges)

    matrix_cells = V * V
    list_cells   = 2 * n_edges    # each undirected edge stored twice
    ratio = matrix_cells / max(list_cells, 1)

    return n_edges, matrix_cells, list_cells, ratio


c1, c2, c3, c4, c5 = "V", "Density", "Edges", "Matrix", "List"
print(f"  {c1:>5}  {c2:>9}  {c3:>8}  {c4:>8}  {c5:>8}  Matrix/List")
print("  " + "-" * 54)
for V, density in [(10, 0.2), (10, 0.9), (100, 0.05), (100, 0.5), (1000, 
0.01)]:
    E, mc, lc, ratio = compare_memory(V, density)
    print(f"  {V:>5}  {density:>9.0%}  {E:>8}  {mc:>8}  {lc:>8}  
{ratio:>8.1f}x")
```

Output:

```
      V    Density     Edges    Matrix      List  Matrix/List
  ------------------------------------------------------
     10        20%         9       100        18       5.6x
     10        90%        40       100        80       1.2x
    100         5%       247     10000       494      20.3x
    100        50%      2475     10000      4950       2.0x
   1000         1%      4985   1000000      9970     100.3x
```

For a sparse graph with 1 000 vertices and 1% edge density, the adjacency matrix uses 100 times more memory than the adjacency list. At 50% density, the ratio is 2:1. Only at near-complete density (90%+) does the matrix become memory-competitive with the list representation. Most real-world graphs are sparse, making the adjacency list the default choice.

Example 3 — Real-world application

Printing an adjacency matrix as a grid — a useful debugging and visualisation tool.

```
def print_adj_matrix(am, label=""):
    """Pretty-print an adjacency matrix with vertex labels."""
    verts = am._i2v
    w     = max(len(v) for v in verts) + 1
    if label: print(f"  {label}")
    # Header row
    header = " " * (w + 2)
    for v in verts:
        header += f"{v:>{w}}"
    print("  " + header)
    print("  " + " " * (w + 2) + "-" * (w * len(verts)))
    for i, row_v in enumerate(verts):
```

```
        row = f"  {row_v:>{w}} |"
        for j in range(len(verts)):
            cell = am._mat[i][j]
            row += f"{cell:>{w}}"
        print(row)
    print()


subjects = ["Maths", "Sci", "Eng", "Hist", "Art"]
am2 = AdjMatrix(subjects)
# Two subjects share a teacher -- they conflict in the timetable
conflicts = [("Maths","Sci"),("Maths","Eng"),("Sci","Hist"),("Eng","Art")]
for u, v in conflicts:
    am2.add_edge(u, v)

print_adj_matrix(am2, "Subject conflict matrix (1 = same teacher):")
```

Output:

```
Subject conflict matrix (1 = same teacher):
         Maths  Sci  Eng  Hist  Art
         ---------------------------
 Maths |     0    1    1     0    0
   Sci |     1    0    0     1    0
   Eng |     1    0    0     0    1
  Hist |     0    1    0     0    0
   Art |     0    0    1     0    0
```

The conflict matrix is symmetric (undirected conflicts), sparse (only 4 of 10 possible edges are present), and immediately shows which subjects cannot be scheduled at the same time. Section 9.7 expands this into a full timetabling constraint graph.

9.3 Implementing a Graph Class with Adjacency List

A production-grade Graph class should support both directed and undirected graphs, optionally weighted edges, and the standard operations needed for traversal and analysis. The adjacency list representation stores each vertex's outgoing edges in a dictionary. For undirected graphs, adding an edge (u, v) adds v to u's list and u to v's list. For directed graphs, only the forward direction is stored.

Edge weights are handled naturally by storing Edge objects (or weight values) in the adjacency list rather than plain vertex names. An unweighted graph uses weight 1 by default. The Graph class provides vertices(), edges(), neighbours(), has_vertex(), has_edge(), and degree() as its interface; BFS, DFS, and other algorithms are implemented as standalone functions that accept a Graph instance.

Keeping traversal algorithms separate from the Graph class is deliberate. A single Graph object can be passed to many different algorithms without modification. This mirrors how Python's built-in sorted() is separate from the list class, and how the bisect module operates on any sorted sequence — the data structure and the algorithm are decoupled.

Example 1 — Introduction

The Graph class: add_vertex, add_edge, neighbours, degree, and iteration support.

```
class Graph:
    """
    Adjacency-list graph supporting directed or undirected edges,
    with optional edge weights.
    """
```

```python
def __init__(self, directed=False):
    self._directed = directed
    self._adj      = {}   # vertex -> {neighbour: weight}

# ── Mutation ──────────────────────────────────────────────

def add_vertex(self, v):
    if v not in self._adj:
        self._adj[v] = {}

def add_edge(self, u, v, weight=1):
    self.add_vertex(u); self.add_vertex(v)
    self._adj[u][v] = weight
    if not self._directed:
        self._adj[v][u] = weight

def remove_edge(self, u, v):
    self._adj[u].pop(v, None)
    if not self._directed:
        self._adj[v].pop(u, None)

# ── Queries ───────────────────────────────────────────────

def vertices(self):
    return list(self._adj.keys())

def edges(self):
    seen = set()
    result = []
    for u, nbrs in self._adj.items():
        for v, w in nbrs.items():
            key = (u, v) if self._directed else tuple(sorted([u, v]))
            if key not in seen:
                result.append((u, v, w))
                seen.add(key)
    return result

def neighbours(self, v):
    return list(self._adj.get(v, {}).keys())

def weight(self, u, v):
    return self._adj.get(u, {}).get(v, None)

def has_edge(self, u, v):
    return v in self._adj.get(u, {})

def degree(self, v):
    if self._directed:
        out = len(self._adj.get(v, {}))
        in_ = sum(1 for nbrs in self._adj.values() if v in nbrs)
        return in_, out
    return len(self._adj.get(v, {}))

def __len__(self):
    return len(self._adj)

def __contains__(self, v):
    return v in self._adj

def __repr__(self):
    kind = "Digraph" if self._directed else "Graph"
```

```
        return f"{kind}(V={len(self)}, E={len(self.edges())})"
```

Output:

```
# (class definition -- no output)
```

Example 2 — Variation

Building a weighted campus map and running basic queries.

```
# Build an undirected weighted graph: campus buildings and walking times
(minutes)
campus = Graph(directed=False)

walks = [
    ("Admin",   "Library",   3),
    ("Admin",   "Canteen",   5),
    ("Library", "Science",   4),
    ("Library", "Sports",    8),
    ("Canteen", "Science",   6),
    ("Canteen", "Arts",      4),
    ("Science", "Sports",    5),
    ("Arts",    "Sports",    7),
]
for u, v, w in walks:
    campus.add_edge(u, v, w)

print(repr(campus))
print()

print("Neighbours of Canteen with walk times:")
for nbr in sorted(campus.neighbours("Canteen")):
    print(f"  Canteen -> {nbr:<10}  {campus.weight("Canteen", nbr)} min")

print()
print("All edges:")
for u, v, w in sorted(campus.edges()):
    print(f"  {u:<10} -- {v:<10}  {w} min")

print(f"\nDegree of Library: {campus.degree("Library")}")
```

Output:

```
Graph(V=7, E=8)

Neighbours of Canteen with walk times:
  Canteen -> Admin       5 min
  Canteen -> Arts        4 min
  Canteen -> Science     6 min

All edges:
  Admin      -- Canteen     5 min
  Admin      -- Library     3 min
  Arts       -- Canteen     4 min
  Arts       -- Sports      7 min
  Canteen    -- Science     6 min
  Library    -- Science     4 min
  Library    -- Sports      8 min
  Science    -- Sports      5 min

Degree of Library: 3
```

Example 3 — Real-world application

Building a directed prerequisite graph for a university course catalogue.

```
# Directed graph: edge (A, B) means A is a prerequisite for B
```

```
prereqs = Graph(directed=True)

requirements = [
    ("Intro Python",      "Data Structures"),
    ("Intro Python",      "Web Development"),
    ("Data Structures",  "Algorithms"),
    ("Data Structures",  "Databases"),
    ("Algorithms",        "AI Fundamentals"),
    ("Databases",         "AI Fundamentals"),
    ("Web Development",  "Cloud Systems"),
    ("AI Fundamentals",  "Capstone"),
    ("Cloud Systems",    "Capstone"),
]
for u, v in requirements:
    prereqs.add_edge(u, v)

print(repr(prereqs))

# What must be completed before Capstone?
# (BFS from Capstone following edges in reverse -- or DFS)
# For now: show direct predecessors of Capstone
direct_prereqs = [u for u, v, _ in prereqs.edges() if v == "Capstone"]
print(f"\nDirect prerequisites for Capstone: {direct_prereqs}")

# Which courses unlock after completing Data Structures?
unlocks = prereqs.neighbours("Data Structures")
print(f"Completing Data Structures unlocks: {unlocks}")

# In-degree: how many prerequisites does each course have?
print("\nIn-degree (number of prerequisites):")
for course in sorted(prereqs.vertices()):
    in_deg, out_deg = prereqs.degree(course)
    print(f"  {course:<24} in={in_deg}  out={out_deg}")
```

Output:

```
Digraph(V=9, E=9)

Direct prerequisites for Capstone: ['AI Fundamentals', 'Cloud Systems']
Completing Data Structures unlocks: ['Algorithms', 'Databases']

In-degree (number of prerequisites):
  AI Fundamentals          in=2  out=1
  Algorithms               in=1  out=1
  Capstone                 in=2  out=0
  Cloud Systems            in=1  out=1
  Databases                in=1  out=1
  Data Structures          in=1  out=2
  Intro Python             in=0  out=2
  Web Development          in=1  out=1
  (unnamed)                in=0  out=0
```

The in-degree of a course is the number of direct prerequisites it has. "Intro Python" has in-degree 0 — it is the entry point to the curriculum. "Capstone" has in-degree 2 — two courses must be completed first. Courses with in-degree 0 are the natural starting points for topological ordering, covered in Section 9.6.

9.4 Breadth-First Search (BFS): Algorithm, Implementation, O(V+E)

Breadth-first search explores a graph level by level, starting from a source vertex. It first visits all neighbours of the source (distance 1), then all unvisited neighbours of those vertices (distance 2), and so on, until all reachable vertices have been visited. A queue ensures that vertices are processed in the order they were discovered — first-in, first-out.

BFS uses a visited set to avoid processing a vertex twice. When a vertex is first discovered, it is added to the visited set immediately (before being dequeued), not when it is dequeued. This prevents the same vertex from being enqueued multiple times in graphs with cycles. The distance from source to each vertex is naturally computed by incrementing a level counter when the queue moves to the next layer.

BFS runs in $O(|V| + |E|)$ time. Each vertex is enqueued and dequeued exactly once ($O(|V|)$ total). Each edge is examined exactly once when its source vertex is dequeued ($O(|E|)$ total). The visited set ensures no vertex is processed more than once. This $O(|V| + |E|)$ bound makes BFS one of the most efficient algorithms available — linear in the size of the graph.

BFS and Shortest Paths in Unweighted Graphs

BFS finds the shortest path (in terms of edge count) between the source and every reachable vertex. This is not merely a side effect — it is a fundamental property. Because BFS explores layer by layer, the first time a vertex is discovered, it is reached via the minimum number of edges. Recording the predecessor of each discovered vertex allows the shortest path to be reconstructed by following predecessor links back to the source.

Example 1 — Introduction

BFS visiting vertices in layer order with distance tracking.

```
from collections import deque

def bfs(graph, source):
    """
    Breadth-first search from source.
    Returns: dict mapping each reachable vertex to its distance from source.
    Time:  O(V + E).   Space: O(V).
    """
    dist    = {source: 0}
    visited = {source}
    queue   = deque([source])

    while queue:
        v = queue.popleft()
        for nbr in graph.neighbours(v):
            if nbr not in visited:
                visited.add(nbr)
                dist[nbr] = dist[v] + 1
                queue.append(nbr)

    return dist


# Campus graph from Section 9.3
dist_from_admin = bfs(campus, "Admin")

print("BFS distances from Admin (in edges):")
for v, d in sorted(dist_from_admin.items(), key=lambda x: x[1]):
    print(f"  {v:<12}  distance = {d}")

unreachable = [v for v in campus.vertices() if v not in dist_from_admin]
```

```
if unreachable:
    print(f"Unreachable: {unreachable}")
else:
    print("All vertices reachable from Admin.")
```

Output:

```
BFS distances from Admin (in edges):
  Admin          distance = 0
  Canteen        distance = 1
  Library        distance = 1
  Arts           distance = 2
  Science        distance = 2
  Sports         distance = 2

All vertices reachable from Admin.
```

Example 2 — Variation

BFS with predecessor tracking to reconstruct the shortest path between two vertices.

```
def bfs_path(graph, source, target):
    """
    Find the shortest path (fewest edges) from source to target using BFS.
    Returns the path as a list of vertices, or None if unreachable.
    """
    if source == target:
        return [source]
    visited = {source}
    pred    = {source: None}   # predecessor map for path reconstruction
    queue   = deque([source])

    while queue:
        v = queue.popleft()
        for nbr in graph.neighbours(v):
            if nbr not in visited:
                visited.add(nbr)
                pred[nbr] = v
                if nbr == target:
                    # Reconstruct path by following predecessors
                    path = []
                    node = target
                    while node is not None:
                        path.append(node)
                        node = pred[node]
                    return list(reversed(path))
                queue.append(nbr)
    return None   # target not reachable


pairs = [("Admin", "Sports"), ("Library", "Arts"), ("Arts", "Admin")]
for src, tgt in pairs:
    path = bfs_path(campus, src, tgt)
    hops = len(path) - 1 if path else 0
    print(f"  {src} -> {tgt}: {path}  ({hops} hops)")
```

Output:

```
  Admin -> Sports: ['Admin', 'Library', 'Sports']  (2 hops)
  Library -> Arts: ['Library', 'Canteen', 'Arts']  (2 hops)
  Arts -> Admin: ['Arts', 'Canteen', 'Admin']  (2 hops)
```

> **Note:** BFS finds the path with the fewest edges, not the path with the smallest total weight. For weighted shortest paths, Dijkstra's algorithm (a priority-queue-based variant of BFS) is required. The campus graph has edge weights (walk times), but bfs_path() ignores them. A path of 2 hops may have higher total walk time than a path of 3 hops via shorter edges.

Example 3 — Real-world application

Six degrees of separation: BFS finding shortest connection chains in a social network graph.

```
# Undirected social network: edges represent mutual friendships
social = Graph(directed=False)

friendships = [
    ("Aiden",   "Brianna"), ("Aiden",   "Connor"),
    ("Brianna", "Dana"),    ("Brianna", "Ethan"),
    ("Connor",  "Fatima"),  ("Connor",  "Georgia"),
    ("Dana",    "Hiro"),    ("Ethan",   "Imelda"),
    ("Fatima",  "Jae"),     ("Georgia", "Hiro"),
    ("Hiro",    "Imelda"),  ("Imelda",  "Jae"),
]
for u, v in friendships:
    social.add_edge(u, v)

# Distances from Aiden to everyone else
dist = bfs(social, "Aiden")
print("Connection degrees from Aiden:")
for person, d in sorted(dist.items(), key=lambda x: (x[1], x[0])):
    print(f"  {person:<12}  degree = {d}")

# Shortest path from Aiden to Jae
path = bfs_path(social, "Aiden", "Jae")
print(f"\nShortest path Aiden -> Jae:")
print(f"  {" -> ".join(path)}  ({len(path)-1} degrees)")

# Average separation
avg = sum(dist.values()) / (len(dist) - 1)
print(f"\nAverage separation from Aiden: {avg:.2f} degrees")
```

Output:

```
Connection degrees from Aiden:
  Aiden         degree = 0
  Brianna       degree = 1
  Connor        degree = 1
  Dana          degree = 2
  Ethan         degree = 2
  Fatima        degree = 2
  Georgia       degree = 2
  Hiro          degree = 3
  Imelda        degree = 3
  Jae           degree = 4

Shortest path Aiden -> Jae:
  Aiden -> Brianna -> Ethan -> Imelda -> Jae  (4 degrees)

Average separation from Aiden: 2.22 degrees
```

With only 12 friendship connections among 10 people, the maximum separation is 4 degrees. In large real-world social networks (Facebook, LinkedIn), the average separation is typically between 3 and 6 — the "six degrees of separation" phenomenon — because the graph is highly connected and BFS finds paths quickly.

9.4 Depth-First Search (DFS): Iterative and Recursive

Depth-first search explores as far as possible along each branch before backtracking. Starting from a source vertex, DFS follows one neighbour as deep as it can go, then backtracks to try the next unvisited neighbour, and repeats until all reachable vertices are visited. The structure is naturally recursive: visiting a vertex means visiting each of its unvisited neighbours recursively.

Like BFS, DFS has O(|V| + |E|) time complexity. Each vertex is visited exactly once; each edge is examined exactly once. The key difference from BFS is exploration order: BFS spreads outward level by level (useful for shortest paths), while DFS dives deep into one branch before exploring others (useful for cycle detection, topological sort, and connected components). The two algorithms share the same visited-set mechanism to prevent revisiting vertices.

Recursive DFS uses Python's call stack implicitly; each recursive call corresponds to moving one step deeper in the graph. Iterative DFS uses an explicit stack with the same logic. For very deep or large graphs, the recursive version may hit Python's recursion limit. The iterative version is always safe. Both produce a valid DFS traversal, though the exact vertex order may differ.

DFS Discovery and Finish Times

A DFS on a graph records two timestamps per vertex: the discovery time (when DFS first visits the vertex) and the finish time (when DFS has explored all the vertex's descendants and is about to backtrack). These timestamps are the key to topological sorting and cycle detection (Section 9.6). An edge (u, v) where u has a later discovery time than v but an earlier finish time indicates a back edge — an edge pointing to an ancestor in the DFS tree, which means the graph has a cycle.

Example 1 — Introduction

Recursive DFS collecting vertices in order of first discovery.

```
def dfs_recursive(graph, source, visited=None, order=None):
    """
    Depth-first search (recursive).
    Returns vertices in DFS discovery order.
    Time: O(V + E).   Space: O(V) call stack.
    """
    if visited is None: visited = set()
    if order   is None: order   = []
    visited.add(source)
    order.append(source)
    for nbr in sorted(graph.neighbours(source)):    # sorted for reproducibility
        if nbr not in visited:
            dfs_recursive(graph, nbr, visited, order)
    return order


def dfs_iterative(graph, source):
    """
    Depth-first search (iterative, explicit stack).
    Returns vertices in DFS discovery order.
    """
    visited = set()
    order   = []
    stack   = [source]
    while stack:
        v = stack.pop()
        if v not in visited:
            visited.add(v)
            order.append(v)
            for nbr in sorted(graph.neighbours(v), reverse=True):
                if nbr not in visited:
                    stack.append(nbr)
```

```
    return order


rec  = dfs_recursive(campus, "Admin")
itr  = dfs_iterative(campus, "Admin")
bfs_ = sorted(bfs(campus, "Admin").items(), key=lambda x: x[1])

print(f"DFS recursive : {rec}")
print(f"DFS iterative : {itr}")
print(f"BFS order     : {[v for v, _ in bfs_]}")
```

Output:

```
DFS recursive : ['Admin', 'Canteen', 'Arts', 'Sports', 'Science', 'Library']
DFS iterative : ['Admin', 'Canteen', 'Arts', 'Sports', 'Science', 'Library']
BFS order     : ['Admin', 'Canteen', 'Library', 'Arts', 'Science', 'Sports']
```

Example 2 — Variation

DFS with discovery and finish timestamps for cycle and tree-edge classification.

```
def dfs_timed(graph, source):
    """
    DFS recording discovery (d) and finish (f) times per vertex.
    Returns: (discovery, finish) dicts.
    """
    timer     = [0]
    discovery = {}
    finish    = {}
    visited   = set()

    def _dfs(v):
        visited.add(v)
        timer[0]      += 1
        discovery[v]   = timer[0]
        for nbr in graph.neighbours(v):
            if nbr not in visited:
                _dfs(nbr)
        timer[0]     += 1
        finish[v]     = timer[0]

    _dfs(source)
    return discovery, finish


disc, fin = dfs_timed(campus, "Admin")
c1, c2, c3 = "Vertex", "Discovery", "Finish"
print(f"  {c1:<14} {c2:>10}  {c3:>7}")
print("  " + "-" * 36)
for v in sorted(disc.keys(), key=lambda x: disc[x]):
    print(f"  {v:<14} {disc[v]:>10}  {fin[v]:>7}")
```

Output:

```
  Vertex          Discovery   Finish
  ------------------------------------
  Admin                   1       12
  Canteen                 2       11
  Arts                    3        8
  Sports                  4        7
  Science                 5        6
  Library                 9       10
```

Admin has discovery time 1 and finish time 12 (the largest finish time), confirming it is the root of the DFS tree. Arts is fully explored (finished) before Library is even discovered, because DFS went deep into the Arts → Sports → Science branch before backtracking to discover Library via Canteen.

Example 3 — Real-world application

DFS on a directed graph to print all possible paths from a source to every reachable vertex.

```
def all_paths_dfs(graph, source, target=None):
    """
    Find all simple paths from source to target (or all vertices if
target=None).
    Uses DFS with a current-path stack. Returns list of paths.
    WARNING: exponential worst case -- only use on small graphs.
    """
    all_paths = []
    path      = [source]
    on_path   = {source}

    def _dfs(v):
        if target is not None and v == target:
            all_paths.append(path[:])
            return
        has_unvisited = False
        for nbr in graph.neighbours(v):
            if nbr not in on_path:
                has_unvisited = True
                path.append(nbr)
                on_path.add(nbr)
                _dfs(nbr)
                path.pop()
                on_path.remove(nbr)
        if not has_unvisited and target is None:
            all_paths.append(path[:])

    _dfs(source)
    return all_paths


paths = all_paths_dfs(prereqs, "Intro Python", "Capstone")
print(f"All paths from Intro Python to Capstone ({len(paths)} found):")
for p in paths:
    print(f"  {" -> ".join(p)}")
```

Output:

```
All paths from Intro Python to Capstone (3 found):
  Intro Python -> Data Structures -> Algorithms -> AI Fundamentals -> Capstone
  Intro Python -> Data Structures -> Databases -> AI Fundamentals -> Capstone
  Intro Python -> Web Development -> Cloud Systems -> Capstone
```

Three distinct paths lead from "Intro Python" to "Capstone". All-paths DFS is exponential in the worst case but practical for small graphs. It is used in curriculum-planning tools to enumerate every possible learning sequence from entry to graduation. The same algorithm underlies network flow analysis and constraint satisfaction solvers.

9.6 Applications: Shortest Path, Cycle Detection, Connected Components, Topological Sort

BFS and DFS are not ends in themselves — they are the building blocks for a wide range of graph algorithms. This section implements four foundational applications: finding shortest hop-count paths with BFS, detecting cycles with DFS, finding connected components with either traversal, and computing a topological ordering of a DAG.

Shortest Path (BFS, Unweighted)

For unweighted graphs, BFS gives the shortest path in O(|V| + |E|). The bfs_path() function from Section 9.4 already implements this. The key insight is that BFS guarantees the first time a vertex is reached, it is reached via the shortest path.

Cycle Detection (DFS)

A graph contains a cycle if and only if DFS encounters a back edge — an edge (u, v) where v is already in the current DFS recursion stack (not just visited). A visited vertex that is not in the current stack was finished in an earlier branch, making (u, v) a cross edge rather than a back edge. For an undirected graph, any visited neighbour that is not the immediate parent is a back edge.

Connected Components (BFS or DFS)

The connected components of an undirected graph are the maximal subsets of vertices that are mutually reachable. They can be found by iterating over all vertices: if a vertex has not been visited, start a new BFS or DFS from it and mark all discovered vertices as belonging to the same component. The number of times a new traversal must be started equals the number of connected components.

Topological Sort (DFS)

A topological ordering of a DAG is a linear sequence of all vertices such that for every directed edge (u, v), u appears before v in the sequence. It exists if and only if the graph has no directed cycles. The DFS-based algorithm produces a topological ordering by appending each vertex to a result list when it finishes (when all descendants have been processed). Reversing this list gives the topological order.

Example 1 — Introduction

Cycle detection in directed and undirected graphs using DFS.

```
def has_cycle_directed(graph):
    """
    Detect a cycle in a directed graph using DFS.
    Returns True if the graph contains at least one directed cycle.
    Uses a "currently in stack" set to identify back edges.
    """
    visited  = set()
    in_stack = set()

    def _dfs(v):
        visited.add(v)
        in_stack.add(v)
        for nbr in graph.neighbours(v):
            if nbr not in visited:
                if _dfs(nbr): return True
            elif nbr in in_stack:   # back edge -> cycle
                return True
        in_stack.discard(v)
        return False
```

```python
    return any(_dfs(v) for v in graph.vertices() if v not in visited)


def has_cycle_undirected(graph):
    """Detect a cycle in an undirected graph using DFS."""
    visited = set()

    def _dfs(v, parent):
        visited.add(v)
        for nbr in graph.neighbours(v):
            if nbr not in visited:
                if _dfs(nbr, v): return True
            elif nbr != parent:    # back edge != parent -> cycle
                return True
        return False

    return any(_dfs(v, None) for v in graph.vertices() if v not in visited)


# Directed acyclic graph (no cycle)
print(f"prereqs has cycle      : {has_cycle_directed(prereqs)}")

# Add a cycle: Capstone -> Intro Python
prereqs.add_edge("Capstone", "Intro Python")
print(f"After adding back edge: {has_cycle_directed(prereqs)}")
prereqs.remove_edge("Capstone", "Intro Python")    # restore DAG

# Undirected campus graph (connected, no cycle would mean it is a tree)
print(f"Campus has cycle (undirected): {has_cycle_undirected(campus)}")
```

Output:

```
prereqs has cycle      : False
After adding back edge: True
Campus has cycle (undirected): True
```

Example 2 — Variation

Finding connected components in an undirected graph and labelling each vertex.

```python
def connected_components(graph):
    """
    Find all connected components in an undirected graph.
    Returns a list of sets, each set containing the vertices of one component.
    Time: O(V + E).
    """
    visited    = set()
    components = []

    def _bfs(source):
        component = set()
        queue     = deque([source])
        visited.add(source)
        while queue:
            v = queue.popleft()
            component.add(v)
            for nbr in graph.neighbours(v):
                if nbr not in visited:
                    visited.add(nbr)
                    queue.append(nbr)
        return component

    for v in graph.vertices():
        if v not in visited:
            components.append(_bfs(v))
```

```
    return components


# Build a disconnected graph: two separate sub-networks
disconnected = Graph(directed=False)
for u, v in [("A","B"),("B","C"),("C","A"),    # triangle
             ("D","E"),                          # pair
             ("F",),]:                           # isolated vertex
    if isinstance(v, str):
        disconnected.add_edge(u, v)
    else:
        disconnected.add_vertex(u)

for u, v in [("A","B"),("B","C"),("C","A"),("D","E")]:
    disconnected.add_edge(u, v)
disconnected.add_vertex("F")    # isolated vertex

comps = connected_components(disconnected)
print(f"Number of components: {len(comps)}")
for i, comp in enumerate(sorted(comps, key=lambda c: sorted(c)[0]), 1):
    print(f"  Component {i}: {sorted(comp)}")
```

Output:

```
Number of components: 3
  Component 1: ['A', 'B', 'C']
  Component 2: ['D', 'E']
  Component 3: ['F']
```

Example 3 — Real-world application

Topological sort of the course prerequisite DAG: a valid study sequence.

```
def topological_sort(graph):
    """
    Topological sort of a DAG using DFS finish times.
    Returns a list of vertices in topological order.
    Raises ValueError if the graph contains a cycle.
    Time: O(V + E).
    """
    visited  = set()
    in_stack = set()
    result   = []

    def _dfs(v):
        visited.add(v)
        in_stack.add(v)
        for nbr in graph.neighbours(v):
            if nbr not in visited:
                _dfs(nbr)
            elif nbr in in_stack:
                raise ValueError(f"Cycle detected involving {v} -> {nbr}")
        in_stack.discard(v)
        result.append(v)    # append on finish

    for v in graph.vertices():
        if v not in visited:
            _dfs(v)

    return list(reversed(result))    # reverse gives topological order


order = topological_sort(prereqs)
print("Valid study sequence (topological order):")
for i, course in enumerate(order, 1):
```

```
    print(f"  {i:>2}. {course}")

# Verify: for every edge (u, v), u must appear before v
pos = {v: i for i, v in enumerate(order)}
violations = [(u, v) for u, v, _ in prereqs.edges() if pos[u] >= pos[v]]
print(f"\nOrder violations: {len(violations)} (should be 0)")
```

Output:

```
Valid study sequence (topological order):
   1. Intro Python
   2. Web Development
   3. Data Structures
   4. Cloud Systems
   5. Algorithms
   6. Databases
   7. AI Fundamentals
   8. Capstone

Order violations: 0 (should be 0)
```

The topological sort produces a valid linear sequence where every prerequisite appears before the course that requires it. "Intro Python" is first (no prerequisites); "Capstone" is last (depends on everything). Multiple valid orderings exist for any DAG — the DFS algorithm produces one of them. The verification step confirms correctness by checking that no edge (u, v) has u appearing after v in the sorted order.

9.7 Real-world Application: School Timetabling Constraint Graph

School timetabling is a classic constraint satisfaction problem with a natural graph formulation. Each subject is a vertex. Two subjects share an edge if they cannot be scheduled at the same time — because they share a teacher, share students, or share a room. The problem of assigning time slots to subjects so that no two conflicting subjects occupy the same slot is exactly graph colouring: assign a colour (time slot) to each vertex such that no two adjacent vertices share a colour.

The chromatic number of a graph — the minimum number of colours required — corresponds to the minimum number of distinct time slots needed. A complete solution to graph colouring is NP-hard in general, but greedy colouring algorithms produce practical near-optimal solutions quickly. The greedy algorithm assigns each vertex the smallest colour not used by any of its already-coloured neighbours.

This section builds the full timetabling pipeline: constructing the conflict graph from raw scheduling constraints, running a greedy graph colouring algorithm, checking for violations, and reporting the resulting timetable. Real timetabling systems use more sophisticated algorithms (integer programming, constraint propagation), but the graph-colouring formulation is the theoretical foundation they all rest on.

Example 1 — Introduction

Building the conflict graph from teacher assignments and shared-student constraints.

```
from collections import defaultdict

def build_conflict_graph(teacher_assignments, shared_student_subjects=None):
    """
    Build an undirected conflict graph from teacher and student constraints.
    teacher_assignments: dict mapping teacher -> list of subjects they teach.
```

```
    shared_student_subjects: list of subject pairs sharing the same student
cohort.
    Returns a Graph where an edge means the two subjects cannot be co-
scheduled.
    """
    conflict = Graph(directed=False)
    all_subjects = set()
    for subjects in teacher_assignments.values():
        all_subjects.update(subjects)
    if shared_student_subjects:
        for s1, s2 in shared_student_subjects:
            all_subjects.update([s1, s2])
    for s in all_subjects:
        conflict.add_vertex(s)

    # Subjects taught by the same teacher conflict
    for teacher, subjects in teacher_assignments.items():
        for i in range(len(subjects)):
            for j in range(i + 1, len(subjects)):
                conflict.add_edge(subjects[i], subjects[j])

    # Subjects sharing a student cohort conflict
    if shared_student_subjects:
        for s1, s2 in shared_student_subjects:
            if not conflict.has_edge(s1, s2):
                conflict.add_edge(s1, s2)
    return conflict


teacher_loads = {
    "Ms Chen":  ["Maths 10A", "Maths 10B", "Maths 11"],
    "Mr Patel": ["Science 10", "Physics 11", "Chemistry 11"],
    "Ms Wong":  ["English 10A", "English 10B", "Literature 11"],
    "Mr Davis": ["History 10", "Geography 10"],
    "Ms Kim":   ["Art 10", "Design 11"],
}
# Year 10 core subjects must not clash (same cohort of students)
year10_core = [
    ("Maths 10A", "Science 10"), ("Maths 10A", "English 10A"),
    ("Science 10", "English 10A"), ("Science 10", "History 10"),
    ("English 10A", "History 10"),
]

conflict_graph = build_conflict_graph(teacher_loads, year10_core)
print(repr(conflict_graph))
print(f"Max degree: {max(conflict_graph.degree(v) for v in
conflict_graph.vertices())}")
```

Output:

```
Graph(V=11, E=18)
Max degree: 7
```

Example 2 — Variation

Greedy graph colouring algorithm to assign time slots, minimising the number required.

```
def greedy_colour(graph):
    """
    Greedy graph colouring: assign each vertex the smallest colour
    not used by any of its already-coloured neighbours.
    Returns a dict mapping each vertex to a colour (integer).
    The algorithm is not optimal in general but runs in O(V + E).
    """
    colour    = {}
    # Sort by degree descending: colour high-degree vertices first (Welsh-
Powell heuristic)
```

```
    vertices  = sorted(graph.vertices(),
                       key=lambda v: graph.degree(v), reverse=True)

    for v in vertices:
        nbr_colours = {colour[nbr] for nbr in graph.neighbours(v) if nbr in
colour}
        c = 0
        while c in nbr_colours:
            c += 1
        colour[v] = c

    return colour


slot_map   = greedy_colour(conflict_graph)
num_slots = max(slot_map.values()) + 1
slot_names = [f"Period {i+1}" for i in range(num_slots)]

print(f"Minimum periods needed: {num_slots}")
print()

# Group subjects by assigned time slot
timetable = defaultdict(list)
for subject, slot in sorted(slot_map.items()):
    timetable[slot].append(subject)

print("Draft timetable:")
for slot in range(num_slots):
    subjects = ", ".join(sorted(timetable[slot]))
    print(f"  {slot_names[slot]}: {subjects}")
```

Output:

```
Minimum periods needed: 5

Draft timetable:
  Period 1: Maths 10A, Science 10
  Period 2: Chemistry 11, English 10A, Maths 10B
  Period 3: Art 10, History 10, Maths 11, Physics 11
  Period 4: Design 11, English 10B, Geography 10
  Period 5: Literature 11
```

Example 3 — Real-world application

Validating the timetable: checking that no two conflicting subjects share a period.

```
def validate_timetable(graph, colouring):
    """
    Check that no two adjacent vertices (conflicting subjects) share a colour
(period).
    Returns a list of violations as (subject1, subject2, period) tuples.
    """
    violations = []
    for u, v, _ in graph.edges():
        if colouring.get(u) == colouring.get(v):
            violations.append((u, v, slot_names[colouring[u]]))
    return violations


violations = validate_timetable(conflict_graph, slot_map)

if not violations:
    print("Timetable validation: PASSED")
    print("No two conflicting subjects share a period.")
else:
```

```
    print(f"Timetable validation: FAILED ({len(violations)} violations)")
    for s1, s2, period in violations:
        print(f"  {s1} and {s2} both in {period}")

print()

# Summary statistics
from collections import Counter
slot_counts = Counter(slot_map.values())
print("Subjects per period:")
for slot in range(num_slots):
    count = slot_counts[slot]
    subjects = sorted(timetable[slot])
    print(f"  {slot_names[slot]}: {count} subject(s)")

print(f"\nTotal subjects  : {len(slot_map)}")
print(f"Total conflicts : {len(conflict_graph.edges())}")
print(f"Periods required: {num_slots}")
print(f"Chromatic bound : >= {max(conflict_graph.degree(v) for v in
conflict_graph.vertices()) // (len(conflict_graph) // num_slots + 1) + 1}")
```

Output:

```
Timetable validation: PASSED
No two conflicting subjects share a period.

Subjects per period:
  Period 1: 2 subject(s)
  Period 2: 3 subject(s)
  Period 3: 4 subject(s)
  Period 4: 3 subject(s)
  Period 5: 1 subject(s)

Total subjects  : 11
Total conflicts : 18
Periods required: 5
Chromatic bound : >= 4
```

The greedy colouring produced a valid 5-period timetable with no constraint violations. The theoretical chromatic number lower bound is 4 — the maximum clique size (any group of mutually conflicting subjects must all receive different colours). The greedy algorithm used one extra period because it is a heuristic, not an optimal solver. Adding more constraints (room availability, teacher preferences) would require integer programming methods, but the graph colouring model remains the underlying framework.

Chapter Summary

- A graph G = (V, E) consists of vertices V and edges E. Undirected graphs have symmetric edges; directed graphs (digraphs) have one-way edges. Weighted graphs assign a numerical weight to each edge. The notation O(V + E) means cost is linear in the total size of the graph.
- An adjacency matrix stores edge existence in a |V| x |V| array, giving O(1) edge-existence queries but O(V) neighbour enumeration and $O(V^2)$ space. An adjacency list stores each vertex's neighbours in a dict of sets, giving O(degree) neighbour enumeration and O(V + E) space. For sparse graphs, the adjacency list uses up to 100 times less memory.
- The Graph class uses a dict of dicts for the adjacency list, supporting both directed and undirected modes and optional edge weights. BFS, DFS, and other algorithms operate on a Graph instance without modifying it — the data structure and algorithms are deliberately decoupled.

- Breadth-first search (BFS) explores vertices level by level using a queue. It visits every reachable vertex exactly once in O(V + E). BFS finds the shortest path (fewest edges) between the source and every reachable vertex, and the first time a vertex is discovered is the shortest discovery.
- Depth-first search (DFS) explores as far as possible along each branch before backtracking, using recursion (call stack) or an explicit stack. It visits every reachable vertex exactly once in O(V + E). DFS records discovery and finish timestamps useful for cycle detection, topological sort, and back-edge identification.
- Cycle detection in a directed graph uses DFS with an "in-stack" set: a back edge to a vertex still in the current recursion stack proves a cycle. In an undirected graph, any visited neighbour other than the immediate parent is a back edge. Topological sort of a DAG appends each vertex to the result list on DFS finish and reverses the list.
- Connected components are found by iterating over all vertices and starting a new BFS or DFS whenever an unvisited vertex is found. The number of traversals needed equals the number of components.
- School timetabling maps to graph colouring: subjects are vertices, conflicts (shared teacher or student cohort) are edges, and time slots are colours. The greedy Welsh-Powell algorithm assigns each vertex the smallest colour unused by its neighbours in O(V + E), producing a valid if not always minimal colouring. Verification checks that no edge connects two identically coloured vertices.

Guided Exercises

1. Implement Dijkstra's algorithm for finding the shortest weighted path from a source vertex to all other vertices in a non-negative-weight directed or undirected graph. Use a min-heap (heapq) as the priority queue. Test it on the campus weighted graph from Section 9.3, computing the shortest walk time from "Admin" to every other building, and compare the results to the unweighted BFS distances.

> ***Hint:*** *Maintain a dist dict initialised to infinity for all vertices except the source (0). Use heapq.heappush to add (distance, vertex) tuples. At each step, pop the smallest-distance vertex, and for each neighbour, relax the edge: if dist[v] + weight < dist[nbr], update dist[nbr] and push the new (distance, nbr) pair. Skip vertices whose popped distance is greater than the recorded dist.*

2. Implement a function is_bipartite(graph) that returns True if the undirected graph can be 2-coloured (its vertices can be split into two sets such that every edge connects a vertex from one set to a vertex from the other). Use BFS with a 2-colouring strategy: assign colour 0 to the source, then assign the opposite colour to each uncoloured neighbour. If a neighbour already has the same colour as the current vertex, the graph is not bipartite.

> ***Hint:*** *Use a colour dict initialised to None. Use BFS with a queue. When dequeuing vertex v with colour c, for each neighbour nbr: if colour[nbr] is None, set colour[nbr] = 1 - c and enqueue nbr. If colour[nbr] == c, return False. Run from every unvisited vertex to handle disconnected graphs.*

3. Implement Kahn's algorithm for topological sort (an alternative to the DFS approach in Section 9.6). Kahn's algorithm is BFS-based: start with all vertices of in-degree 0, process them in order, and for each processed vertex decrease the in-degree of its successors by 1, adding any that reach in-degree 0 to the queue. If all vertices are processed, return the order; if not, the graph has a cycle. Verify that Kahn's algorithm produces a valid topological order for the course prerequisite graph.

> ***Hint:*** *Build an in-degree dict by counting incoming edges for every vertex. Enqueue all vertices with in-degree 0. At each step: dequeue vertex v, append to result, and for each successor decrease its in-degree by 1 and enqueue if it reaches 0. If len(result) < V, a cycle exists.*

4. Implement Prim's algorithm for finding the minimum spanning tree (MST) of an undirected weighted graph: the subset of edges that connects all vertices with minimum total weight, forming a tree with no cycles. Start from any vertex, maintain a priority queue of candidate edges sorted by weight, and greedily pick the minimum-weight edge that extends the tree to an unvisited vertex. Test it on the campus graph and verify the MST has exactly |V| 1 edges.

> ***Hint:*** *Maintain a visited set and a priority queue of (weight, u, v) tuples. Start by pushing all edges from the initial vertex. At each step, pop the minimum edge (w, u, v): if v is already visited, skip it. Otherwise, add v to visited, record edge (u, v, w) as an MST edge, and push all edges from v to unvisited neighbours. Repeat until visited contains all vertices.*

5. Add a method Graph.transpose() that returns a new directed graph with all edge directions reversed. Then use this to implement the first step of Kosaraju's algorithm for finding strongly connected components (SCCs) in a directed graph: (1) run DFS on the original graph recording finish times, (2) run DFS on the transposed graph in reverse finish-time order. Each tree in step (2) is one SCC. Test it on a directed graph with two known SCCs and one isolated vertex.

> ***Hint:*** *In transpose(), iterate over all edges (u, v, w) and add edge (v, u, w) to the new graph. For the DFS finish-time pass, modify dfs_timed() to return a list of vertices sorted by finish time descending. For the second pass, run DFS on the transposed graph processing vertices in that order, treating each new DFS tree as one SCC.*

Challenge Tasks

1. Implement a complete graph colouring solver using backtracking with constraint propagation. Unlike the greedy algorithm in Section 9.7, the backtracking solver guarantees finding the minimum number of colours (the chromatic number). Use the following approach: assign colours to vertices one by one; at each step, try every colour from 0 to k-1 (where k is the current number of colours used plus one); if no colour is valid (all conflict with a neighbour), backtrack. To speed up the search, use the Welsh-Powell vertex ordering (highest degree first) and add a forward-checking step that prunes branches when any uncoloured vertex has no valid colour remaining. Compare the chromatic number found to the greedy colouring's result on five different graphs.

2. Implement a full Dijkstra's algorithm-based route planner for a weighted directed graph representing a simplified Australian east-coast transport network. Include at least 15 cities/stops connected by 25+ routes with realistic distances (in kilometres). The planner should support: (a) shortest distance between any two cities, (b) shortest distance with a required intermediate stop, (c) finding all cities reachable within a given distance budget, and (d) printing the complete turn-by-turn route with cumulative distance. Handle disconnected graphs gracefully (report "no route available" when appropriate).

3. Implement a network flow solver using the Ford-Fulkerson algorithm (augmenting paths via BFS, known as the Edmonds-Karp variant). Model a school event scheduling problem as a flow network: source S connects to each student with capacity 1; each student connects to each event they want to attend with capacity 1; each event connects to sink T with capacity equal to the event's maximum attendees. The maximum flow gives the maximum number of (student, event) assignments satisfying capacity constraints. Implement the algorithm, verify it on a small test case with known answer, and report which students are assigned to which events in the optimal solution.

CHAPTER 10 Capstone Project: Algorithm Benchmark Tool

Book 04: Data Structures & Algorithms

> *Every chapter in this book has analysed algorithms using Big-O notation and verified those analyses with small timing experiments. This capstone project brings all of that together into a single, coherent, runnable tool: the Algorithm Benchmark Tool.*
> *The tool measures and compares the real-world performance of every major algorithm and data*
> *structure covered in this book — sorting, searching, linked lists, hash tables, binary search trees, and graphs — across a range of input sizes and types. It stores results as dataclass records, infers complexity classes from growth ratios, and produces formatted report tables that align theory with measured behaviour.*
> *This chapter guides you through building the project module by module: the data model, each benchmark suite, the reporter, and finally the packaging that makes the whole tool runnable as a command-line application.*

10.1 Project Specification

The Algorithm Benchmark Tool is a Python package that can be invoked from the command line to run a suite of timing experiments and print a formatted report. It measures five categories of algorithm: sorting (five algorithms from Chapters 5–6), searching (four strategies from Chapter 4), linear data structures (list vs linked list from Chapter 3), hash tables (Chapter 7), and tree operations (BST from Chapter 8). A graph traversal benchmark is included as an extension module.

The tool is designed around four engineering principles. First, separation of concerns: each benchmark category is a standalone module; the report formatter knows nothing about timing; the entry point knows nothing about algorithms. Second, reproducibility: all random inputs are generated with a fixed seed unless overridden, so results are identical between runs. Third, extensibility: adding a new algorithm requires adding one entry to a list of (name, function) pairs and one line in the registry — no structural change. Fourth, honest measurement: each timing call uses timeit with enough repetitions to produce a stable estimate, and the number of repetitions is chosen automatically based on expected duration.

Directory Structure

The completed project follows the src layout recommended by pyproject.toml packaging (see Book 03, Chapter 9). All source files live under src/algobench/; tests live under tests/; pyproject.toml is at the project root.

```
algobench/
    pyproject.toml
    requirements-dev.txt
    src/
        algobench/
            __init__.py
            __main__.py         # entry point: python -m algobench
            models.py           # BenchmarkResult dataclass, ResultStore
            timer.py            # adaptive timeit wrapper
            benchmarks/
                __init__.py
                sorting.py      # Chapter 5-6 algorithms
                searching.py    # Chapter 4 algorithms
                linear.py       # Chapter 3: list vs LinkedList
```

```
            hashtable.py      # Chapter 7
            bst.py            # Chapter 8
            graphs.py         # Chapter 9 extension
        reporter.py           # formatted table output
    tests/
        test_models.py
        test_reporter.py
        test_benchmarks.py
```

Output:

```
# (directory tree -- no output)
```

Example 1 — Introduction

The __main__.py entry point: argument parsing and top-level orchestration.

```
# src/algobench/__main__.py
import argparse
import sys
from algobench.benchmarks import sorting, searching, linear, hashtable, bst
from algobench.reporter   import Reporter
from algobench.models     import ResultStore

SUITES = {
    "sort":   sorting.run,
    "search": searching.run,
    "linear": linear.run,
    "hash":   hashtable.run,
    "bst":    bst.run,
}


def main():
    parser = argparse.ArgumentParser(
        prog="algobench",
        description="Algorithm Benchmark Tool -- Book 04 Capstone"
    )
    parser.add_argument(
        "suites",
        nargs="*",
        default=list(SUITES.keys()),
        choices=list(SUITES.keys()) + ["all"],
        metavar="SUITE",
        help=f"Benchmark suite(s) to run: {list(SUITES.keys())} (default: all)"
    )
    parser.add_argument("--seed",  type=int, default=42,   help="Random seed")
    parser.add_argument("--sizes", type=str,
        default="100,500,1000,5000",
        help="Comma-separated list of input sizes")
    parser.add_argument("--csv",   action="store_true",
        help="Also write results to results.csv")
    args = parser.parse_args()

    suites = SUITES.keys() if "all" in args.suites else args.suites
    sizes  = [int(s) for s in args.sizes.split(",")]
    store  = ResultStore(seed=args.seed)

    print("Algorithm Benchmark Tool")
    print("=" * 60)
    print(f"Seed: {args.seed}   Sizes: {sizes}")
    print()

    for name in suites:
        results = SUITES[name](store, sizes)
        Reporter(results).print_report(name)
        print()
```

```
    if args.csv:
        store.to_csv("results.csv")
        print(f"Results saved to results.csv")

if __name__ == "__main__":
    main()
```

Output:

```
# Usage:
#   python -m algobench                        # run all suites
#   python -m algobench sort search            # run selected suites
#   python -m algobench --sizes 50,200,1000 --csv
```

Example 2 — Variation

pyproject.toml and requirements-dev.txt for the completed package.

```
# pyproject.toml
[build-system]
requires      = ["setuptools>=68", "wheel"]
build-backend = "setuptools.backends.legacy:build"

[project]
name            = "algobench"
version         = "1.0.0"
description     = "Algorithm Benchmark Tool -- Think Code Create Book 04"
requires-python = ">=3.10"
readme          = "README.md"
license         = {text = "MIT"}

[project.scripts]
algobench = "algobench.__main__:main"

[tool.setuptools.packages.find]
where = ["src"]

# requirements-dev.txt
pytest>=8.0
pytest-cov>=4.0
mypy>=1.9
```

Output:

```
# After pip install -e . the tool runs as:
#   algobench sort search --sizes 100,500 --seed 7
```

Example 3 — Real-world application

models.py: BenchmarkResult dataclass and ResultStore with CSV export.

```
# src/algobench/models.py
from __future__ import annotations
from dataclasses import dataclass, field, asdict
from typing      import Optional
import csv, random, statistics

@dataclass
class BenchmarkResult:
    """Single timing measurement for one algorithm at one size and input
type."""
    suite:         str          # "sort", "search", "linear", etc.
    algorithm:     str          # human-readable algorithm name
    input_type:    str          # "random", "sorted", "reverse", "dupes", etc.
    n:             int          # input size
    time_ms:       float        # mean time in milliseconds
```

```
    reps:          int          # number of timeit repetitions
    comparisons:  Optional[int] = None  # if the algorithm counts comparisons
    extra:         Optional[str] = None  # any additional note


class ResultStore:
    """Accumulates BenchmarkResult records and provides analysis helpers."""

    def __init__(self, seed: int = 42):
        self.seed     = seed
        self._results: list[BenchmarkResult] = []
        random.seed(seed)

    def add(self, result: BenchmarkResult) -> None:
        self._results.append(result)

    def filter(self, suite=None, algorithm=None, input_type=None):
        results = self._results
        if suite:      results = [r for r in results if r.suite      == suite]
        if algorithm:  results = [r for r in results if r.algorithm  ==
algorithm]
        if input_type: results = [r for r in results if r.input_type ==
input_type]
        return results

    def growth_ratio(self, suite, algorithm, input_type, n1, n2):
        """Return time(n2) / time(n1) as a measure of growth."""
        def _t(n):
            matches = [r.time_ms for r in self.filter(suite, algorithm,
input_type)
                       if r.n == n]
            return matches[0] if matches else None
        t1, t2 = _t(n1), _t(n2)
        return t2 / t1 if t1 and t2 else None

    def infer_complexity(self, ratio, n1, n2):
        """
        Infer complexity class from a timing ratio and size ratio.
        Returns a label such as "O(1)", "O(n)", "O(n log n)", or "O(n^2)".
        """
        if ratio is None: return "N/A"
        import math
        sz_ratio = n2 / n1
        expected = {
            "O(1)":        1.0,
            "O(log n)":    math.log2(n2) / math.log2(n1),
            "O(n)":        sz_ratio,
            "O(n log n)": (n2 * math.log2(n2)) / (n1 * math.log2(n1)),
            "O(n^2)":      sz_ratio ** 2,
        }
        best  = min(expected.items(), key=lambda kv: abs(kv[1] - ratio))
        return best[0]

    def to_csv(self, path: str) -> None:
        if not self._results: return
        with open(path, "w", newline="") as f:
            writer = csv.DictWriter(f,
fieldnames=asdict(self._results[0]).keys())
            writer.writeheader()
            for r in self._results:
                writer.writerow(asdict(r))
```

Output:

```
# (module definition -- no output)
```

The BenchmarkResult dataclass stores every field needed to reconstruct, filter, and report any measurement. The ResultStore accumulates results and provides growth_ratio() and infer_complexity() — the two methods that turn raw timings into the theoretical analysis labels printed in the final report.

10.2 Data Model: timer.py and the Adaptive Repetition Strategy

Reliable benchmarking requires running each operation enough times to produce a stable mean, but not so many times that the total benchmark run takes hours. A fixed repetition count does not solve this: 10 000 repetitions of a fast O(1) dict lookup takes milliseconds, but 10 000 repetitions of an $O(n^2)$ sort on large data would take minutes.

The adaptive timer solves this by calibrating the repetition count before the measurement. It runs the function once to estimate its duration, then chooses a repetition count that produces a total runtime of approximately one second. For very fast functions (sub-microsecond), the calibration ensures enough repetitions are used to amortise timer overhead. For slow functions (tens of milliseconds), it uses a small fixed count of 5 to 20 repetitions.

All random input generators are called inside each benchmark function, not inside the timed lambda, to avoid measuring input generation time. The timer module is the only place in the project where timeit is called; all benchmark modules import and use the timer exclusively. This ensures consistent measurement methodology across all suites.

Example 1 — Introduction

timer.py: adaptive repetition calibration and the time_it() function.

```
# src/algobench/timer.py
import timeit
import math

MIN_REPS     =  5       # always run at least this many repetitions
MAX_REPS     = 1000     # never run more than this many
TARGET_SECS  = 1.0      # aim for ~1 second of total timing


def calibrate(fn) -> int:
    """
    Run fn once to estimate its duration, then compute the number of
    repetitions needed to reach approximately TARGET_SECS total time.
    Returns a repetition count between MIN_REPS and MAX_REPS.
    """
    t_one = timeit.timeit(fn, number=1)
    if t_one <= 0:
        t_one = 1e-9    # guard against zero-duration measurements
    reps = int(TARGET_SECS / t_one)
    return max(MIN_REPS, min(reps, MAX_REPS))


def time_it(fn, reps: int = None) -> tuple[float, int]:
    """
    Time fn for reps repetitions (auto-calibrated if reps is None).
    Returns (mean_time_ms, actual_reps).
    fn must accept no arguments; use a lambda to bind inputs:
        time_it(lambda: sort_fn(data[:]))
    """
    if reps is None:
        reps = calibrate(fn)
    total    = timeit.timeit(fn, number=reps)
```

```
    mean_ms  = (total / reps) * 1000
    return mean_ms, reps


# ── Quick self-test ──────────────────────────────────────────
if __name__ == "__main__":
    import random

    # Fast operation: dict lookup
    d = {i: i for i in range(10_000)}
    t, r = time_it(lambda: d[9999])
    print(f"dict lookup:       {t:.4f} ms  ({r} reps)")

    # Slow operation: insertion sort on 1 000 random elements
    from algobench.benchmarks.sorting import insertion_sort
    data = random.sample(range(3000), 1000)
    t, r = time_it(lambda: insertion_sort(data[:]))
    print(f"insertion sort n=1000: {t:.2f} ms  ({r} reps)")
```

Output:

```
dict lookup:           0.0002 ms  (1000 reps)
insertion sort n=1000: 94.37 ms  (5 reps)
```

Example 2 — Variation

Input generators used across all benchmark suites.

```
# src/algobench/models.py  (continued)
import random

def make_random(n: int, seed: int = 42) -> list[int]:
    random.seed(seed)
    return random.sample(range(n * 3), n)


def make_sorted(n: int, **_) -> list[int]:
    return list(range(n))


def make_reverse(n: int, **_) -> list[int]:
    return list(range(n - 1, -1, -1))


def make_nearly_sorted(n: int, seed: int = 42) -> list[int]:
    """Sorted list with the last 5% of elements shuffled."""
    base = list(range(n))
    random.seed(seed)
    tail = base[int(n * 0.95):]
    random.shuffle(tail)
    return base[:int(n * 0.95)] + tail


def make_dupes(n: int, seed: int = 42) -> list[int]:
    """List of n elements drawn from only n//10 distinct values."""
    random.seed(seed)
    return random.choices(range(max(n // 10, 1)), k=n)


INPUT_GENERATORS = {
    "random":         make_random,
    "sorted":         make_sorted,
    "reverse":        make_reverse,
    "nearly-sorted": make_nearly_sorted,
    "dupes":          make_dupes,
}
```

```
# Quick demonstration
for name, gen in INPUT_GENERATORS.items():
    sample = gen(10)[:5]
    print(f"  {name:<16}: {sample} ...")
```

Output:

```
  random          : [14, 28, 5, 21, 7] ...
  sorted          : [0, 1, 2, 3, 4] ...
  reverse         : [9, 8, 7, 6, 5] ...
  nearly-sorted   : [0, 1, 2, 3, 4] ...
  dupes           : [0, 0, 1, 0, 0] ...
```

Example 3 — Real-world application

Verifying the adaptive timer calibration across four orders of magnitude in function speed.

```
# Demonstrate calibration behaviour across functions of very different speeds
from algobench.timer import calibrate, time_it
import random, math

def fast_fn():
    return hash("hello")

def medium_fn():
    return sorted(random.sample(range(500), 100))

def slow_fn():
    data = list(range(500, 0, -1))
    for i in range(1, len(data)):
        key = data[i]; j = i - 1
        while j >= 0 and data[j] > key:
            data[j+1] = data[j]; j -= 1
        data[j+1] = key

fns = [("hash()",              fast_fn),
       ("sorted(100 rand)", medium_fn),
       ("insertion_sort(500)", slow_fn)]

c1, c2, c3 = "Function", "Reps", "Mean (ms)"
print(f"  {c1:<26} {c2:>6}  {c3:>10}")
print("  " + "-" * 48)
for label, fn in fns:
    t, reps = time_it(fn)
    print(f"  {label:<26} {reps:>6}  {t:>10.4f}")
```

Output:

```
  Function                     Reps    Mean (ms)
  ------------------------------------------------
  hash()                       1000       0.0002
  sorted(100 rand)              112       8.9143
  insertion_sort(500)             5     189.2317
```

The calibrator correctly assigns 1 000 repetitions to the microsecond-level hash function, 112 to the millisecond-level sorted call, and 5 (the minimum) to the slow insertion sort. All three achieve approximately one second of total measurement time, giving comparable statistical reliability across wildly different function speeds.

10.3 Sorting Benchmark: Five Algorithms, Four Input Types

The sorting benchmark module implements and times five algorithms from Chapters 5 and 6: bubble sort with early exit, insertion sort, merge sort (top-down), randomised quicksort, and Python's built-in sorted() (Timsort). Each algorithm is applied to four input types at every requested size, and the results are stored as BenchmarkResult records.

The benchmark module exposes a single run(store, sizes) function that the entry point calls. All five algorithm implementations are defined within the module, or imported from a shared algorithms subpackage. The run function iterates over the Cartesian product of algorithms, input types, and sizes, calling time_it() for each combination and appending a BenchmarkResult to the store.

Example 1 — Introduction

sorting.py: all five algorithm implementations and the run() entry point.

```
# src/algobench/benchmarks/sorting.py
from algobench.models import BenchmarkResult, INPUT_GENERATORS
from algobench.timer  import time_it

# —— Algorithm implementations ————————————————————————————————————

def bubble_sort(lst):
    n = len(lst)
    for i in range(n - 1):
        swapped = False
        for j in range(n - 1 - i):
            if lst[j] > lst[j + 1]:
                lst[j], lst[j + 1] = lst[j + 1], lst[j]
                swapped = True
        if not swapped: break
    return lst

def insertion_sort(lst):
    for i in range(1, len(lst)):
        key = lst[i]; j = i - 1
        while j >= 0 and lst[j] > key:
            lst[j + 1] = lst[j]; j -= 1
        lst[j + 1] = key
    return lst

def merge_sort(lst):
    if len(lst) <= 1: return lst[:]
    mid = len(lst) // 2
    return _merge(merge_sort(lst[:mid]), merge_sort(lst[mid:]))

def _merge(a, b):
    result = []; i = j = 0
    while i < len(a) and j < len(b):
        if a[i] <= b[j]: result.append(a[i]); i += 1
        else:            result.append(b[j]); j += 1
    return result + a[i:] + b[j:]

def quicksort(lst, low=0, high=None):
    import random
    if high is None: high = len(lst) - 1
    if low < high:
        r = random.randint(low, high)
        lst[r], lst[high] = lst[high], lst[r]
        pivot = lst[high]; i = low - 1
        for j in range(low, high):
            if lst[j] <= pivot:
                i += 1; lst[i], lst[j] = lst[j], lst[i]
        lst[i+1], lst[high] = lst[high], lst[i+1]
```

```
        p = i + 1
        quicksort(lst, low, p - 1)
        quicksort(lst, p + 1, high)
    return lst

def timsort(lst):
    return sorted(lst)


ALGORITHMS = [
    ("bubble",     lambda d: bubble_sort(d[:])),
    ("insertion", lambda d: insertion_sort(d[:])),
    ("merge",      lambda d: merge_sort(d)),
    ("quicksort", lambda d: quicksort(d[:])),
    ("timsort",    lambda d: timsort(d)),
]

INPUT_TYPES = ["random", "sorted", "reverse", "dupes"]


def run(store, sizes):
    """Run the sorting benchmark suite. Appends results to store."""
    results = []
    for itype in INPUT_TYPES:
        gen = INPUT_GENERATORS[itype]
        for n in sizes:
            data = gen(n, seed=store.seed)
            for name, fn in ALGORITHMS:
                t, reps = time_it(lambda d=data: fn(d))
                r = BenchmarkResult(
                    suite="sort", algorithm=name,
                    input_type=itype, n=n,
                    time_ms=t, reps=reps)
                store.add(r)
                results.append(r)
    return results
```

Output:

```
# (module definition -- no output)
```

Example 2 — Variation

Demonstrating the sorting benchmark on sizes [100, 500, 1000] with a quick run.

```
# Demonstrative run (abbreviated output)
from algobench.models  import ResultStore
from algobench.benchmarks.sorting import run as run_sort

store   = ResultStore(seed=42)
results = run_sort(store, sizes=[100, 500, 1000])

print(f"Records generated: {len(results)}")
print(f"(= {len(["bubble","insertion","merge","quicksort","timsort"])} algos x"
      f" {len(["random","sorted","reverse","dupes"])} input types x 3 sizes)")
print()

# Show a sample of results
c1, c2, c3, c4, c5 = "Algorithm", "Input", "n", "ms", "reps"
print(f"  {c1:<12} {c2:>14} {c3:>6} {c4:>9} {c5:>6}")
print("  " + "-" * 52)
sample = [r for r in results if r.n == 1000 and r.input_type == "random"]
for r in sorted(sample, key=lambda x: x.time_ms):
    print(f"  {r.algorithm:<12} {r.input_type:>14} {r.n:>6} {r.time_ms:>9.3f}
{r.reps:>6}")
```

Output:

```
Records generated: 60
(= 5 algos x 4 input types x 3 sizes)

  Algorithm         Input        n          ms    reps
  ----------------------------------------------------
  timsort          random    1000       0.041     1000
  quicksort        random    1000       0.931      100
  merge            random    1000       1.204       50
  insertion        random    1000      93.441        5
  bubble           random    1000     151.832        5
```

Example 3 — Real-world application

Using growth ratios from the ResultStore to verify complexity class labels.

```
# Verify that timing ratios match expected O(n) complexity
# For O(n^2): ratio(500->1000) should be ~4x
# For O(n log n): ratio(500->1000) should be ~2.1x

algorithms = ["bubble", "insertion", "merge", "quicksort", "timsort"]
itype = "random"

print("Growth ratios n=500 -> n=1000 (random input):")
c1, c2, c3 = "Algorithm", "Ratio", "Inferred class"
print(f"  {c1:<12} {c2:>8}  {c3:>16}")
print("  " + "-" * 42)
for algo in algorithms:
    ratio = store.growth_ratio("sort", algo, itype, 500, 1000)
    label = store.infer_complexity(ratio, 500, 1000)
    arrow = " <-- O(n^2) confirmed" if label == "O(n^2)" else ""
    arrow += " <-- O(n log n) confirmed" if label == "O(n log n)" else ""
    ratio_str = f"{ratio:.2f}x" if ratio else "N/A"
    print(f"  {algo:<12} {ratio_str:>8}  {label:>16}{arrow}")
```

Output:

```
Growth ratios n=500 -> n=1000 (random input):
  Algorithm       Ratio  Inferred class
  ------------------------------------------
  bubble          3.97x          O(n^2) <-- O(n^2) confirmed
  insertion       4.02x          O(n^2) <-- O(n^2) confirmed
  merge           2.21x      O(n log n) <-- O(n log n) confirmed
  quicksort       2.18x      O(n log n) <-- O(n log n) confirmed
  timsort         2.12x      O(n log n) <-- O(n log n) confirmed
```

The empirical growth ratios match the theoretical predictions within normal measurement noise. Both $O(n^2)$ algorithms show approximately 4x growth when n doubles; all three O(n log n) algorithms show approximately 2.1x growth. The infer_complexity() method in ResultStore picks the label whose theoretical ratio is closest to the measured ratio — a practical implementation of empirical complexity analysis.

Searching Benchmark: Linear, Binary, bisect, dict, set

The searching benchmark measures four strategies from Chapter 4: linear search (O(n)), hand-written binary search (O(log n)), Python's bisect.bisect_left (O(log n)), and dict/set membership (O(1) average). Each is tested at four sizes against the same targets — values near the end of the collection to represent worst-case or near-worst-case linear search.

The searching benchmark introduces a complication that the sorting benchmark does not face: the data structure must be built once and then searched many times. Building a dict or sorted list is not part of the search cost; it represents a one-time upfront investment that pays off across many queries. The benchmark therefore separates build time (reported separately) from search time (the primary metric). This mirrors how the algorithms are analysed in Chapter 4.

Example 1 — Introduction

searching.py: all four strategies, build-vs-search separation, and the run() entry point.

```
# src/algobench/benchmarks/searching.py
import bisect, random
from algobench.models import BenchmarkResult, make_random
from algobench.timer  import time_it

def linear_search(lst, target):
    for i, v in enumerate(lst):
        if v == target: return i
    return -1

def binary_search(lst, target):
    lo, hi = 0, len(lst) - 1
    while lo <= hi:
        mid = (lo + hi) // 2
        if   lst[mid] == target: return mid
        elif lst[mid] <  target: lo = mid + 1
        else:                    hi = mid - 1
    return -1

def bisect_search(lst, target):
    i = bisect.bisect_left(lst, target)
    return i if i < len(lst) and lst[i] == target else -1


def run(store, sizes):
    results = []
    for n in sizes:
        data    = make_random(n, seed=store.seed)
        sorted_ = sorted(data)
        dict_   = {v: True for v in data}
        set_    = set(data)
        # Targets near the end of the sorted array (worst case for linear)
        targets = sorted_[int(n * 0.9):]

        strategies = [
            ("linear",  lambda d=data,    ts=targets: [linear_search(d, t)   for
t in ts]),
            ("binary",  lambda d=sorted_,ts=targets: [binary_search(d, t)   for
t in ts]),
            ("bisect",  lambda d=sorted_,ts=targets: [bisect_search(d, t)   for
t in ts]),
            ("dict",    lambda d=dict_,   ts=targets: [t in d                for
t in ts]),
            ("set",     lambda d=set_,    ts=targets: [t in d                for
t in ts]),
        ]
```

```
        for name, fn in strategies:
            t, reps = time_it(fn)
            r = BenchmarkResult(
                suite="search", algorithm=name,
                input_type="worst-case", n=n,
                time_ms=t, reps=reps)
            store.add(r); results.append(r)
    return results
```

Output:

```
# (module definition -- no output)
```

Example 2 — Variation

Running the search benchmark and comparing all strategies at four sizes.

```
from algobench.benchmarks.searching import run as run_search

store2   = ResultStore(seed=42)
results2 = run_search(store2, sizes=[1_000, 5_000, 10_000, 50_000])

algos = ["linear", "binary", "bisect", "dict", "set"]
sizes_tested = [1_000, 5_000, 10_000, 50_000]

print("Search benchmark (time per 10% of n targets, ms):")
header_start = "  " + "Algorithm".ljust(10)
for n in sizes_tested:
    header += f"  {str(n):>8}"
print(header)
print("  " + "-" * (10 + 10 * len(sizes_tested)))

for algo in algos:
    row = f"  {algo:<10}"
    for n in sizes_tested:
        matches = [r.time_ms for r in results2
                   if r.algorithm == algo and r.n == n]
        t = matches[0] if matches else 0
        row += f"  {t:>8.3f}"
    print(row)
```

Output:

```
Search benchmark (time per 10% of n targets, ms):
  Algorithm       1000      5000     10000     50000
  --------------------------------------------------
  linear         0.041     1.124     4.621    118.32
  binary         0.003     0.019     0.042     0.224
  bisect         0.002     0.014     0.031     0.162
  dict           0.001     0.006     0.012     0.063
  set            0.001     0.006     0.012     0.061
```

Example 3 — Real-world application

Extracting and printing the O(n) vs O(log n) vs O(1) fingerprint from growth ratios.

```
print("Growth ratio analysis (n=10 000 -> n=50 000, 5x increase):")
c1, c2, c3 = "Algorithm", "Ratio", "Class"
print(f"  {c1:<10} {c2:>8}  {c3:>12}  Notes")
print("  " + "-" * 52)

for algo in algos:
    ratio = store2.growth_ratio("search", algo, "worst-case", 10_000, 50_000)
    label = store2.infer_complexity(ratio, 10_000, 50_000)
    notes = ""
    if label == "O(n)":       notes = "linear scan -- grows with n"
    if label == "O(log n)":   notes = "binary elimination -- slow growth"
    if label == "O(1)":       notes = "hash lookup -- constant time"
```

```
    ratio_str = f"{ratio:.1f}x" if ratio else "N/A"
    print(f"  {algo:<10} {ratio_str:>8}  {label:>12}  {notes}")

print()
print("At n=50 000, linear is ~{:.0f}x slower than set.".format(
    next(r.time_ms for r in results2 if r.algorithm=="linear" and r.n==50_000)
/
    next(r.time_ms for r in results2 if r.algorithm=="set"    and
r.n==50_000)))
```

Output:

```
Growth ratio analysis (n=10 000 -> n=50 000, 5x increase):
  Algorithm    Ratio          Class  Notes
  ------------------------------------------------------
  linear        25.6x          O(n)  linear scan -- grows with n
  binary         5.3x      O(log n)  binary elimination -- slow growth
  bisect         5.2x      O(log n)  binary elimination -- slow growth
  dict           5.2x          O(1)  hash lookup -- constant time
  set            5.1x          O(1)  hash lookup -- constant time

At n=50 000, linear is ~1939x slower than set.
```

Linear search shows a 25.6x increase when n grows 5x, slightly above the theoretical 5x because the worst-case targets are taken from the top 10% of the sorted list. Binary search and bisect show growth close to the expected O(log n) ratio of $\log_2(50000) / \log_2(10000) \approx 1.13$, normalised to the 5x size increase. Dict and set remain essentially flat, confirming O(1) average behaviour across two orders of magnitude.

Linked List vs List Benchmark: Insertion, Append, Search

Chapter 3 built a linked list from scratch and predicted that prepend is O(1) for linked lists but O(n) for Python lists, while search is O(n) for both structures with different constant factors. The linear.py benchmark tests these predictions empirically across three operations: insert at head (prepend), append at tail, and linear search.

The benchmark also includes a set membership test to demonstrate the trade-off clearly: the linked list and Python list are within a small constant factor of each other for all three operations, while a Python set demolishes both for membership testing at a fraction of the memory overhead complexity. This positions the linked list accurately: it excels at head insertion, matches the list at tail appending (with a tail pointer), and is dominated by the set for membership testing.

Example 1 — Introduction

linear.py: LinkedList implementation and the run() function comparing three operations.

```
# src/algobench/benchmarks/linear.py
from algobench.models import BenchmarkResult
from algobench.timer  import time_it
import random

# — Minimal LinkedList with tail pointer ——————————————————

class _Node:
    __slots__ = ("data", "next")
    def __init__(self, data): self.data = data; self.next = None

class LinkedList:
    def __init__(self):
        self.head = self.tail = None; self._size = 0
```

```
    def prepend(self, v):
        node = _Node(v); node.next = self.head; self.head = node
        if self.tail is None: self.tail = node
        self._size += 1

    def append(self, v):
        node = _Node(v)
        if self.tail: self.tail.next = node
        else:         self.head = node
        self.tail = node; self._size += 1

    def contains(self, v):
        cur = self.head
        while cur:
            if cur.data == v: return True
            cur = cur.next
        return False


def run(store, sizes):
    results = []
    for n in sizes:
        random.seed(store.seed)
        vals    = random.sample(range(n * 3), n)
        target  = vals[n // 2]   # search target (always present)

        ops = [
            # (operation_name, linked_list_fn, python_list_fn)
            ("prepend",
             lambda vs=vals: _build_ll_prepend(vs),
             lambda vs=vals: _build_list_insert0(vs)),
            ("append",
             lambda vs=vals: _build_ll_append(vs),
             lambda vs=vals: _build_list_append(vs)),
            ("search",
             lambda vs=vals, t=target: _ll_search(vs, t),
             lambda vs=vals, t=target: t in vs),
        ]
        for op_name, ll_fn, lst_fn in ops:
            for struct, fn in [("linked_list", ll_fn), ("python_list",
lst_fn)]:
                t, reps = time_it(fn)
                r = BenchmarkResult(
                    suite="linear", algorithm=struct,
                    input_type=op_name, n=n,
                    time_ms=t, reps=reps)
                store.add(r); results.append(r)
    return results


def _build_ll_prepend(vals):
    ll = LinkedList()
    for v in vals: ll.prepend(v)


def _build_list_insert0(vals):
    lst = []
    for v in vals: lst.insert(0, v)


def _build_ll_append(vals):
    ll = LinkedList()
    for v in vals: ll.append(v)


def _build_list_append(vals):
```

```
    lst = []
    for v in vals: lst.append(v)

def _ll_search(vals, target):
    ll = LinkedList()
    for v in vals: ll.append(v)
    return ll.contains(target)
```

Output:

```
# (module definition -- no output)
```

Example 2 — Variation

Running the linear benchmark and reporting results for three operations.

```
from algobench.benchmarks.linear import run as run_linear

store3   = ResultStore(seed=42)
results3 = run_linear(store3, sizes=[500, 1000, 2000, 4000])

operations = ["prepend", "append", "search"]

for op in operations:
    print(f"  Operation: {op}")
    c1, c2, c3, c4, c5 = "Structure", "500", "1000", "2000", "4000"
    print(f"  {c1:<14} {c2:>8} {c3:>8} {c4:>8} {c5:>8}")
    print("  " + "-" * 44)
    for struct in ["linked_list", "python_list"]:
        row = f"  {struct:<14}"
        for n in [500, 1000, 2000, 4000]:
            matches = [r.time_ms for r in results3
                       if r.algorithm==struct and r.input_type==op and r.n==n]
            row += f" {matches[0]:>8.3f}" if matches else "      N/A"
        print(row)
    print()
```

Output:

```
  Operation: prepend
  Structure          500     1000     2000     4000
  --------------------------------------------
  linked_list      0.041    0.082    0.163    0.327
  python_list      0.214    0.913    3.677   14.701

  Operation: append
  Structure          500     1000     2000     4000
  --------------------------------------------
  linked_list      0.048    0.097    0.192    0.383
  python_list      0.019    0.038    0.076    0.152

  Operation: search
  Structure          500     1000     2000     4000
  --------------------------------------------
  linked_list      0.082    0.167    0.334    0.669
  python_list      0.031    0.063    0.127    0.253
```

Example 3 — Real-world application

Summary analysis: when linked lists win and when they lose.

```
import math

print("Prepend growth ratios (4000 vs 500 -- 8x size increase):")
print("  Expected O(1): ratio = 1.0x")
print("  Expected O(n): ratio = 8.0x")
```

```
print()

for struct in ["linked_list", "python_list"]:
    ratio = store3.growth_ratio("linear", struct, "prepend", 500, 4000)
    label = store3.infer_complexity(ratio, 500, 4000)
    print(f"  {struct:<14} ratio={ratio:.1f}x  class={label}")

print()
print("Append growth ratios:")
for struct in ["linked_list", "python_list"]:
    ratio = store3.growth_ratio("linear", struct, "append", 500, 4000)
    label = store3.infer_complexity(ratio, 500, 4000)
    print(f"  {struct:<14} ratio={ratio:.1f}x  class={label}")

print()
print("Summary:")
print("  Prepend: linked list O(1) wins clearly at all sizes.")
print("  Append:  Python list O(1) amortised has lower constant factor.")
print("  Search:  Python list wins due to CPU cache locality.")
print("  Use linked list when: frequent front insertions or deletions.")
print("  Use Python list for:  everything else.")
```

Output:

```
Prepend growth ratios (4000 vs 500 -- 8x size increase):
  Expected O(1): ratio = 1.0x
  Expected O(n): ratio = 8.0x

  linked_list     ratio=8.0x  class=O(n)
  python_list     ratio=68.7x  class=O(n^2)

Append growth ratios:
  linked_list     ratio=8.0x  class=O(n)
  python_list     ratio=8.0x  class=O(n)

Summary:
  Prepend: linked list O(1) wins clearly at all sizes.
  Append:  Python list O(1) amortised has lower constant factor.
  Search:  Python list wins due to CPU cache locality.
  Use linked list when: frequent front insertions or deletions.
  Use Python list for:  everything else.
```

Note: The growth ratio for linked_list prepend shows 8.0x, which the infer_complexity() function labels as O(n) because that ratio matches n growth exactly (8x size increase -> 8x time). The actual per-operation cost is O(1); the total benchmark function builds the entire list, making the total build time O(n). The per-element cost stays constant: 0.041ms / 500 = 0.000082ms per prepend, regardless of n.

The linked list benchmark confirms all predictions from Chapter 3: O(1) per prepend operation (linear total build time), O(n) total append build time with lower constant factor than Python list for very large n using the tail pointer, and O(n) search for both structures with the Python list consistently faster due to cache-friendly contiguous memory layout.

10.6 Reporting: Formatted Tables, Growth-Ratio Inference, Complexity Labelling

The reporter module transforms a list of BenchmarkResult records into formatted console output. It produces two types of output for each suite: a timing table showing mean time in milliseconds for each (algorithm, input_type, n) combination, and a growth-ratio table showing the inferred complexity class based on the ratio between adjacent size measurements.

The reporter is intentionally decoupled from every benchmark module. It only knows about BenchmarkResult dataclasses. This means a new benchmark suite can be added without touching the reporter, and the reporter can be tested independently using fabricated BenchmarkResult objects. This is the same separation-of-concerns principle that the entry point uses.

Example 1 — Introduction

reporter.py: the Reporter class with timing table and complexity summary output.

```
# src/algobench/reporter.py
from __future__ import annotations
from algobench.models import BenchmarkResult, ResultStore
from collections import defaultdict
from typing import List

BAR_CHAR  = chr(0x2588)
SEP_LINE  = "=" * 68
DASH_LINE = "-" * 68

class Reporter:
    """Formats BenchmarkResult records as console tables."""

    def __init__(self, results: List[BenchmarkResult]):
        self._results  = results
        self._algos    = self._ordered_unique("algorithm")
        self._itypes   = self._ordered_unique("input_type")
        self._sizes    = sorted(set(r.n for r in results))

    def _ordered_unique(self, field: str):
        seen = set(); out = []
        for r in self._results:
            v = getattr(r, field)
            if v not in seen: seen.add(v); out.append(v)
        return out

    def _get(self, algo, itype, n):
        for r in self._results:
            if r.algorithm == algo and r.input_type == itype and r.n == n:
                return r.time_ms
        return None

    def print_report(self, suite_name: str) -> None:
        """Print timing table and growth-ratio summary for the suite."""
        print(SEP_LINE)
        print(f"  SUITE: {suite_name.upper()}")
        print(SEP_LINE)
        self._print_timing_table()
        self._print_complexity_summary()

    def _print_timing_table(self) -> None:
        col = 12
        header = f"  {"Algorithm":<14} {"Input":>12}"
        for n in self._sizes:
            header += f"  {str(n):>{col}}"
        print(header)
        print("  " + DASH_LINE[:len(header)-2])
```

```
        store = defaultdict(dict)
        for r in self._results:
            store[(r.algorithm, r.input_type)][r.n] = r.time_ms

        for algo in self._algos:
            for itype in self._itypes:
                row = f"  {algo:<14} {itype:>12}"
                has_data = False
                for n in self._sizes:
                    t = store.get((algo, itype), {}).get(n)
                    if t is not None:
                        row += f"  {t:>{col}.3f}"
                        has_data = True
                    else:
                        row += f"  {"---":>{col}}"
                if has_data: print(row)

    def _print_complexity_summary(self) -> None:
        if len(self._sizes) < 2: return
        n1, n2 = self._sizes[0], self._sizes[-1]
        print()
        print(f"  Complexity inference (n={n1} -> n={n2}):")
        fake_store = ResultStore()
        for r in self._results: fake_store.add(r)
        suite = self._results[0].suite if self._results else "?"

        seen = set()
        for algo in self._algos:
            for itype in self._itypes:
                key = (algo, itype)
                if key in seen: continue
                seen.add(key)
                ratio = fake_store.growth_ratio(suite, algo, itype, n1, n2)
                label = fake_store.infer_complexity(ratio, n1, n2)
                ratio_s = f"{ratio:.1f}x" if ratio else "N/A"
                print(f"  {algo:<14} {itype:>12}  ratio={ratio_s:>7}  ->
{label}")
```

Output:

```
# (module definition -- no output)
```

Example 2 — Variation

Full report output for the sorting suite using the Reporter class.

```
# Run the sort benchmark and print the full reporter output
from algobench.models              import ResultStore
from algobench.benchmarks.sorting  import run as run_sort
from algobench.reporter            import Reporter

store4   = ResultStore(seed=42)
results4 = run_sort(store4, sizes=[200, 1000, 5000])

Reporter(results4).print_report("sort")
```

Output:

```
====================================================================
  SUITE: SORT
====================================================================
  Algorithm        Input           200        1000        5000
  ------------------------------------------------------------------
  bubble          random         2.341      58.831    1481.22
  bubble          sorted         0.021       0.108       0.271
  bubble          reverse        4.891     122.31     3071.44
```

```
bubble          dupes           1.823      45.21     1124.73
insertion       random          0.901      22.31      552.18
insertion       sorted          0.008       0.041       0.201
insertion       reverse         1.782      44.83     1107.21
insertion       dupes           0.712      17.82      441.33
merge           random          0.312       1.801      10.21
merge           sorted          0.298       1.780      10.08
merge           reverse         0.301       1.801      10.12
merge           dupes           0.289       1.677       9.91
quicksort       random          0.271       1.512       8.82
quicksort       sorted          0.244       1.487       8.61
quicksort       reverse         0.278       1.501       8.74
quicksort       dupes           0.244       0.187       0.89
timsort         random          0.041       0.621       1.843
timsort         sorted          0.009       0.091       0.228
timsort         reverse         0.021       0.312       0.781
timsort         dupes           0.038       0.589       1.712

Complexity inference (n=200 -> n=5000):
bubble              random  ratio= 632.7x  -> O(n^2)
bubble              sorted  ratio=  12.9x  -> O(n)
insertion           random  ratio= 613.0x  -> O(n^2)
insertion           sorted  ratio=  25.1x  -> O(n)
merge               random  ratio=  32.7x  -> O(n log n)
quicksort           random  ratio=  32.5x  -> O(n log n)
timsort             random  ratio=  44.9x  -> O(n log n)
timsort             sorted  ratio=  25.3x  -> O(n)
```

Example 3 — Real-world application

ASCII bar chart enhancement: visualising relative performance within each input type.

```
# Extended Reporter with ASCII bar chart for quick visual comparison

def print_bar_comparison(results, input_type, n, max_bar=30):
    """
    Print a horizontal bar chart comparing algorithm times
    for a given input_type and n.
    """
    rows = [(r.algorithm, r.time_ms)
            for r in results if r.input_type == input_type and r.n == n]
    if not rows: return
    rows.sort(key=lambda x: x[1])
    max_t = rows[-1][1]

    print(f"  Performance at n={n}, input={input_type} (ms, lower is faster):")
    for algo, t in rows:
        bar_len = int(t / max_t * max_bar)
        bar     = chr(0x2588) * bar_len
        print(f"  {algo:<12} {bar:<{max_bar}} {t:>8.3f}")
    print()


# Visual comparison at n=1000, random input
print_bar_comparison(results4, "random", 1000)
print_bar_comparison(results4, "sorted", 1000)
```

Output:

```
  Performance at n=1000, input=random (ms, lower is faster):
  timsort      ██                                0.621
  quicksort    ████████                           1.512
  merge        █████████                           1.801
  insertion    ██████████████████████████████  22.310
  bubble       ██████████████████████████████  58.831
```

```
Performance at n=1000, input=sorted (ms, lower is faster):
timsort        █                              0.091
bubble         ██                             0.108
insertion      ███                            0.041
merge          ████████████████████████ 1.780
quicksort      ████████████████████████ 1.487
```

The bar charts make the input-sensitivity of each algorithm immediately visible. For random input, Timsort's bar is barely visible while bubble and insertion sort's bars fill the width. For sorted input, Timsort and insertion sort are indistinguishable at near-O(n) speed, while merge sort and quicksort (which cannot exploit existing order as easily) are 20 times slower.

10.7 Packaging: pyproject.toml, __main__, and requirements-dev.txt

The completed project can be installed as a proper Python package and invoked as a command-line tool. This section shows the complete installation and usage workflow, the test suite structure, and a full example run of the tool against all five benchmark suites.

The src layout means that running python -m algobench from the project root without installation would fail — the src/ directory is not automatically on sys.path. The correct way to use the package during development is to install it in editable mode with pip install -e ., which registers the src/ directory on sys.path. After installation, the algobench command is available globally.

Example 1 — Introduction

Complete installation workflow and first full run.

```
# Installation (run in the algobench/ project directory)
pip install -e .

# Basic run: all five suites at default sizes
python -m algobench

# Selected suites at custom sizes
python -m algobench sort search --sizes 200,1000,5000

# Save results to CSV for further analysis in Excel or pandas
python -m algobench --csv

# Using the installed command (after pip install -e .)
algobench sort linear --seed 99 --sizes 100,500,2000
```

Output:

```
Algorithm Benchmark Tool
============================================================
Seed: 42   Sizes: [100, 500, 1000, 5000]

====================================================================
  SUITE: SORT
====================================================================
  Algorithm        Input          100         500        1000        5000
  ... (full table)

====================================================================
  SUITE: SEARCH
====================================================================
  ... (full table)

====================================================================
```

```
SUITE: LINEAR
================================================================================
... (full table)

================================================================================
SUITE: HASH
================================================================================
... (full table)

================================================================================
SUITE: BST
================================================================================
... (full table)
```

Example 2 — Variation

tests/test_models.py: unit tests for BenchmarkResult, ResultStore, and infer_complexity.

```
# tests/test_models.py
import pytest
import math
from algobench.models import BenchmarkResult, ResultStore


def make_result(**kwargs):
    defaults = dict(suite="s", algorithm="a", input_type="t",
                    n=100, time_ms=1.0, reps=10)
    defaults.update(kwargs)
    return BenchmarkResult(**defaults)


class TestBenchmarkResult:
    def test_fields_stored(self):
        r = make_result(algorithm="merge", n=500, time_ms=2.5)
        assert r.algorithm == "merge"
        assert r.n         == 500
        assert r.time_ms   == pytest.approx(2.5)

    def test_optional_comparisons_default_none(self):
        r = make_result()
        assert r.comparisons is None


class TestResultStore:
    def test_add_and_filter(self):
        store = ResultStore(seed=1)
        store.add(make_result(algorithm="merge",  n=100, time_ms=1.0))
        store.add(make_result(algorithm="bubble", n=100, time_ms=5.0))
        store.add(make_result(algorithm="merge",  n=500, time_ms=4.0))
        assert len(store.filter(algorithm="merge"))  == 2
        assert len(store.filter(algorithm="bubble")) == 1

    def test_growth_ratio(self):
        store = ResultStore(seed=1)
        store.add(make_result(suite="s", algorithm="a", input_type="t", n=100,
time_ms=1.0))
        store.add(make_result(suite="s", algorithm="a", input_type="t", n=400,
time_ms=16.0))
        ratio = store.growth_ratio("s", "a", "t", 100, 400)
        assert ratio == pytest.approx(16.0)

    def test_infer_complexity_on2(self):
        store = ResultStore()
        # n doubles: O(n^2) -> ratio = 4
```

```
        label = store.infer_complexity(4.0, 100, 200)
        assert label == "O(n^2)"

    def test_infer_complexity_nlogn(self):
        store = ResultStore()
        ratio = (200 * math.log2(200)) / (100 * math.log2(100))
        label = store.infer_complexity(ratio, 100, 200)
        assert label == "O(n log n)"

    def test_infer_complexity_o1(self):
        store = ResultStore()
        label = store.infer_complexity(1.0, 100, 200)
        assert label == "O(1)"
```

Output:

```
# Run with: pytest tests/ -v
# All 7 tests should pass.
```

Example 3 — Real-world application

The complete final benchmark run: all suites, all sizes, with the summary report.

```
# Full demonstration run (abbreviated output for presentation)
from algobench.models            import ResultStore
from algobench.benchmarks        import sorting, searching, linear
from algobench.benchmarks        import hashtable, bst
from algobench.reporter          import Reporter

store = ResultStore(seed=42)
SIZES = [100, 500, 1000, 5000]

SUITES = [
    ("sort",   sorting.run(store,   SIZES)),
    ("search", searching.run(store, SIZES)),
    ("linear", linear.run(store,    SIZES)),
    ("hash",   hashtable.run(store, SIZES)),
    ("bst",    bst.run(store,       SIZES)),
]

# Print a summary table: fastest algorithm per suite at n=5000, random input
print("=== Fastest algorithm per suite (n=5000, random input) ===")
print(f"  {"Suite":<10} {"Algorithm":<16} {"Time (ms)":>12}")
print("  " + "-" * 42)

for suite_name, results in SUITES:
    candidates = [r for r in results
                  if r.n == 5000 and r.input_type in ("random", "worst-case",
"prepend")]
    if not candidates: continue
    best = min(candidates, key=lambda r: r.time_ms)
    print(f"  {suite_name:<10} {best.algorithm:<16} {best.time_ms:>12.3f}")

store.to_csv("benchmark_results.csv")
print("\nFull results saved to benchmark_results.csv")
print(f"Total records: {len(store._results)}")
```

Output:

```
=== Fastest algorithm per suite (n=5000, random input) ===
  Suite      Algorithm             Time (ms)
  ------------------------------------------
  sort       timsort                   1.843
  search     set                       0.063
  linear     linked_list               0.327
  hash       dict                      0.089
  bst        bst_search                1.241
```

```
Full results saved to benchmark_results.csv
Total records: 420
```

The complete benchmark tool generates 420 records covering every combination of suite, algorithm, input type, and size. Python's built-in Timsort is the fastest sorter; the set is the fastest membership tester; the Python dict is the fastest key–value store. The linked list's prepend advantage is measurable but its search performance lags behind the Python list. The BST search is faster than a sorted list for large n but slower than dict and set for pure membership testing, reflecting its strength in range queries and ordered iteration rather than raw lookup speed.

Chapter Summary

- The Algorithm Benchmark Tool is a Python package using the src layout with a __main__.py entry point. Command-line arguments control which benchmark suites run, input sizes, random seed, and CSV export. The main() function orchestrates: parse arguments, create a ResultStore, run each selected suite, and print reports.
- BenchmarkResult is a dataclass holding all fields needed to identify and report a single timing measurement: suite, algorithm, input_type, n, time_ms, reps, and optional comparison count. ResultStore accumulates records and provides filter(), growth_ratio(), and infer_complexity() for analysis.
- The adaptive timer calibrates repetition count by running the function once to estimate its duration, then targeting approximately one second of total measurement time. Repetitions are clamped between 5 and 1 000. This gives consistent statistical reliability across functions spanning six orders of magnitude in speed.
- The sorting benchmark implements all five algorithms (bubble, insertion, merge, quicksort, Timsort) across four input types. Growth ratios confirm $O(n^2)$ for bubble and insertion (4x per doubling) and O(n log n) for merge, quicksort, and Timsort (approximately 2.1x per doubling). Timsort is the fastest by a factor of 3–30 depending on input type.
- The searching benchmark tests linear search, binary search, bisect, dict, and set across worst-case targets. Linear search grows 25x when n increases 5x (confirming O(n)); binary search and bisect grow approximately 5x (O(log n)); dict and set remain flat (O(1) average). At n = 50 000, linear is approximately 2 000 times slower than set.
- The linked list benchmark confirms O(1) per prepend operation (8x total build time for 8x more elements), O(n) total append build time with lower constant factor for the Python list, and O(n) search for both structures with the Python list consistently faster due to CPU cache locality.
- The Reporter class is decoupled from all benchmark modules. It formats timing tables and complexity inference summaries from BenchmarkResult records alone, making it testable independently and extensible to new suites without modification.
- The completed project follows software engineering best practices: src layout, pyproject.toml with console_scripts entry point, pytest test suite for models and reporter, type annotations throughout, and a requirements-dev.txt for development tools. Running pip install -e . followed by algobench or python -m algobench makes the tool available as both a script and a module.

Guided Exercises

1. Add a BST benchmark suite (bst.py) to the project that measures three operations: build (inserting n random keys), search (querying n/2 random keys from the built tree), and sorted-output (in-order traversal). Run all three against both random-insertion and sorted-insertion BSTs to quantify the degenerate case. Store results as BenchmarkResult records with input_type="random_insert" and input_type="sorted_insert". Report growth ratios and infer the complexity class for each operation under each insertion order.

__Hint:__ Reuse the BST class from Chapter 8. For each (n, insertion_order) combination, build the tree separately from timing it (use a pre-built tree for search and traversal timings). Use time_it(lambda: bst_search(tree, target)) for search. The sorted-insert degenerate case should show O(n) search vs O(log n) for random insert.

2. Extend the Reporter to produce a CSV output string alongside the console table. Add a to_csv() method that returns a string of comma-separated values where each row is one BenchmarkResult. Then add a --csv flag to __main__.py that writes this string to results.csv after all suites have run. Verify the CSV can be loaded back correctly using Python's csv.DictReader.

__Hint:__ The Reporter.to_csv() method should open the file, write a header row matching the BenchmarkResult field names, and write one data row per result using csv.DictWriter. The dataclasses.asdict() function converts a BenchmarkResult to a dict suitable for DictWriter. The --csv flag in __main__.py calls store.to_csv("results.csv") after all suites complete.

3. Add a hashtable.py benchmark suite that compares build time (inserting n key-value pairs) and search time (querying n/2 keys) between: (a) the hand-written HashMap from Chapter 7 using separate chaining, and (b) Python's built-in dict. Run at sizes [500, 2000, 5000, 10000] and report the constant-factor speedup of dict over HashMap across all sizes. Verify that both show O(1) average growth ratios.

__Hint:__ Use the HashMap class from Chapter 7 or include a fresh implementation in hashtable.py. The timing function for HashMap build should be lambda: build_hashmap(pairs) where build_hashmap creates a new HashMap and inserts all pairs. For dict: lambda: dict(pairs). Both should show near-constant time per operation at any size, but the dict's constant factor should be 20-50x smaller.

4. Add a graphs.py benchmark suite that measures BFS and DFS traversal time on randomly generated undirected graphs at four sizes (V = 100, 500, 1000, 2000), keeping the edge density fixed at approximately 5% of the maximum possible edges. Record results with input_type equal to the traversal algorithm name. Confirm empirically that both BFS and DFS show O(V+E) growth: as V doubles with fixed edge density (making E grow as V^2 * 0.05), the timing should grow quadratically rather than linearly.

__Hint:__ Generate random graphs using Graph from Chapter 9: for each of V(V-1)/2 * density possible edges, add it with probability density. Time bfs(graph, source) and dfs_recursive(graph, source) separately. With 5% density on V=2000, E ≈ 0.05 * 2000*1999/2 ≈ 100 000. The O(V+E) complexity with quadratically growing E means growth ratios will track O(E) = O(V^2) for dense graphs.*

5. Write a complete test file tests/test_benchmarks.py with at least ten tests covering: (a) that sorting.run() produces the correct number of records (n_algos * n_input_types * n_sizes), (b) that all sort results for the same (algorithm, input_type, n) are in ascending time order relative to n, (c) that the sorted output of all five sort algorithms matches sorted() for three random inputs, (d) that searching.run() dict results are always faster than linear results at the same n, and (e) that the linked list prepend time is less than Python list insert(0) time at n=2000.

__Hint:__ Use pytest fixtures to avoid repeating benchmark setup. A @pytest.fixture(scope="module") named store that builds one ResultStore and runs all suites once is efficient for the test file. Use store.filter() to retrieve results for specific comparisons. For correctness tests, call the algorithm functions directly on known inputs and compare to sorted().

Challenge Tasks

1. Extend the benchmark tool with a visualisation module that exports an HTML report. The HTML report should include: one collapsible section per benchmark suite, a data table showing all timing

results, an inline bar chart (rendered using HTML and CSS, no external libraries) showing relative performance of each algorithm at the largest tested size, and a complexity inference table. The HTML should be self-contained in a single file. Generate it by building an HTML string in a new reporter_html.py module and writing it to benchmark_report.html when the --html flag is passed. Test that the file opens correctly in a browser and that all data tables are accurate.
2. Add a memory profiling module to the benchmark tool. Use Python's tracemalloc module to measure peak memory allocation during each benchmark operation. Record the peak memory (in kilobytes) alongside the timing in an extended BenchmarkResult, and add a memory table column to the Reporter output. Profile and compare the memory footprint of: merge sort vs quicksort (merge sort allocates O(n) auxiliary; quicksort uses O(log n) call stack), a Python list vs a linked list of 5 000 elements (absolute memory usage), and a Python dict vs the hand-written HashMap at the same fill level. Report the memory-per-element cost for each structure.
3. Build a benchmarking dashboard as an interactive terminal application using Python's curses module (or the blessed package as a cross-platform alternative). The dashboard should display a live-updating screen as benchmarks run: a progress bar showing which suite and size is currently being measured, a scrollable results table that updates after each measurement, and a "fastest so far" summary line. When all benchmarks are complete, the user should be able to press arrow keys to scroll through results by suite or input type, and press Q to quit. This combines the benchmarking logic from all sections with the event-driven programming concepts covered in Book 10 (GUI Programming).

Appendix A Python Installation & Setup Guide

This appendix walks you through installing Python and setting up a workspace suitable for the exercises in this book. Every code example in Book 04 was written and tested on Python 3.10 or later; any version from 3.10 up to the latest release will run the code unchanged. If you already have a working Python 3.10+ installation, skip to Section A.4.

A.1 Installing Python on Windows

Download the latest stable installer from python.org. Select the 64-bit Windows installer (most modern computers). When you launch the installer, tick the checkbox labelled "Add python.exe to PATH" at the bottom of the first screen — this step is easy to miss and will save you a great deal of trouble later. Choose "Install Now" for the default setup, which is suitable for this book.

Verify the installation by opening Command Prompt (press Win+R, type cmd, press Enter) and running:

```
python --version
```

You should see output similar to Python 3.12.2. If the command is not recognised, re-run the installer and ensure the PATH checkbox is ticked.

A.2 Installing Python on macOS

macOS ships with a system Python, but it is often out of date. Install a recent version using one of two methods. The simpler option is the official installer from python.org: download the macOS installer, open the .pkg file, and follow the prompts. The second option, popular with developers, uses Homebrew:

```
/bin/bash -c "$(curl -fsSL
https://raw.githubusercontent.com/Homebrew/install/HEAD/install.sh)"
brew install python@3.12
```

Verify the installation by opening Terminal (Applications → Utilities → Terminal) and running:

```
python3 --version
```

On macOS the command is python3, not python — the latter may still point at the old system Python 2.

A.3 Installing Python on Linux

Most Linux distributions come with Python 3 pre-installed, but the version may be older than 3.10. To check, open a terminal and run python3 --version. If you need a newer version, use your distribution's package manager:

```
# Ubuntu / Debian
sudo apt update
sudo apt install python3 python3-pip python3-venv

# Fedora
sudo dnf install python3 python3-pip

# Arch Linux
sudo pacman -S python python-pip
```

If your distribution's repositories do not offer Python 3.10 or later, consider using pyenv (github.com/pyenv/pyenv) to install and switch between multiple Python versions without affecting the system Python.

A.4 Choosing an Editor or IDE

Any plain-text editor will work for writing Python, but an editor with syntax highlighting, auto-indentation and an integrated terminal will make working through the exercises substantially easier. Three good choices:

- IDLE — bundled with every Python installation. Simple, lightweight, and ideal for trying out short scripts. Launch it by typing idle at a terminal or searching for it in your Start menu / Applications folder.
- Thonny — a free, beginner-focused IDE available from thonny.org. It includes a visual debugger that steps through code one line at a time and displays variables as they change — particularly useful when studying the recursive traversals in Chapters 8 and 9.
- Visual Studio Code — free, powerful, and widely used in industry. Install the Python extension from Microsoft once VS Code is installed to enable syntax highlighting, linting, and the built-in debugger. Available from code.visualstudio.com.

A.5 Creating a Workspace for This Book

Create a dedicated folder for your work on this book. A consistent layout makes the capstone project in Chapter 10 much easier to manage:

```
book04/
    chapter_01/
        1_1_algorithm_demo.py
        1_2_bigO_comparison.py
        ...
    chapter_02/
        ...
    capstone/
        benchmark_suite/
```

At the command line, create this structure in one step:

```
mkdir book04
cd book04
mkdir chapter_01 chapter_02 chapter_03 chapter_04 chapter_05
mkdir chapter_06 chapter_07 chapter_08 chapter_09 chapter_10
mkdir capstone
```

A.6 Creating and Using a Virtual Environment

A virtual environment is an isolated Python installation that keeps a project's dependencies separate from the system Python. This is the standard professional practice and is well worth adopting from the start. Inside your book04 folder, create and activate a virtual environment:

```
# Create the environment (one-time setup)
python -m venv .venv

# Activate – Windows
.venv\Scripts\activate

# Activate – macOS / Linux
source .venv/bin/activate
```

When the environment is active, the command prompt is prefixed with (.venv). Any package you install with pip now lives inside the environment only. Deactivate with the deactivate command when you are finished.

This book's exercises use only the Python standard library, so no extra packages are strictly required. However, when you work through Booklet 09 (Data Analysis) later, pandas and matplotlib will install cleanly into this same virtual environment.

A.7 Running Your First Program

Create a file called hello.py in chapter_01 with the following contents:

```
print("Book 04 is ready to run.")

name = input("What is your name? ")
print(f"Welcome, {name}.")
```

Run it from the terminal (with the virtual environment activated if you created one):

```
python hello.py
```

If the program prompts for your name and prints a welcome message, your setup is complete. You are ready to begin Chapter 1.

Appendix B Big-O Complexity Cheat Sheet

This appendix summarises the time and space complexity of every data structure and algorithm covered in Book 04, together with a small number of additional operations that appear frequently in Python code. All entries assume the average-case complexity unless a worst case is shown separately in brackets.

The complexity classes used throughout this book, ordered from fastest to slowest, are: O(1), O(log n), O(n), O(n log n), $O(n^2)$, $O(2^n)$, O(n!). The practical impact of each class is demonstrated in Chapter 1, Section 1.3.

B.1 Python Built-in Data Structures

Operation	list	tuple	dict	set	deque
Index access lst[i]	O(1)	O(1)	—	—	O(n)
Membership x in c	O(n)	O(n)	O(1)	O(1)	O(n)
Append to end	O(1)*	—	—	—	O(1)
Insert at front	O(n)	—	—	—	O(1)
Delete from end	O(1)	—	—	—	O(1)
Delete from front	O(n)	—	—	—	O(1)
Get by key	—	—	O(1)	—	—
Insert / update	—	—	O(1)	O(1)	—
Iteration (full)	O(n)	O(n)	O(n)	O(n)	O(n)
Length (len)	O(1)	O(1)	O(1)	O(1)	O(1)

* list append is O(1) amortised; individual appends occasionally trigger an O(n) resize, but the cost averaged across many appends remains constant.

B.2 Searching Algorithms

Algorithm	Best	Average	Worst	Space	Covered in
Linear search	O(1)	O(n)	O(n)	O(1)	Chapter 4, §4.1
Binary search (iterative)	O(1)	O(log n)	O(log n)	O(1)	Chapter 4, §4.3
Binary search (recursive)	O(1)	O(log n)	O(log n)	O(log n)	Chapter 4, §4.4
Hash table lookup	O(1)	O(1)	O(n)	O(n)	Chapter 7, §7.3
BST search (balanced)	O(1)	O(log n)	O(log n)	O(1)	Chapter 8, §8.3
BST search (degenerate)	O(1)	O(n)	O(n)	O(1)	Chapter 8, §8.6

B.3 Sorting Algorithms

Algorithm	Best	Average	Worst	Space	Stable	Covered in
Bubble sort	O(n)	$O(n^2)$	$O(n^2)$	O(1)	Yes	Chapter 5, §5.2
Selection sort	$O(n^2)$	$O(n^2)$	$O(n^2)$	O(1)	No	Chapter 5, §5.3
Insertion sort	O(n)	$O(n^2)$	$O(n^2)$	O(1)	Yes	Chapter 5, §5.4
Merge sort	O(n log n)	O(n log n)	O(n log n)	O(n)	Yes	Chapter 6, §6.2
Quicksort (avg pivot)	O(n log n)	O(n log n)	$O(n^2)$	O(log n)	No	Chapter 6, §6.4

Python sorted() / .sort()	O(n)	O(n log n)	O(n log n)	O(n)	Yes	Chapter 5, §5.6

Python's built-in sort uses Timsort — a hybrid of merge sort and insertion sort designed to exploit naturally occurring runs of sorted data in real-world input. Its O(n) best case applies when the input is already sorted or nearly so.

B.4 Linear Data Structures

Operation	Stack (list)	Queue (deque)	Singly linked list	Doubly linked list
Push / enqueue	O(1)	O(1)	O(1) at head	O(1) at head/tail
Pop / dequeue	O(1)	O(1)	O(1) at head	O(1) at head/tail
Peek	O(1)	O(1)	O(1)	O(1)
Search by value	—	—	O(n)	O(n)
Access by index	O(1)	O(n)	O(n)	O(n)
Insert in middle	—	—	O(n)	O(n)
Delete in middle	—	—	O(n)	O(1) given node

B.5 Tree and Graph Algorithms

Algorithm	Time	Space	Covered in
BST insert / search / delete (balanced)	O(log n)	O(1) iter / O(log n) rec	Chapter 8
BST insert / search / delete (worst)	O(n)	O(n)	Chapter 8, §8.6
In-order / pre-order / post-order traversal	O(n)	O(h)	Chapter 8, §8.5
Level-order traversal	O(n)	O(w)	Chapter 8
Breadth-first search (BFS)	O(V + E)	O(V)	Chapter 9, §9.4
Depth-first search (DFS)	O(V + E)	O(V)	Chapter 9, §9.5
Topological sort	O(V + E)	O(V)	Chapter 9, §9.6
Dijkstra's shortest paths	O((V + E) log V)	O(V)	Chapter 9, Exercise 1

In the table above, V is the number of vertices, E is the number of edges, h is the height of a tree, and w is the maximum width of a tree (the largest number of nodes at any single level).

B.6 How to Read a Complexity Class

Big-O describes how the work an algorithm performs grows as the input grows, not how long it takes at any one input size. An $O(n^2)$ algorithm is not "slow" in absolute terms — at n = 10 it is usually faster than an O(n log n) algorithm on the same problem, because constant factors and initialisation costs dominate. The O(n log n) algorithm wins as n grows because its growth rate is smaller. Choose an algorithm by asking two questions: how large will n become in the worst realistic case, and how often will this code run?

B.7 Master Theorem (Recursion Summary)

Many divide-and-conquer algorithms in this book (merge sort, quicksort, recursive binary search) have complexities that follow a common pattern described by the Master Theorem. Without going into full detail, the shortcut for three common cases is:

- If the algorithm splits the input into two halves and does O(1) work to combine them (binary search), the recurrence $T(n) = T(n/2) + O(1)$ gives $T(n) = O(\log n)$.
- If it splits into two halves and does O(n) work to combine them (merge sort), the recurrence $T(n) = 2T(n/2) + O(n)$ gives $T(n) = O(n \log n)$.

- If it reduces the input by one and does $O(1)$ work per step (linear recursion), the recurrence $T(n) = T(n-1) + O(1)$ gives $T(n) = O(n)$.

Appendix C Solutions to Guided Exercises

This appendix provides worked solutions to all fifty guided exercises from Chapters 1 to 10. Each solution is presented as a runnable code block with a short explanation of the approach and the resulting complexity. Many problems admit more than one correct solution; where this is the case, the solution shown is the one that most closely follows the hint given in the chapter. If your own solution differs but produces correct results within the expected complexity class, it is also correct.

Challenge tasks are intentionally left without solutions — they are open-ended, often admit several equally good approaches, and are suited for classroom discussion, peer review, and assessment.

C.1 Solutions for Chapter 1

Exercise 1.1 Linear Search Timing

```
import timeit


def linear_search(students, target):
    for name, score in students:
        if name == target:
            return score
    return None


for n in [100, 1_000, 10_000]:
    students = [(f"S{i}", i % 100) for i in range(n)]
    target = f"S{n - 1}"
    t = timeit.timeit(lambda: linear_search(students, target), number=100)
    print(f"n = {n:>6}:  {t * 1000:6.2f} ms")
```

Search time grows linearly with n: doubling the list roughly doubles the total time. This confirms O(n) behaviour.

Exercise 1.2 Dictionary Lookup Timing

```
import timeit


for n in [100, 1_000, 10_000]:
    roll = dict((f"S{i}", i % 100) for i in range(n))
    target = f"S{n - 1}"
    t = timeit.timeit(lambda: roll.get(target), number=100_000)
    print(f"n = {n:>6}:  {t * 1000:6.2f} ms")
```

The time is effectively flat across all three sizes: the dictionary hashes the key and goes straight to the bucket, regardless of n. This confirms O(1) behaviour.

Exercise 1.3 Operation Counter

```
_ops = 0


def linear_count(lst, target):
    global _ops
    _ops = 0
    for x in lst:
        _ops += 1
        if x == target:
            return True
    return False


def duplicates_count(lst):
    global _ops
```

```
    _ops = 0
    for i in range(len(lst)):
        for j in range(i + 1, len(lst)):
            _ops += 1
            if lst[i] == lst[j]:
                return True
    return False

for n in [10, 50, 100]:
    data = list(range(n))
    linear_count(data, -1)
    linear_ops = _ops
    duplicates_count(data)
    dup_ops = _ops
    print(f"n = {n:>3}:  linear = {linear_ops:>5}   nested = {dup_ops:>5}   ratio =
{dup_ops / linear_ops:.1f}")
```

The ratio grows in proportion to n: for n = 10 it is about 5, for n = 100 it is about 50. This matches the $O(n^2) / O(n) = O(n)$ relative growth.

Exercise 1.4 append vs insert(0, ...)

```
import timeit

def build_append(n):
    lst = []
    for i in range(n):
        lst.append(i)
    return lst

def build_insert(n):
    lst = []
    for i in range(n):
        lst.insert(0, i)
    return lst

for n in [2_000, 4_000, 8_000]:
    t_app = timeit.timeit(lambda: build_append(n), number=5) / 5
    t_ins = timeit.timeit(lambda: build_insert(n), number=5) / 5
    print(f"n = {n:>5}:  append = {t_app*1000:7.2f} ms   insert(0) = {t_ins*1000:7.2f} ms
ratio = {t_ins/t_app:5.1f}x")
```

append is O(1) amortised, so total work is O(n). insert(0, v) is O(n) per call because all existing elements must shift one position right, so total work is $O(n^2)$. Doubling n roughly quadruples the insert total time while only doubling the append total time.

Exercise 1.5 find_duplicates — $O(n^2)$ vs O(n)

```
import timeit

def duplicates_nested(items):
    for i in range(len(items)):
        for j in range(i + 1, len(items)):
            if items[i] == items[j]:
                return True
    return False

def duplicates_set(items):
    seen = set()
    for x in items:
```

```
        if x in seen:
            return True
        seen.add(x)
    return False

for n in [500, 1_000, 2_000]:
    data = list(range(n))  # duplicate-free — worst case for both
    t_nested = timeit.timeit(lambda: duplicates_nested(data), number=3) / 3
    t_set    = timeit.timeit(lambda: duplicates_set(data),    number=3) / 3
    print(f"n = {n:>4}:  nested = {t_nested*1000:7.2f} ms   set = {t_set*1000:7.2f} ms
speed-up = {t_nested/t_set:6.0f}x")
```

The speed-up factor roughly doubles each time n doubles, matching the $O(n^2)/O(n) = O(n)$ growth ratio. At n = 2000 the set version is hundreds of times faster.

C.2 Solutions for Chapter 2

Exercise 2.1 Stack.peek_all()

```
class Stack:
    def __init__(self):
        self._data = []

    def push(self, item):
        self._data.append(item)

    def pop(self):
        return self._data.pop()

    def peek(self):
        return self._data[-1] if self._data else None

    def size(self):
        return len(self._data)

    def peek_all(self):
        return self._data[::-1]  # top-to-bottom without mutation

s = Stack()
for x in [1, 2, 3, 4]:
    s.push(x)

before = s.size()
print(s.peek_all())  # [4, 3, 2, 1]
print(s.size() == before)  # True — unchanged
print(s.peek() == 4)       # True — top still 4
```

Slicing with [::-1] creates a reversed copy and never touches the stack. All tests pass because the internal list is read, not mutated.

Exercise 2.2 is_palindrome Using a Stack

```
def is_palindrome(word):
    stack = []
    for ch in word.lower():
        stack.append(ch)
    for ch in word.lower():
        if ch != stack.pop():
            return False
    return True

for w in ["racecar", "python", "level", "noon", "hello"]:
    print(f"{w:>8}: {is_palindrome(w)}")
```

Pushing every character then popping reverses the order. Comparing left-to-right against the pops gives the forward-vs-reverse equality check without using slicing or reversed().

Exercise 2.3 Queue From Two Stacks

```
class TwoStackQueue:
    def __init__(self):
        self._in, self._out = [], []

    def enqueue(self, item):
```

```
        self._in.append(item)

    def dequeue(self):
        if not self._out:
            while self._in:
                self._out.append(self._in.pop())
        return self._out.pop() if self._out else None

    def __len__(self):
        return len(self._in) + len(self._out)

q = TwoStackQueue()
for x in "ABC":
    q.enqueue(x)
print(q.dequeue())      # A
q.enqueue("D")
print(q.dequeue())      # B
print(q.dequeue())      # C
print(q.dequeue())      # D  — FIFO preserved
```

Each element is transferred between stacks at most once, so dequeue is O(1) amortised even though any single dequeue might do O(n) work during the transfer.

Exercise 2.4 Hot-Potato Simulation

```
from collections import deque

def hot_potato(players, k):
    q = deque(players)
    while len(q) > 1:
        for _ in range(k - 1):       # k-1 passes around the circle
            q.append(q.popleft())
        eliminated = q.popleft()      # the player holding the potato goes
        print(f"Eliminated: {eliminated}")
    return q[0]

winner = hot_potato(["Alice", "Bob", "Charlie", "Diana", "Ed"], 3)
print(f"Winner: {winner}")
```

Rotating the queue k-1 times simulates the potato being passed; the front of the queue then holds the player who is eliminated. The last remaining player is the winner.

Exercise 2.5 TopK Tracker With a Min-Heap

```
import heapq, random

class TopK:
    def __init__(self, k):
        self.k = k
        self._heap = []

    def add(self, x):
        if len(self._heap) < self.k:
            heapq.heappush(self._heap, x)
        elif x > self._heap[0]:
            heapq.heapreplace(self._heap, x)

    def items(self):
        return sorted(self._heap, reverse=True)
```

```
random.seed(42)
tracker = TopK(5)
stream = [random.randint(1, 1000) for _ in range(50)]
for x in stream:
    tracker.add(x)
print("Top 5:", tracker.items())
print("Verified:", tracker.items() == sorted(stream, reverse=True)[:5])
```

The min-heap keeps the smallest of the current top-k at its root. Any incoming value that beats the root is the new k-th largest — swap it in. Total cost: O(n log k), which is better than sorting everything at O(n log n) when k is small.

C.3 Solutions for Chapter 3

Exercise 3.1 LinkedList.reverse() In-Place

```
def reverse(self):
    prev, current = None, self.head
    self.tail = self.head    # old head becomes new tail
    while current is not None:
        next_node = current.next
        current.next = prev
        prev = current
        current = next_node
    self.head = prev


# Demonstration
lst = LinkedList()
for x in [1, 2, 3, 4, 5]:
    lst.append(x)
lst.reverse()
print(lst)            # 5 -> 4 -> 3 -> 2 -> 1
lst.reverse()
print(lst)            # 1 -> 2 -> 3 -> 4 -> 5
```

One pass through the list with three pointers. O(n) time and O(1) extra space — no new nodes are created.

Exercise 3.2 LinkedList.remove_duplicates()

```
def remove_duplicates(self):
    seen, prev, current = set(), None, self.head
    while current is not None:
        if current.data in seen:
            prev.next = current.next
            if current is self.tail:
                self.tail = prev
            self.size -= 1
        else:
            seen.add(current.data)
            prev = current
        current = current.next
```

O(n) time (single pass, set membership is O(1) average) and O(n) extra space for the set of seen values.

Exercise 3.3 merge_sorted(list1, list2)

```
def merge_sorted(list1, list2):
    result = LinkedList()
    a, b = list1.head, list2.head
    while a and b:
        if a.data <= b.data:
            result.append(a.data); a = a.next
        else:
            result.append(b.data); b = b.next
    while a:
        result.append(a.data); a = a.next
    while b:
        result.append(b.data); b = b.next
    return result
```

Single traversal of both lists — O(n + m) time where n and m are the two list lengths. This is the merge step of merge sort (Chapter 6).

Exercise 3.4 Stack Backed by a Singly Linked List

```
class LinkedStack:
    class _Node:
        __slots__ = ("data", "next")
        def __init__(self, data, next=None):
            self.data, self.next = data, next

    def __init__(self):
        self._head = None
        self._size = 0

    def push(self, item):
        self._head = self._Node(item, self._head)
        self._size += 1

    def pop(self):
        if self._head is None:
            raise IndexError("pop from empty stack")
        data, self._head = self._head.data, self._head.next
        self._size -= 1
        return data

    def peek(self):
        return self._head.data if self._head else None

    def __len__(self):
        return self._size

s = LinkedStack()
for x in [10, 20, 30]:
    s.push(x)
print(s.pop(), s.pop(), s.pop())   # 30 20 10 — LIFO
```

Only the head pointer is touched, so push and pop are O(1). No Python list is used internally.

Exercise 3.5 find_middle() With Fast and Slow Pointers

```
def find_middle(self):
    if self.head is None:
        return None
    slow = fast = self.head
    while fast is not None and fast.next is not None:
        slow = slow.next
        fast = fast.next.next
    return slow.data

# Odd length 1->2->3->4->5  → middle = 3
# Even length 1->2->3->4    → middle = 3 (second middle)
```

The fast pointer moves twice as quickly as the slow one. When fast reaches the end, slow has traversed exactly half. Single pass, O(n) time, O(1) space.

C.4 Solutions for Chapter 4

Exercise 4.1 binary_search With Insertion Point

```
def binary_search(lst, target):
    low, high = 0, len(lst) - 1
    while low <= high:
        mid = (low + high) // 2
        if lst[mid] == target:
            return (True, mid)
        elif lst[mid] < target:
            low = mid + 1
        else:
            high = mid - 1
    return (False, low)   # low is the insertion point


data = [1, 3, 5, 7, 9, 11, 13, 15, 17, 19]
for t in [5, 17, 1, 0, 4, 20]:
    print(f"{t:>3}: {binary_search(data, t)}")
```

When the loop exits without finding the target, low has advanced to the index where the target would be inserted to keep the list sorted — identical to bisect.bisect_left.

Exercise 4.2 count_in_range Using bisect

```
from bisect import bisect_left, bisect_right


def count_in_range(sorted_lst, lo, hi):
    return bisect_right(sorted_lst, hi) - bisect_left(sorted_lst, lo)


data = [2, 3, 5, 7, 11, 13, 17, 19, 23, 29, 31, 37, 41, 43, 47, 53, 59, 61, 67, 71]
print(count_in_range(data, 10, 30))   # 5
print(count_in_range(data, 40, 60))   # 4
print(count_in_range(data, 0, 100))   # 20 — all
```

Two O(log n) binary searches. No loops, no slicing. Total complexity O(log n).

Exercise 4.3 two_sum — $O(n^2)$ vs O(n)

```
import timeit, random

def two_sum_nested(lst, target):
    for i in range(len(lst)):
        for j in range(i + 1, len(lst)):
            if lst[i] + lst[j] == target:
                return (i, j)
    return None


def two_sum_dict(lst, target):
    seen = {}
    for j, v in enumerate(lst):
        if target - v in seen:
            return (seen[target - v], j)
        seen[v] = j
    return None


random.seed(1)
data = random.sample(range(100_000), 10_000)
target = data[-1] + data[-2]
```

```python
t_n = timeit.timeit(lambda: two_sum_nested(data, target), number=1)
t_d = timeit.timeit(lambda: two_sum_dict(data, target),   number=1)
print(f"nested = {t_n*1000:8.2f} ms   dict = {t_d*1000:6.2f} ms   speed-up =
{t_n/t_d:.0f}x")
```

The dict-based version performs a single pass with O(1) lookups, giving O(n) total; the nested version is $O(n^2)$. At n = 10 000 the speed-up is typically a thousand-fold.

Exercise 4.4 search_sorted_2d — Staircase Search

```python
def search_sorted_2d(matrix, target):
    if not matrix or not matrix[0]:
        return (-1, -1)
    row, col = 0, len(matrix[0]) - 1
    while row < len(matrix) and col >= 0:
        v = matrix[row][col]
        if v == target:
            return (row, col)
        elif v > target:
            col -= 1
        else:
            row += 1
    return (-1, -1)


grid = [
    [ 1,  4,  7, 11],
    [ 2,  5,  8, 12],
    [ 3,  6,  9, 16],
    [10, 13, 14, 17],
]
print(search_sorted_2d(grid, 5))    # (1, 1)
print(search_sorted_2d(grid, 15))   # (-1, -1)
```

Each comparison eliminates one entire row or column, so the worst case is m + n steps. Complexity: O(m + n) time, O(1) space.

Exercise 4.5 PhoneBook With Adaptive Strategy

```python
from bisect import bisect_left, insort


class PhoneBook:
    THRESHOLD = 30


    def __init__(self):
        self._entries = []


    def add(self, name, number):
        insort(self._entries, (name, number))   # keeps the list sorted


    def search(self, name):
        if len(self._entries) < self.THRESHOLD:
            for n, num in self._entries:
                if n == name:
                    return num
            return None
        idx = bisect_left(self._entries, (name,))
        if idx < len(self._entries) and self._entries[idx][0] == name:
            return self._entries[idx][1]
        return None
```

```
pb = PhoneBook()
for n, num in [("Alice", "0401"), ("Bob", "0402"), ("Charlie", "0403")]:
    pb.add(n, num)
print(pb.search("Bob"))          # 0402 (below threshold → linear)
print(pb.search("Zoe"))          # None
```

Below 30 entries, linear scan is competitive because cache behaviour and low constant factors dominate. Above the threshold, bisect gives O(log n) lookup.

C.5 Solutions for Chapter 5

Exercise 5.1 Cocktail Shaker Sort

```
def cocktail_sort(lst):
    left, right = 0, len(lst) - 1
    while left < right:
        swapped = False
        for i in range(left, right):
            if lst[i] > lst[i + 1]:
                lst[i], lst[i + 1] = lst[i + 1], lst[i]
                swapped = True
        right -= 1
        if not swapped: break
        swapped = False
        for i in range(right, left, -1):
            if lst[i] < lst[i - 1]:
                lst[i], lst[i - 1] = lst[i - 1], lst[i]
                swapped = True
        left += 1
        if not swapped: break
    return lst

print(cocktail_sort([5, 1, 4, 2, 8, 0, 9, 3]))
```

Bidirectional passes place both the current maximum and current minimum each cycle, halving the number of passes on many inputs. Worst-case complexity remains $O(n^2)$.

Exercise 5.2 Binary-Insertion Sort

```
from bisect import bisect_left

def binary_insertion_sort(lst):
    comparisons = shifts = 0
    for i in range(1, len(lst)):
        key = lst[i]
        p = bisect_left(lst, key, 0, i)
        comparisons += (i.bit_length())       # ~ log2 i comparisons by bisect
        for j in range(i, p, -1):
            lst[j] = lst[j - 1]
            shifts += 1
        lst[p] = key
    return lst, comparisons, shifts

# Averaged over 100 random lists of size 50, comparisons ~ 300, shifts ~ 600
```

Comparisons drop to $O(n \log n)$, but shifts remain $O(n^2)$ because the array still moves one element at a time to make room. Total complexity is still $O(n^2)$.

Exercise 5.3 sort_by_frequency

```
from collections import Counter

def sort_by_frequency(lst):
    count = Counter(lst)
    return sorted(lst, key=lambda x: (-count[x], x))

print(sort_by_frequency([4, 2, 4, 3, 2, 4, 1]))
# [4, 4, 4, 2, 2, 1, 3]
```

Negating the count makes higher frequencies sort first; the second key (x) breaks ties with the smaller value first. Counter construction is O(n), sorted() is O(n log n).

Exercise 5.4 is_sorted + sort_if_needed

```
def is_sorted(lst, key=None, reverse=False):
    if key is None: key = lambda x: x
    for i in range(len(lst) - 1):
        a, b = key(lst[i]), key(lst[i + 1])
        if reverse and a < b: return False
        if not reverse and a > b: return False
    return True


def sort_if_needed(lst, key=None, reverse=False):
    if is_sorted(lst, key=key, reverse=reverse):
        return lst
    return sorted(lst, key=key, reverse=reverse)
```

is_sorted is a single O(n) pass. Calling sort_if_needed on already-sorted input avoids the O(n log n) work of sorted(). On fully random input the extra check costs only O(n) and is insignificant compared to the sort.

Exercise 5.5 Instrumenting Insertion Sort With SortRecorder

```
class SortRecorder:
    def __init__(self, initial):
        self.frames = [(list(initial), "start")]

    def snapshot(self, label, data):
        self.frames.append((list(data), label))

def insertion_sort_recorded(lst):
    rec = SortRecorder(lst)
    for i in range(1, len(lst)):
        key = lst[i]
        j = i - 1
        while j >= 0 and lst[j] > key:
            lst[j + 1] = lst[j]
            j -= 1
        lst[j + 1] = key
        rec.snapshot(f"placed {key} at {j + 1}", lst)
    return lst, rec


_, rec = insertion_sort_recorded([5, 2, 4, 6, 1, 3])
for snap, label in rec.frames:
    print(f"{label:>18}: {snap}")
```

Each snapshot shows the sorted prefix growing by exactly one element — a direct visual confirmation of the insertion sort invariant.

C.6 Solutions for Chapter 6

Exercise 6.1 Hybrid Merge Sort With Insertion Cutoff

```
def insertion_sort_range(lst, lo, hi):
    for i in range(lo + 1, hi + 1):
        key = lst[i]
        j = i - 1
        while j >= lo and lst[j] > key:
            lst[j + 1] = lst[j]; j -= 1
        lst[j + 1] = key


def hybrid_merge_sort(lst, lo=0, hi=None, cutoff=16):
    if hi is None: hi = len(lst) - 1
    if hi - lo + 1 <= cutoff:
        insertion_sort_range(lst, lo, hi)
        return
    mid = (lo + hi) // 2
    hybrid_merge_sort(lst, lo, mid, cutoff)
    hybrid_merge_sort(lst, mid + 1, hi, cutoff)
    _merge_in_place(lst, lo, mid, hi)
```

Small subarrays use insertion sort, whose low constant factor beats merge sort's recursion overhead below about 16 elements. Timsort uses this exact idea.

Exercise 6.2 Quicksort With Median-of-Three Pivot

```
def median_of_three(lst, low, high):
    mid = (low + high) // 2
    a, b, c = lst[low], lst[mid], lst[high]
    if (a - b) * (c - a) >= 0:       # a is the median
        lst[low], lst[high] = lst[high], lst[low]
    elif (b - a) * (c - b) >= 0:     # b is the median
        lst[mid], lst[high] = lst[high], lst[mid]
    # else c is already at high


def quicksort_m3(lst, low=0, high=None):
    if high is None: high = len(lst) - 1
    if low < high:
        median_of_three(lst, low, high)
        p = _partition(lst, low, high)
        quicksort_m3(lst, low, p - 1)
        quicksort_m3(lst, p + 1, high)
```

On sorted input, the naive "last element" pivot triggers worst-case $O(n^2)$. Median-of-three almost always selects a reasonable pivot, keeping behaviour at $O(n \log n)$ in practice without the overhead of random number generation.

Exercise 6.3 merge_k_sorted — Naive vs Divide-and-Conquer

```
def _merge(a, b):
    out, i, j = [], 0, 0
    while i < len(a) and j < len(b):
        if a[i] <= b[j]: out.append(a[i]); i += 1
        else:            out.append(b[j]); j += 1
    out.extend(a[i:]); out.extend(b[j:])
    return out


def merge_k_naive(lists):
    result = []
    for lst in lists:
```

```
        result = _merge(result, lst)
    return result

def merge_k_divide(lists):
    if len(lists) == 1: return lists[0]
    mid = len(lists) // 2
    return _merge(merge_k_divide(lists[:mid]), merge_k_divide(lists[mid:]))
```

Naive merging processes each element roughly k times (every pairwise merge re-reads earlier elements), giving O(nk). Divide-and-conquer touches each element $\log_2 k$ times, giving O(n log k) — at k = 16 this is a 4× speed-up.

Exercise 6.4 Quickselect — k-th Smallest in O(n) Average

```
def quickselect(lst, k, low=0, high=None):
    if high is None: high = len(lst) - 1
    if low == high: return lst[low]
    pivot = lst[high]
    p = low
    for i in range(low, high):
        if lst[i] < pivot:
            lst[p], lst[i] = lst[i], lst[p]; p += 1
    lst[p], lst[high] = lst[high], lst[p]
    if p == k: return lst[p]
    if k < p:  return quickselect(lst, k, low, p - 1)
    return quickselect(lst, k, p + 1, high)

data = [7, 2, 9, 4, 1, 8, 3, 6, 5]
print(quickselect(data[:], 0))                   # 1 – minimum
print(quickselect(data[:], len(data) - 1))       # 9 – maximum
print(quickselect(data[:], len(data) // 2))      # 5 – median
```

Each recursion discards one side of the partition rather than sorting both, giving O(n) average total work. Worst case is still $O(n^2)$, but rare in practice with a reasonable pivot.

Exercise 6.5 Comparison-Counting Benchmark

```
def bubble_counted(lst, counter):
    n = len(lst)
    for i in range(n):
        for j in range(n - i - 1):
            counter[0] += 1
            if lst[j] > lst[j + 1]:
                lst[j], lst[j + 1] = lst[j + 1], lst[j]

def merge_counted(lst, counter):
    if len(lst) <= 1: return lst
    mid = len(lst) // 2
    L = merge_counted(lst[:mid], counter)
    R = merge_counted(lst[mid:], counter)
    out, i, j = [], 0, 0
    while i < len(L) and j < len(R):
        counter[0] += 1
        if L[i] <= R[j]: out.append(L[i]); i += 1
        else:            out.append(R[j]); j += 1
    out.extend(L[i:]); out.extend(R[j:])
    return out

import random
data = random.sample(range(10_000), 500)
```

```
c1 = [0]; bubble_counted(data[:], c1)
c2 = [0]; merge_counted(data[:], c2)
print(f"bubble n=500: {c1[0]:>7} cmp  (theory ~ 124 750)")
print(f"merge  n=500: {c2[0]:>7} cmp  (theory ~ {500 * 9:>5})")
```

Empirical counts match the theoretical predictions closely: bubble sort is near n(n-1)/2; merge sort is near n $\log_2$ n.

C.7 Solutions for Chapter 7

Exercise 7.1 HashMap.update() and setdefault()

```
def update(self, other):
    if hasattr(other, "items"):
        for k, v in other.items():
            self[k] = v
    else:
        for k, v in other:
            self[k] = v


def setdefault(self, key, default=None):
    if key not in self:
        self[key] = default
    return self[key]
```

Both methods mirror the built-in dict API exactly. update accepts any object exposing an items() method — HashMap, dict, or any other mapping.

Exercise 7.2 Two-Sum With a Dict

```
def two_sum(lst, target):
    seen = {}
    for j, v in enumerate(lst):
        complement = target - v
        if complement in seen:
            return (seen[complement], j)
        seen[v] = j
    return None


import timeit, random
random.seed(0)
data = random.sample(range(200_000), 20_000)
target = data[-1] + data[0]
t = timeit.timeit(lambda: two_sum(data, target), number=10) / 10
print(f"O(n) dict version on n=20 000: {t * 1000:.2f} ms")
```

Single pass, O(1) lookups and inserts into the dict. Total O(n). Compared with the $O(n^2)$ nested-loop approach, the speed-up at n = 20 000 is typically several thousand-fold.

Exercise 7.3 group_anagrams

```
from collections import defaultdict


def group_anagrams(words):
    groups = defaultdict(list)
    for w in words:
        key = "".join(sorted(w))
        groups[key].append(w)
    return list(groups.values())


print(group_anagrams(["eat", "tea", "tan", "ate", "nat", "bat"]))
# [['eat', 'tea', 'ate'], ['tan', 'nat'], ['bat']]
```

Complexity: $O(n \cdot k \log k)$ where n is the word count and k is the average word length. The sorted characters act as a canonical form for all anagrams of a word.

Exercise 7.4 LFU Cache

```
from collections import defaultdict, OrderedDict
```

```python
class LFUCache:
    def __init__(self, capacity):
        self.cap = capacity
        self.data = {}                              # key -> value
        self.freq = {}                              # key -> count
        self.buckets = defaultdict(OrderedDict)     # count -> ordered keys
        self.min_freq = 0

    def _bump(self, key):
        f = self.freq[key]
        del self.buckets[f][key]
        if not self.buckets[f] and self.min_freq == f:
            self.min_freq += 1
        self.freq[key] = f + 1
        self.buckets[f + 1][key] = None

    def get(self, key):
        if key not in self.data: return None
        self._bump(key)
        return self.data[key]

    def put(self, key, value):
        if self.cap == 0: return
        if key in self.data:
            self.data[key] = value
            self._bump(key)
            return
        if len(self.data) >= self.cap:
            oldest, _ = self.buckets[self.min_freq].popitem(last=False)
            del self.data[oldest]; del self.freq[oldest]
        self.data[key] = value
        self.freq[key] = 1
        self.buckets[1][key] = None
        self.min_freq = 1
```

All operations are O(1). The OrderedDict per frequency bucket gives LRU tie-breaking within each frequency level for free.

Exercise 7.5 SubstitutionCipher

```python
import string, random

class SubstitutionCipher:
    def __init__(self, seed=None):
        rng = random.Random(seed)
        lower = list(string.ascii_lowercase)
        shuffled = lower[:]; rng.shuffle(shuffled)
        self._enc = dict(zip(lower, shuffled))
        self._enc.update({k.upper(): v.upper() for k, v in self._enc.items()})
        self._dec = {v: k for k, v in self._enc.items()}

    def encode(self, text):
        return "".join(self._enc.get(c, c) for c in text)

    def decode(self, text):
        return "".join(self._dec.get(c, c) for c in text)
```

```
c = SubstitutionCipher(seed=42)
for msg in ["Hello, World!", "Meet at 3:15 PM.", "Python 3.12 — Data Structures"]:
    enc = c.encode(msg)
    assert c.decode(enc) == msg
    print(f"{msg!r:<40}  →  {enc!r}")
```

Each character is one dict lookup — O(n) total. Non-alphabetic characters pass through unchanged via the dict.get default.

C.8 Solutions for Chapter 8

Exercise 8.1 BST maximum(), floor(), ceiling()

```
def maximum(self):
    node = self.root
    if node is None: return None
    while node.right is not None:
        node = node.right
    return (node.key, node.value)

def floor(self, k):
    best, node = None, self.root
    while node is not None:
        if node.key == k: return node.key
        if node.key < k:
            best = node.key
            node = node.right
        else:
            node = node.left
    return best

def ceiling(self, k):
    best, node = None, self.root
    while node is not None:
        if node.key == k: return node.key
        if node.key > k:
            best = node.key
            node = node.left
        else:
            node = node.right
    return best
```

All three run in O(h) where h is the tree height — O(log n) for a balanced tree.

Exercise 8.2 rank(k) and select(r) With Size-Augmented BST

```
def _size(node):
    return 0 if node is None else node.size

def rank(self, k):
    def _rank(node, k):
        if node is None: return 0
        if k == node.key: return _size(node.left)
        if k < node.key:  return _rank(node.left, k)
        return _size(node.left) + 1 + _rank(node.right, k)
    return _rank(self.root, k)

def select(self, r):
    def _select(node, r):
        if node is None: return None
        left_size = _size(node.left)
        if r < left_size:   return _select(node.left, r)
        if r == left_size:  return node.key
        return _select(node.right, r - left_size - 1)
    return _select(self.root, r)
```

Both operations take O(h) comparisons using the stored subtree sizes. Every insert and delete must update sizes along the path back to the root — also O(h).

Exercise 8.3 Level-Order Traversal

```
from collections import deque

def level_order(self):
    if self.root is None: return
    q = deque([(0, self.root)])
    current_level, bucket = 0, []
    while q:
        level, node = q.popleft()
        if level != current_level:
            yield current_level, bucket
            current_level, bucket = level, []
        bucket.append(node.key)
        if node.left:  q.append((level + 1, node.left))
        if node.right: q.append((level + 1, node.right))
    yield current_level, bucket
```

For a perfect BST of height h, level k holds exactly 2^k nodes — yielding 1, 2, 4, 8, ... as output. Complexity O(n) time, O(w) space where w is the widest level.

Exercise 8.4 build_balanced_bst(sorted_list)

```
def build_balanced_bst(sorted_list):
    def _build(lo, hi):
        if lo > hi: return None
        mid = (lo + hi) // 2
        node = BSTNode(sorted_list[mid], None)
        node.left  = _build(lo, mid - 1)
        node.right = _build(mid + 1, hi)
        return node
    t = BST()
    t.root = _build(0, len(sorted_list) - 1)
    return t

# Heights: n=7 → 2,  n=15 → 3,  n=31 → 4,  n=63 → 5  (i.e. ⌊log2 n⌋)
```

Recursively choosing the middle element as root gives a perfectly balanced tree of height $\lfloor \log_2 n \rfloor$. Construction is O(n) total.

Exercise 8.5 Lowest Common Ancestor (LCA)

```
def lca(self, u_key, v_key):
    node = self.root
    while node is not None:
        if u_key < node.key and v_key < node.key:
            node = node.left
        elif u_key > node.key and v_key > node.key:
            node = node.right
        else:
            return node.key
    return None
```

The BST property is exactly right for LCA: walk down the tree, turning left or right only while both keys lie on the same side. The first node where they diverge — or where one of them equals the node — is the LCA. O(h) time, O(1) space.

C.9 Solutions for Chapter 9

Exercise 9.1 Dijkstra's Algorithm

```
import heapq

def dijkstra(graph, source):
    dist = {v: float("inf") for v in graph.vertices()}
    dist[source] = 0
    pq = [(0, source)]
    while pq:
        d, u = heapq.heappop(pq)
        if d > dist[u]:
            continue
        for nbr, w in graph.neighbours_weighted(u):
            alt = d + w
            if alt < dist[nbr]:
                dist[nbr] = alt
                heapq.heappush(pq, (alt, nbr))
    return dist
```

Total complexity O((V + E) log V) with a binary heap. Unlike BFS, Dijkstra returns true shortest walk times, not hop counts.

Exercise 9.2 is_bipartite

```
from collections import deque

def is_bipartite(graph):
    colour = {v: None for v in graph.vertices()}
    for start in graph.vertices():
        if colour[start] is not None: continue
        colour[start] = 0
        q = deque([start])
        while q:
            v = q.popleft()
            for nbr in graph.neighbours(v):
                if colour[nbr] is None:
                    colour[nbr] = 1 - colour[v]
                    q.append(nbr)
                elif colour[nbr] == colour[v]:
                    return False
    return True
```

BFS with 2-colouring. The outer for loop handles disconnected graphs. O(V + E) time.

Exercise 9.3 Kahn's Algorithm — Topological Sort

```
from collections import deque

def topo_kahn(graph):
    in_deg = {v: 0 for v in graph.vertices()}
    for u in graph.vertices():
        for v in graph.neighbours(u):
            in_deg[v] += 1
    q = deque(v for v, d in in_deg.items() if d == 0)
    order = []
    while q:
        v = q.popleft()
        order.append(v)
        for nbr in graph.neighbours(v):
```

```python
            in_deg[nbr] -= 1
            if in_deg[nbr] == 0:
                q.append(nbr)
    if len(order) != len(in_deg):
        raise ValueError("graph contains a cycle")
    return order
```

Linear in V + E. If the final order is shorter than V, a cycle exists — Kahn's algorithm doubles as a cycle detector.

Exercise 9.4 Prim's Minimum Spanning Tree

```python
import heapq

def prim(graph, start):
    visited = {start}
    edges = []
    pq = [(w, start, v) for v, w in graph.neighbours_weighted(start)]
    heapq.heapify(pq)
    mst = []
    while pq and len(visited) < len(graph.vertices()):
        w, u, v = heapq.heappop(pq)
        if v in visited: continue
        visited.add(v)
        mst.append((u, v, w))
        for nbr, w2 in graph.neighbours_weighted(v):
            if nbr not in visited:
                heapq.heappush(pq, (w2, v, nbr))
    return mst     # exactly |V| - 1 edges
```

Greedy — always extend the tree by the cheapest edge crossing out of it. With a binary heap, total cost is O(E log V).

Exercise 9.5 Graph.transpose() and Kosaraju's SCC

```python
def transpose(self):
    g = Graph(directed=True)
    for v in self.vertices(): g.add_vertex(v)
    for u in self.vertices():
        for v, w in self.neighbours_weighted(u):
            g.add_edge(v, u, w)
    return g

def kosaraju(graph):
    # Pass 1: DFS on original, record finish order
    visited, order = set(), []
    def dfs1(u):
        visited.add(u)
        for v in graph.neighbours(u):
            if v not in visited: dfs1(v)
        order.append(u)
    for u in graph.vertices():
        if u not in visited: dfs1(u)

    # Pass 2: DFS on transpose in reverse finish order
    gt = graph.transpose()
    seen, sccs = set(), []
    def dfs2(u, comp):
        seen.add(u); comp.append(u)
        for v in gt.neighbours(u):
            if v not in seen: dfs2(v, comp)
```

```
    for u in reversed(order):
        if u not in seen:
            comp = []; dfs2(u, comp); sccs.append(comp)
    return sccs
```

Two linear DFS passes — O(V + E) total. Each tree formed in the second pass is exactly one strongly connected component.

C.10 Solutions for Chapter 10

Exercise 10.1 BST Benchmark Suite

```
# bst.py
from random import Random
from bst import BST
from framework import BenchmarkResult, time_it

def run(store, sizes=(500, 2_000, 5_000, 10_000)):
    rng = Random(42)
    for n in sizes:
        keys = rng.sample(range(1_000_000), n)
        queries = rng.sample(keys, n // 2)

        # Random-insert BST
        tree_r = BST()
        t_build = time_it(lambda: [tree_r.insert(k, None) for k in keys])
        t_search = time_it(lambda: [tree_r.search(k) for k in queries])
        t_sorted = time_it(lambda: list(tree_r.in_order()))
        store.add(BenchmarkResult("bst_build",  "random_insert", n, t_build))
        store.add(BenchmarkResult("bst_search", "random_insert", n, t_search))
        store.add(BenchmarkResult("bst_sorted", "random_insert", n, t_sorted))

        # Sorted-insert BST — degenerate
        tree_s = BST()
        sorted_keys = sorted(keys)
        t_build_s  = time_it(lambda: [tree_s.insert(k, None) for k in sorted_keys])
        t_search_s = time_it(lambda: [tree_s.search(k) for k in queries])
        store.add(BenchmarkResult("bst_build",  "sorted_insert", n, t_build_s))
        store.add(BenchmarkResult("bst_search", "sorted_insert", n, t_search_s))
```

Random-insert search shows O(log n) growth (ratios near 1); sorted-insert search shows O(n) growth (ratios near 2 when n doubles) — the degenerate-tree case in action.

Exercise 10.2 Reporter.to_csv() With --csv Flag

```
# reporter.py (addition)
import csv, io, dataclasses

def to_csv(self):
    buf = io.StringIO()
    if not self.results: return ""
    fields = [f.name for f in dataclasses.fields(self.results[0])]
    w = csv.DictWriter(buf, fieldnames=fields)
    w.writeheader()
    for r in self.results:
        w.writerow(dataclasses.asdict(r))
    return buf.getvalue()

# __main__.py (addition)
if args.csv:
    with open("results.csv", "w", newline="") as f:
        f.write(store.to_csv())

# Round-trip verification
with open("results.csv") as f:
    loaded = list(csv.DictReader(f))
assert len(loaded) == len(store.results)
```

Uses dataclasses.asdict to flatten each record. io.StringIO gives the same CSV data as an in-memory string for testing without file I/O.

Exercise 10.3 hashtable.py — HashMap vs dict

```
# hashtable.py
from random import Random
from hashmap import HashMap      # from Chapter 7
from framework import BenchmarkResult, time_it


def run(store, sizes=(500, 2_000, 5_000, 10_000)):
    rng = Random(7)
    for n in sizes:
        pairs = [(f"k{i}", i) for i in rng.sample(range(1_000_000), n)]
        queries = [k for k, _ in rng.sample(pairs, n // 2)]

        t_hm_build  = time_it(lambda: _build_hashmap(pairs))
        hm = _build_hashmap(pairs)
        t_hm_search = time_it(lambda: [hm[k] for k in queries])

        t_dict_build  = time_it(lambda: dict(pairs))
        d = dict(pairs)
        t_dict_search = time_it(lambda: [d[k] for k in queries])

        store.add(BenchmarkResult("build", "hashmap", n, t_hm_build))
        store.add(BenchmarkResult("build", "dict",    n, t_dict_build))
        store.add(BenchmarkResult("search","hashmap", n, t_hm_search))
        store.add(BenchmarkResult("search","dict",    n, t_dict_search))


def _build_hashmap(pairs):
    hm = HashMap()
    for k, v in pairs: hm[k] = v
    return hm
```

Both show flat (O(1) per op) growth ratios. The built-in dict wins on constant factor by 20–50× because it is implemented in C while HashMap is pure Python.

Exercise 10.4 graphs.py — BFS/DFS at Increasing V

```
# graphs.py
import random
from graph import Graph
from traversal import bfs, dfs_recursive
from framework import BenchmarkResult, time_it


def run(store, sizes=(100, 500, 1_000, 2_000), density=0.05):
    rng = random.Random(13)
    for V in sizes:
        g = Graph(directed=False)
        for v in range(V): g.add_vertex(v)
        for u in range(V):
            for v in range(u + 1, V):
                if rng.random() < density:
                    g.add_edge(u, v, 1)
        t_bfs = time_it(lambda: bfs(g, 0))
        t_dfs = time_it(lambda: dfs_recursive(g, 0))
        store.add(BenchmarkResult("traverse", "bfs", V, t_bfs))
        store.add(BenchmarkResult("traverse", "dfs", V, t_dfs))
```

Edge count grows quadratically with V at fixed density, so timing growth tracks $O(V^2)$. This confirms the $O(V + E)$ complexity empirically — for dense graphs, E dominates V.

Exercise 10.5 tests/test_benchmarks.py

```
# tests/test_benchmarks.py
import pytest, random
from framework import ResultStore
import sorting, searching, linked_list

@pytest.fixture(scope="module")
def store():
    s = ResultStore()
    sorting.run(s, sizes=[200, 400])
    searching.run(s, sizes=[200, 400])
    linked_list.run(s, sizes=[2_000])
    return s

def test_sorting_record_count(store):
    results = store.filter(suite="sort")
    assert len(results) == 5 * 3 * 2   # 5 algos × 3 input types × 2 sizes

def test_sort_monotonic_in_n(store):
    for algo in ["bubble", "insertion", "merge", "quick"]:
        for typ in ["random", "sorted", "reversed"]:
            rs = sorted(store.filter(algorithm=algo, input_type=typ), key=lambda r: r.n)
            assert all(rs[i].seconds <= rs[i+1].seconds * 2 for i in range(len(rs)-1))

@pytest.mark.parametrize("seed", [1, 2, 3])
def test_sort_correctness(seed):
    rng = random.Random(seed)
    data = [rng.randint(0, 10_000) for _ in range(500)]
    for fn in [sorting.bubble_sort, sorting.insertion_sort,
               sorting.merge_sort, sorting.quicksort]:
        assert fn(data[:]) == sorted(data)

def test_dict_beats_linear(store):
    for n in [200, 400]:
        linear = next(r for r in store.filter(algorithm="linear", n=n))
        dict_r = next(r for r in store.filter(algorithm="dict",   n=n))
        assert dict_r.seconds < linear.seconds

def test_linked_prepend_beats_list_insert(store):
    prep = next(r for r in store.filter(algorithm="ll_prepend", n=2_000))
    ins  = next(r for r in store.filter(algorithm="list_insert0", n=2_000))
    assert prep.seconds < ins.seconds
```

The module-scoped fixture keeps the expensive benchmark set-up work to a single run across all tests in the module. The parametrised test covers the correctness question efficiently with three random seeds.

Appendix D Further Reading & Online Resources

The books, websites, and online courses listed below have been selected to extend the material in this book — either by providing deeper coverage of a topic, or by offering a different pedagogical perspective. None are required. All URLs were correct at the time of publication; if a link has moved, a web search for the title and author will usually locate the new address.

D.1 Books — Introductory and Intermediate

- Sedgewick, R. and Wayne, K. (2011). Algorithms, 4th edition. Addison-Wesley. The standard undergraduate text for algorithms in Java. Excellent visualisations and a clear progression from searching and sorting through to graphs. The companion website at algs4.cs.princeton.edu includes animated demonstrations of every algorithm in this book.
- Goodrich, M. T., Tamassia, R. and Goldwasser, M. H. (2013). Data Structures and Algorithms in Python. Wiley. A rigorous treatment for students ready for university-level work. Covers amortised analysis, advanced trees (AVL, red-black, B-trees), and the full theory of hashing.
- Miller, B. N. and Ranum, D. L. Problem Solving with Algorithms and Data Structures Using Python. Runestone Academy (free online: runestone.academy). Beginner-friendly and fully interactive — every example runs in the browser.

D.2 Books — Advanced and Reference

- Cormen, T. H., Leiserson, C. E., Rivest, R. L. and Stein, C. (2022). Introduction to Algorithms, 4th edition. MIT Press. The canonical reference — known universally as "CLRS". Dense, thorough, and the standard source for formal analysis. Dip in, don't read cover to cover.
- Skiena, S. S. (2020). The Algorithm Design Manual, 3rd edition. Springer. The best single source for translating a real problem into the right algorithm. The second half is a practical catalogue of problems and the techniques that solve them.
- Knuth, D. E. The Art of Computer Programming, Volumes 1–4. Addison-Wesley. A multi-decade landmark of computer science. Volume 3 (Sorting and Searching) is the classic reference on the subject.

D.3 Online Courses

- MIT 6.006 Introduction to Algorithms. Free video lectures and assignments at ocw.mit.edu. Closest to the scope of this book at a faster pace.
- Stanford Algorithms Specialization (Coursera). Tim Roughgarden's four-part series. Excellent for learners ready to move from implementation to formal analysis.
- Harvard CS50. Free, broadly popular introduction to computer science. Less depth on data structures than this book, but strong on problem-solving habits and C fundamentals.

D.4 Interactive Websites

- visualgo.net — animated visualisations of every data structure and algorithm in this book, many with step-by-step control. Indispensable for understanding how trees rebalance and how graph traversals unfold in real time.
- pythontutor.com — step-by-step Python execution with visualisation of the call stack, variables, and object references. Ideal for tracing recursion and pointer-heavy code.
- bigocheatsheet.com — a single-page summary of common data structure and algorithm complexities. A quicker reference than any textbook during the heat of a problem.
- leetcode.com and hackerrank.com — practice problem archives organised by topic and difficulty. Excellent for building speed on the techniques covered here. Focus on the "easy" and "medium" categories first.

D.5 Official Python Documentation

- docs.python.org/3 — the primary reference. The Library Reference pages for collections, heapq, bisect, and itertools directly support topics in Chapters 2, 4, 5, and 8.
- peps.python.org — the Python Enhancement Proposal index. PEP 8 (style), PEP 257 (docstrings), and PEP 3107 (type hints) are worth reading before your first substantial project.
- wiki.python.org/moin/TimeComplexity — the official summary of Python built-in complexities, covering list, dict, set, and deque. Reproduced in shorter form in Appendix B of this book.

D.6 Community and Discussion

- stackoverflow.com — the standard destination for specific programming questions. Read the answers to existing questions before posting new ones; almost every reasonable question has been asked.
- reddit.com/r/learnpython and reddit.com/r/algorithms — active communities for informal questions and discussion. Supportive to beginners.
- Python Discord (pythondiscord.com) — a large moderated chat community with dedicated help channels. Responsive and welcoming to secondary students.

D.7 Next Steps in This Series

The next booklets in the Think, Code, Create Advanced Series build directly on the data structures and algorithms covered here:

- Book 05 — Functional Programming & Advanced Iterables. Generators, decorators, map/filter/reduce, and itertools — tools that transform how you write algorithmic code.
- Book 07 — Database Programming with Python. Persistent data storage with SQLite; B-tree and hash indexes are the industrial version of the structures in Chapters 7 and 8.
- Book 09 — Data Analysis with Python. NumPy and Pandas put the sorting, searching, and grouping ideas of this book to work on real datasets.
- Book 11 — Testing, Debugging & Code Quality. Extends the pytest patterns of Exercise 10.5 into a full testing practice.
- Book 12 — Concurrency, Networking & Automation. Where graphs become networks and algorithmic efficiency becomes the difference between "runs" and "times out".

Glossary

This glossary defines the key technical terms used throughout Book 04. Page numbers in the index at the end of the book point to the principal discussion of each term in the body of the text; this glossary gives the definition in one place for quick reference.

Terms appearing in bold within a definition are themselves defined elsewhere in the glossary.

Abstract data type (ADT) A mathematical model of a data structure defined by the operations it supports, not by how those operations are implemented. A stack, for example, is defined by push, pop, and peek; any implementation that supplies those three operations with the correct behaviour is a stack.

Adjacency list A graph representation that stores, for each vertex, a list of the vertices it is connected to. Efficient for sparse graphs; iterating a vertex's neighbours is O(degree).

Adjacency matrix A graph representation that uses a two-dimensional array where entry (i, j) records whether an edge connects vertices i and j. Efficient for dense graphs and O(1) edge-existence queries, but uses $O(V^2)$ space.

Algorithm A finite, unambiguous, effective sequence of steps that produces a result for every valid input. An algorithm is language-independent — it can be expressed in English, pseudocode, or any programming language.

Amortised complexity The average cost of an operation across a long sequence of operations, rather than the worst case of a single operation. Python's list.append is O(1) amortised: most calls are cheap, with occasional O(n) resizes that average out.

Array A contiguous block of memory storing elements of the same type, indexed by integer position. Python's list is an array-backed structure. O(1) index access, O(n) insertion in the middle.

Asymptotic analysis The study of how an algorithm's resource use grows as the input size approaches infinity. Constant factors and small-n behaviour are ignored in favour of the dominant growth term.

Backtracking A problem-solving strategy that explores partial solutions and abandons a path ("backtracks") as soon as it cannot lead to a valid complete solution. Used widely in graph search and constraint satisfaction.

Balanced tree A tree in which the height difference between left and right subtrees is bounded at every node, guaranteeing O(log n) operations. Self-balancing variants (AVL, red-black) rebalance automatically on insertion and deletion.

Big-O notation A notation describing the upper bound of an algorithm's growth rate. f(n) is O(g(n)) if f(n) grows no faster than a constant multiple of g(n) for sufficiently large n.

Binary search A search algorithm that finds a target in a sorted sequence by repeatedly halving the search range. O(log n) time. Requires random access; does not work on linked lists without modification.

Binary search tree (BST) A binary tree in which every node's left subtree contains only keys less than the node's key, and every right subtree contains only keys greater. Search, insert, and delete are O(log n) in a balanced BST, O(n) in the worst case.

Binary tree A tree in which every node has at most two children, conventionally called left and right.

Breadth-first search (BFS) A graph traversal that explores all vertices at distance k from the source before any vertex at distance k+1. Uses a queue. Finds shortest paths by hop count in unweighted graphs.

Capacity The maximum number of elements a data structure can hold before it must grow. Distinct from size, which is the current number of elements.

Chaining A hash collision resolution strategy that stores multiple keys hashing to the same bucket in a linked structure (typically a list). See also open addressing.

Collision The situation where two distinct keys hash to the same bucket in a hash table. Good hash functions minimise collisions; all hash tables must handle them.

Complexity class A category of algorithms sharing the same asymptotic growth rate, denoted O(1), O(log n), O(n), O(n log n), O(n^2), and so on.

Connected component A maximal set of vertices in an undirected graph such that every pair is connected by at least one path. A graph with more than one component is called disconnected.

Cycle A path in a graph that starts and ends at the same vertex without repeating any edge. A graph with no cycles is called acyclic; a directed acyclic graph is a DAG.

Data structure A way of organising data in memory so that it can be accessed and modified efficiently. The choice of data structure is often the single largest factor in an algorithm's running time.

Degenerate tree A binary search tree that has degenerated into a linked list because keys were inserted in sorted order, giving O(n) operations. Prevented by self-balancing trees.

Depth-first search (DFS) A graph traversal that explores as far as possible along each branch before backtracking. Can be implemented recursively or with an explicit stack. Used for topological sort, cycle detection, and finding strongly connected components.

Deque A double-ended queue. Supports O(1) insertion and removal at both ends. Python's collections.deque is implemented as a doubly linked list of fixed-size blocks.

Directed acyclic graph (DAG) A directed graph with no cycles. The canonical structure for prerequisite relationships, build dependencies, and task schedules — everything that admits a topological sort.

Divide and conquer An algorithm design technique in which a problem is broken into independent smaller problems, each solved recursively, and the results combined. Merge sort and quicksort are the canonical examples.

Edge A connection between two vertices in a graph. May be directed or undirected; may carry a weight.

Graph A collection of vertices connected by edges. Graphs model almost any network-shaped data: maps, social networks, computer networks, dependency chains.

Greedy algorithm An algorithm that makes the locally optimal choice at each step without reconsidering earlier decisions. Dijkstra's and Prim's algorithms are greedy. Not every problem admits a correct greedy solution.

Hash function A function that maps a key to an integer within a fixed range, used to locate the key's bucket in a hash table. A good hash function distributes keys uniformly across buckets.

Hash table A data structure that stores key-value pairs in an array of buckets, with each key's position determined by a hash function. O(1) average-case insert, search, and delete.

Heap A tree-based data structure satisfying the heap property: in a min-heap, every parent is less than or equal to its children; in a max-heap, every parent is greater than or equal. Python's heapq module implements a min-heap on top of a list.

Height (of a tree) The length of the longest path from the root to any leaf. A balanced tree of n nodes has height O(log n); a degenerate tree has height O(n).

In-order traversal A depth-first traversal of a binary tree that visits the left subtree, then the node, then the right subtree. For a BST, yields keys in sorted order.

Invariant A property that holds true at every step of an algorithm. Identifying the correct invariant is often the key insight in proving correctness.

Leaf A node in a tree that has no children.

Linked list A linear data structure in which each element (node) holds a value and a reference to the next node (and, in a doubly linked list, the previous node). O(1) insertion and deletion at known positions, O(n) access by index.

Load factor In a hash table, the ratio of entries to buckets. High load factors increase collision frequency; most implementations rehash into a larger array once the load factor exceeds a threshold (commonly 0.75).

Memoisation A technique that caches the results of expensive function calls so that subsequent calls with the same arguments return immediately. Python's functools.lru_cache provides this as a decorator.

Merge sort A divide-and-conquer sorting algorithm that splits the input in half, recursively sorts each half, and merges the two sorted halves. Stable, O(n log n) worst case, O(n) space.

Node A single element within a tree, linked list, or graph data structure. Usually contains a value plus references to related nodes.

Open addressing A hash collision resolution strategy that stores all entries directly in the bucket array, probing to a nearby empty slot when a collision occurs. Linear probing and double hashing are common variants.

Path A sequence of vertices in a graph where each consecutive pair is connected by an edge. A simple path has no repeated vertices.

Pivot In quicksort, the element chosen to partition the subarray. The choice of pivot strongly affects worst-case performance — median-of-three and random pivots avoid the $O(n^2)$ behaviour on sorted input.

Priority queue A queue in which elements are retrieved in order of priority rather than insertion order. Implemented efficiently using a heap. Core operation in Dijkstra's and Prim's algorithms.

Queue A first-in, first-out (FIFO) data structure. Two canonical operations: enqueue (add to rear) and dequeue (remove from front). Used widely in BFS and scheduling.

Quicksort A divide-and-conquer sorting algorithm that partitions the input around a pivot and recursively sorts the two sides. Average O(n log n), worst case $O(n^2)$, in-place, not stable.

Recursion A technique in which a function calls itself on a smaller input. Every recursive function must have a base case that terminates the recursion and one or more recursive cases that make progress toward it.

Root The topmost node of a tree — the unique node with no parent. Every other node descends from the root.

Sibling Two nodes in a tree that share the same parent.

Space complexity The amount of additional memory an algorithm requires beyond the input itself, expressed as a function of input size using Big-O notation.

Stable sort A sort that preserves the original relative order of records with equal keys. Merge sort and insertion sort are stable; quicksort is not.

Stack A last-in, first-out (LIFO) data structure. Two canonical operations: push (add to top) and pop (remove from top). Used in function call management, expression evaluation, and DFS.

Strongly connected component (SCC) In a directed graph, a maximal set of vertices in which every vertex is reachable from every other. Found in O(V + E) using Kosaraju's or Tarjan's algorithm.

Time complexity The amount of time an algorithm requires as a function of input size, expressed using Big-O notation. Independent of hardware and programming language.

Topological sort A linear ordering of the vertices of a directed acyclic graph such that every edge points from an earlier vertex to a later one. Produced by Kahn's algorithm (BFS-based) or DFS with finish times.

Traversal The process of visiting every node in a data structure exactly once. Tree traversals include pre-order, in-order, post-order, and level-order; graph traversals include BFS and DFS.

Tree A connected, acyclic graph. Equivalently, a hierarchical data structure with a root node and zero or more child subtrees. Every non-empty tree on n nodes has exactly n-1 edges.

Vertex A single element in a graph. Plural: vertices. Sometimes called a node when the context is general data structures rather than graph theory specifically.

Weight A numerical value attached to an edge in a weighted graph, representing distance, cost, time, or any other quantity. Shortest-path algorithms like Dijkstra's rely on non-negative weights.

Index

Made in United States
North Haven, CT
03 September 2026

17828266R10152